SPORT COMPACT TURBOS & BLOWERS

JOE PETTITT

CarTech®

Copyright © 2005 by Joe Pettitt

All rights reserved. No part of this publication may be reproduced or utilized in any form or by any means, electronic or mechanical, including photocopying, recording, or by any information storage and retrieval system, without prior permission from the Publisher. All text, photographs, and artwork are the property of the Author unless otherwise noted or credited.

The information in this work is true and complete to the best of our knowledge. However, all information is presented without any guarantee on the part of the Author or Publisher, who also disclaim any liability incurred in connection with the use of the information and any implied warranties of merchantability or fitness for a particular purpose. Readers are responsible for taking suitable and appropriate safety measures when performing any of the operations or activities described in this work.

All trademarks, trade names, model names and numbers, and other product designations referred to herein are the property of their respective owners and are used solely for identification purposes. This work is a publication of CarTech, Inc., and has not been licensed, approved, sponsored, or endorsed by any other person or entity. The publisher is not associated with any product, service, or vendor mentioned in this book, and does not endorse the products or services of any vendor mentioned in this book.

Edited By Travis Thompson

Layout By Bruce Leckie

ISBN 978-1-61325-004-4

Order No. SA89P

CarTech®
CarTech®, Inc.,
39966 Grand Avenue
North Branch, MN 55056
Telephone (651) 277-1200 • (800) 551-4754 • Fax: (651) 277-1203
www.cartechbooks.com

Front Cover: *Just imagine a Roots blower like this tucked away in the engine compartment of your sport compact. Sounds like fun, doesn't it?*

Front Cover, Inset: *This Honda S2000 is fitted with a Vortech centrifugal supercharger and an air-to-water aftercooler. A setup like this can make big power, without necessitating a lot of other changes.*

Title Page: *Injecting nitrous oxide at low RPM can help a turbo spool up and create boost. That allows you to run a larger turbine for less backpressure at high RPM. Though you'll get the turbo lag back when not running the nitrous, since you only have to use the nitrous in very short duration, it'll last a reasonably long time.*

Back Cover, Upper Left: *Here's Lisa Kubo at the wheel of the Saturn Motorsports of San Diego Ion Coupe with a turbocharged 2.2-liter Ecotec engine. She has a best e.t. of 8.06 seconds and a best speed of 185.36 mph.*

Back Cover, Upper Right: *One reason that supercharging has become so popular is that with today's complete street kits, a blower is true bolt-on horsepower. You don't have to change anything else in the engine to get a substantial performance increase. Best of all, as demonstrated by this Jackson Racing supercharger kit, a moderate package like this is completely streetable and emissions legal too.*

Back Cover, Lower: *The only real problem with street super/turbocharging is that it's easy to get carried away. The temptation is always there to dial in a little more boost for more horsepower. This isn't what we'd call a street motor, but if it fits your definition, just be sure you have a strong bottom end for this level of excess.*

Chapter 1:	**Introduction to Superchargers and Turbochargers: Exotic or Practical?........6**
	What is a Supercharger?..7
	Superchargers and Turbochargers: Pressurize the Intake 8
	Types of Superchargers 10
	What is a Turbocharger?..11

Chapter 2:	**Supercharging Theory 14**
	The Imperfect World of Supercharging and Turbocharging........................14
	Density, Volume, and Pressure 15
	The Gas Law...15
	The Problem of Heat..15
	Blower Efficiency...17
	The Limits of Supercharging..23
	Expansion Ratio and Thermal Efficiency 24
	Horsepower-Rich Tuning Tips...25

Chapter 3:	**Roots Blowers for Sport Compacts 26**
	Eaton in Aftermarket Supercharger Kits...27
	GM Performance Parts 28
	Jackson Racing 28
	Stillen Superchargers 31
	Toyota Racing Development..31
	The Lysholm Screw-Type Compressor 34
	Whipple Industries..35
	Comptech 37
	Kenne Bell 37

Chapter 4:	**Centrifugal Blowers for Sport Compacts 38**
	Vortech 42
	VF-Engineering 44
	ProCharger 46
	HKS Rotrex Supercharger Kits 47

Chapter 5:	**Turbocharging Theory 48**
	Turbo Lag...50
	The Case Against Turbochargers 51
	The Case for Turbochargers 52
	Turbo Sizing: How to Get a Turbo That Fits Your Performance Needs........53

Chapter 6:	**Turbos for Sport Compacts 63**
	HKS...63
	Garrett..65
	GReddy..66
	BorgWarner...68
	Turbonetics...69
	Edelbrock 71

Sport Compact Turbos & Blowers

Contents

Chapter 7: **Supertuning Turbo and Supercharged Engines** 72
    Intercoolers: Do they Really Make Power? 73
    Intercooler Flow Charts 76
    The Power Recipe: More Mass Flow 77
    Adjusting Cam Timing 78
    Supercharged Exhaust 78
    Turbocharged Exhaust 79
    Fuel Delivery 79
    How to Design a Fuel System 80
    Now Let's do the Math 82
    Ignition 85
    Boost Electronics 88

Chapter 8: **Engine Building Tactics that Survive Under Pressure** 94
    Block, Crank, and Rods 98
    Compression Ratio, Pistons, and Rings 99
    Cylinder Heads 106
    Camshafts 107
    The Cooling System 109

Chapter 9: **History of Turbocharging and Supercharging** 112
    Turbo History 112
    A Short History of Automotive Supercharging 117

Appendix A: **Source Guide** 126

ABOUT THE AUTHOR

Joe Pettitt is a freelance high-performance automotive journalist, photographer, and car-fi guy. He's written hundreds of articles for the performance press including *Hot Rod, Sport Compact Car, Drag Racer, Car Craft, Circle Track,* and *Motor Trend* magazines. His adventures as a high-performance journalist include piloting IROC cars around the famous ovals of Daytona and Talladega, and strapping into the world's fastest open road racer as a passenger. This mind-warping experience offered 27 minutes of sheer terror at over 220 miles per hour while making the 90-mile Silver State Challenge run from Ely, Nevada, to Lund, Nevada, with an average speed of over 194 mph. It was at that time he developed a serious need for high speed, and he has driven the course in a highly modified Buick Grand National, with a top speed (so far) of 204 mph. As a car audio journalist, he has also written for *Autotronics* magazine, where he indulged his passion for great cars and great music. Currently, Joe is the editor of *Sport Truck* magazine.

An avid do-it-yourselfer, Pettitt modified and tuned numerous sports cars, hot rods, and street machines, installing sound systems in all of them. His favorite was a '59 XK 150 Jag. "Every time you build a car," says Pettitt, "you learn something new. You learn how to do it a little smarter and a little easier; and you learn how to find the right people to answer your questions." Finding good information about super tuning your engine isn't easy; but once you have it, it makes your high-performance projects run much more smoothly.

That's why CarTech asked Mr. Pettitt to write this book – to help you cut through some of the marketing hype to get the truth.

Joe Pettitt currently lives in Southern California with wife Patricia and daughters Vanessa and Jordan.

CHAPTER 1

INTRODUCTION TO SUPERCHARGERS AND TURBOCHARGERS
Exotic or Practical?

No single performance modification made to an internal combustion engine is more practical or effective than the addition of a crankshaft or exhaust-driven supercharger.

The foregoing statement may sound like typical technological bragging or advertising hype to some readers. Somebody's always claiming that something is the best new high-performance trick, right? But in the case of superchargers, you will get little argument from engineers, engine builders, or racecar drivers. The supercharger's effectiveness has been known almost since the engine was invented.

If this is true, some skeptics may ask, then why don't the Detroit auto manufacturers put blowers on all cars? It is simply a matter of economics. Other, less-efficient methods of boosting engine output, such as increasing displacement or raising the compression ratio, cost considerably less on a mass-production basis. In addition, even though most superchargers have only one or two basic moving parts, Detroit would view them as an extra mechanical component on the engine that would have to be warranted and serviced.

Despite such bottom-line thinking, however, a surprising number of production cars have come equipped with superchargers in the past, both in the United States and in Europe. Often this was done as a last resort to produce results to boost the performance of an undernourished or poorly designed engine to keep up with the competition. Now that Detroit is finally learning that smaller, more efficient cars are better, more and more manufacturers have been installing turbochargers on the little motors to make them act bigger and

People used to think that blowers were temperamental or unreliable on street engines, but don't forget that most types were initially designed to run thousands of miles on fleet vehicles, such as the ubiquitous GMC 71 series, as shown here on a 6-71 diesel.

stronger without using up a whole lot more fuel. Since the late 1980s, several OEM applications of belt-driven, positive-displacement superchargers have been seen as their efficiency levels have been significantly improved.

Don't forget that the ubiquitous GMC supercharger – the big, impressive, whining, air-gulping windmill that immediately comes to mind when the term "blower" is mentioned to any old-school hot-rodder – is in fact a regular production item. They have been installed by General Motors on millions of hard-working, cross-country-hauling diesel trucks, buses, and other forms of heavy equipment since the 1950s. Although superchargers have almost always been considered an exotic addition to production cars, they can and should be as practical, efficient, and reliable to run every day on the street as any other working component of your engine. Superchargers and turbochargers have not only been used regularly on diesel trucks for years, but also on aircraft engines, diesel trains, stationary engines, boats, and many other applications.

There are only two serious reasons that I can think of why all performance enthusiasts haven't installed superchargers on their engines: (1) ignorance – an ignorance bred and fostered by the Detroit mentality of economics described above; and (2) cost. Both of these reasons may be refuted by the same argument, however. Instead of bolting a blower onto our motor, tradition tells us to bore and stroke, port and polish, change the cam, buy a new manifold, add bigger injectors and pump up the fuel pressure, install headers, and so on. What many of us fail to realize, or have never been taught, is that a properly installed and tuned supercharger can do the same job as all of these other speed parts, and it can usually do it better. Although a complete supercharger kit can be very expensive these days, the total cost should look less "exotic" when you compare it to the accumulated prices of the several traditional performance parts or operations it can replace.

In the following pages, we'll discuss some of the history and theory of supercharger and turbocharger development, but we will be primarily interested in the several varieties of superchargers, turbochargers, and complete kits currently available for street performance engines. We're going to look at how a given package can be tuned for maximum performance and efficiency. We'll also study the types of changes that should be made to a typical street motor (and those that shouldn't) before a supercharger or turbocharger is installed, as well as a rundown on the best ancillary components for both the engine and the power adder (drive systems, linkage, ignition systems, camshafts, exhaust system, water injection, and so on).

What is a Supercharger?

If we are going to spend the rest of this book talking about superchargers, we had better start by determining exactly what a supercharger, or blower, is. In the broadest sense, a supercharger is anything that will force more air, or air/fuel mixture, into the cylinders than would be drawn into the cylinders naturally by the suction of the pistons during the intake stroke. By this definition, turbochargers are superchargers, and we will, for the sake of brevity, use the terms interchangeably in the general discussion on performance dynamics. We'll reserve the specific usages of the terms when discussing issues influenced by the drive mechanism.

In short, superchargers pressurize the intake above the ambient air pressure. At sea level, atmospheric pressure is approximately 14.7 pounds per square inch (psi) – air exerts this much pressure naturally on everything near the surface of the earth (because of the air's weight). When an engine is normally or naturally aspirated, (not supercharged or turbocharged), it must rely on this pressure to push the air into the intake, through the manifold, into the intake port, and then into the cylinder as the piston "opens" the cylinder to maximum volume by moving downward on the intake stroke.

Because of restrictions and bends along the path – friction, turbulence, incomplete evacuation of exhaust from the cylinder, and several other factors – the naturally aspirated cylinder is never able to completely draw in a full charge of air/fuel mix. Let's say the total volume of the cylinder is 40 cubic inches. If you turned the engine to bottom dead center on the intake stroke, by hand, and left it there, the cylinder would fill with 40 cubic inches of air through the open intake valve. Atmospheric pressure pushes the air in (which is exactly the same thing as saying the downward-moving piston sucks the air in, whenever you create a space that has nothing in it – that is, create a vacuum – atmospheric pressure will immediately push air into that space through any available opening. The force pushing the air in will be approximately 14.7 psi at sea level, but less at higher altitudes. However, when the engine is running at speed, atmospheric pressure is not great enough to push 40 cubic inches of fresh air/fuel mixture into the cylinder before the compression stroke begins.

What we are describing is the volumetric efficiency (VE) of the engine, which is a comparison of the total amount of air/fuel charge a naturally aspirated engine *could* draw in (total cylinder volume), to the amount (volume) that it *actually does* draw in under given operating conditions. Other factors being equal, an engine's power output is directly proportional to its volumetric efficiency, and the vast majority of our traditional hop-up tricks are directed at increasing this figure: bigger carburetors or throttle bodies, better intake manifolds, porting, polishing, bigger valves, better camshaft design, exhaust scavenging, and so on.

However, no naturally aspirated engine can attain 100% volumetric efficiency (except in rare cases when a perfectly tuned, ram-induction intake manifold can accelerate the intake charge sufficiently to completely fill the cylinders at a certain narrow span in the RPM range). By increasing throttle body or carburetor and port sizes, streamlining passages, and evacuating exhaust, we can reduce losses and increase the efficiency to a certain point. But as long as we are relying on atmospheric pressure to push the air/fuel

Chapter 1

If you have any doubts whether blowers work or not, take a look at professional Top Fuel dragsters or Funny Cars. These 470-inch, 5,000-plus-horsepower wonders make more power per cubic inch than any other type of motor, and they owe most of it to the big, tight, Teflon-lined, magnesium-case 10-71 to 14-71 GMC Roots-style blowers.

charge into the cylinder – if that remains a constant – we can very rarely reach 100% efficiency. After you've done everything you can to help the engine draw as much air into the cylinders as possible by normal suction, there remains only one way to get more air/fuel charge in – and it's a simple deduction: increase the pressure pushing the air into the motor – i.e., force the air in. This is what a supercharger does.

So again, in the broadest sense, a supercharger is any device or means for increasing the cylinder filling (volumetric efficiency) in an engine beyond that possible by the normal suction of the pistons; that is, beyond that possible under the force of atmospheric pressure.

Given this broad definition, we could say that any sort of pump, fan, or wind-blowing device that can force a greater volume of air through the intake system, and/or get a greater volume of air/fuel charge into the cylinder, than is possible under atmospheric pressure, is a supercharger. Under this definition, we might say that a tuned ram-induction intake manifold, or even a good air scoop on a fast-moving racecar, is a sort of supercharging device. Likewise, it might be argued that nitrous oxide injection is a form of supercharging. (Running your car on a cold night, or at low altitude, produces the same effect in smaller proportion.) Mickey Thompson once even tried feeding his funny car engine with very highly compressed air carried in onboard tanks – with some success!

However, none of these methods is strictly considered supercharging. For the purposes of this book, we will define a supercharger as a mechanical air pump (driven mechanically or by the exhaust) capable of producing a positive boost pressure in the manifold of the engine at some point in its operating range.

SUPERCHARGERS AND TURBOCHARGERS: PRESSURIZE THE INTAKE

Obviously, we have already discussed to some degree what a supercharger does. It pumps air, or air/fuel mixture, into the engine at a rate faster than the engine can draw it in under atmospheric pressure. Therefore, instead of loading the cylinder with a partial air/fuel charge before compression and combustion, a boosted engine can fill its cylinders with a "super charge" that can attain or actually exceed 100% volumetric efficiency.

As we stated, the supercharger can, therefore, do the job of several other traditional performance modifications aimed at increasing the engine's volumetric efficiency. If you are going to add a supercharger to an engine for street use, you will very likely be able to pump in all the extra performance you need without changing the throttle body or intake manifold (other than to accept the blower), porting or polishing the heads, enlarging the valves, changing the camshaft, raising the compression, or installing headers. (You'll need to tune the fuel and ignition timing, however, but more on that later.) If you are building an all-out race motor, or if the intake passages of your engine are particularly restrictive, you will want to make sure that no one component in the intake or exhaust systems "fights" the supercharger by overly constricting airflow either into or out of the cylinders. Most modern engines are ripe for supercharging just the way they are.

Since the blower pressurizes the entire intake manifold, there is less need to streamline, tune, or otherwise enhance intake flow. In fact, the air/fuel mixture no longer really flows through the manifold in a blown engine; instead, you might think of the manifold as a pressurized reservoir of air/fuel mix ready to burst through the valve as soon as it opens. For modern port-injected engines, the intake manifold is the same pressurized reservoir, minus the fuel. In fact, some supercharged engines have problems keeping the intake valves shut and require stronger valvesprings to do so.

Since the intake charge is so eager to get into the cylinder of a supercharged engine, there is also less need to increase valve timing or lift with a special camshaft. Naturally, certain camshaft profiles will work better than others in supercharged or turbocharged engines, and we'll discuss some of these fine points later. In general, a boosted motor is far less touchy about camshaft profile than a naturally aspirated engine (the worst thing for a blown motor is a super long-duration, big-overlap "race" cam, since it will allow much of the blower's forced induction to go right out the exhaust port). With standard cam timing, however, the supercharger will still help to blow residual exhaust gases out of the cylinder as it forces fresh air/fuel mix in to take its place. Therefore exhaust valve size, port size and shape, and tuned headers are much less touchy on a blown engine. The supercharger will actually help pump the exhaust out of the engine.

By pumping a greater amount of air/fuel charge into the cylinder, the supercharger effectively raises the compression ratio of the engine (since a larger volume of air/fuel will be compressed into the same combustion chamber volume when the piston is at top dead center). Consequently, the static compression ratio (the physical ratio of the open cylinder volume at bottom dead center to the closed cylinder volume at top dead center) in a supercharged engine must be considerably lower than that in a naturally aspirated performance engine. Adding a blower to an engine with 10 or 12:1 compression will literally blow the engine because of excessively high cylinder pressures. However, many modern emission motors come with compression ratios in the 8 to 9:1 range, which is just right for supercharging. Even some of the high-performance engines with 10 to 10.5:1 compression ratios are able to run a properly tuned supercharger. The only consideration is whether the factory pistons and rings are strong enough to withstand higher pressure and heat levels produced in the cylinder by the blower.

Some readers may wonder about the logic of reducing the static compression ratio of an unblown high-performance engine so that you can raise the compression back up to a comparable level with a supercharger. If raising the compression was all the blower did, it would be a waste of money (and engine horsepower to turn it), since a set of high-compression pistons costs far less than a blower. But don't forget that the naturally aspirated engine, no matter what its compression ratio, can only draw so much air into the cylinders

Superchargers come in several sizes, shapes, and designs. The centrifugal Paxton/McCulloch blower works on a completely different principle than the GMC or other Roots types, but it produces the same result — forcing a greater amount of air and fuel into a given engine. This blower setup was used as factory equipment on several cars (Ford, Studebaker, Packard, Avanti) in the 1950s and 1960s.

under atmospheric pressure. It cannot achieve 100 percent volumetric efficiency. Higher compression just squeezes the same volume of air into a smaller space with a taller piston dome. Consequently, the more highly compressed charge will fire with a bigger bang, producing more power than the same charge in a lower-compression motor. In a blown motor of the same displacement, however, you start with a larger volume of air/fuel in the cylinder, and then you compress it into a larger combustion chamber, arriving at the same proportional compression ratio. Therefore, you get the same bang as in the high-compression engine, but you have a larger charge to expand and push the piston down. The more fuel and air you put into each cylinder, and burn, during each cycle of the engine, the more power that engine will make. This is what a supercharger or turbocharger does.

Using this same reasoning, you can also think of the supercharger as a device that effectively increases the displacement of an engine. That is, if you compare an unblown 3-liter engine with a supercharged 1.5-liter engine, you would very likely find that the smaller engine is pumping the same mass of air/fuel charge into its cylinders as the

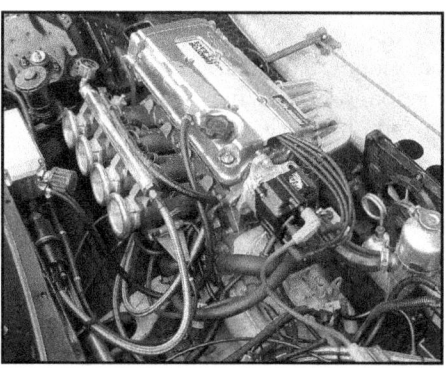

Engines like these look impressive and run strong, but they can never equal the performance potential of a supercharged motor. What's worse, they cost nearly as much to build as a mild blown engine, but they run very poorly at typical street-driving speeds. Blowers are actually more practical and efficient for the price.

One reason that supercharging has become so popular is that, with today's complete street kits, a blower is true bolt-on horsepower. You don't have to change anything else in the engine to get a substantial performance increase. Best of all, as demonstrated by this Jackson Racing supercharger kit, a moderate package like this is completely street-drivable and emissions legal, too.

larger engine is drawing in naturally. The power produced by an engine is directly proportional to the mass (or weight) of air/fuel mixture it can ingest, compress, and ignite per cycle, other things being equal. That's why larger-displacement engines make more power than smaller ones. But rather than making the cylinders bigger, we can use a supercharger to pump more air/fuel charge into the smaller motor, thereby making it perform like a much larger engine. Better yet, the smaller displacement motor can be smaller externally, and lighter, thereby allowing for a smaller and lighter vehicle package, which will increase performance, economy, and overall efficiency tremendously. This is exactly the kind of performance we are looking for today, and superchargers and turbochargers are certainly playing a major role in the tuner-car era.

However, we must be fair and point out that not all contributions made by a supercharger are positive. To begin with, all belt-driven superchargers necessarily consume a certain portion of the engine's power, since they're driven by the crankshaft. At high boost levels, this power drain can be considerable, but the extra power produced by the blower more than offsets the drain. A good supercharger gives much more than it takes. Turbocharger devotees point out that turbos deliver "free" horsepower, unlike belt-driven blowers, but the truth is that turbos do cost something – they add backpressure. But the cost in horsepower lost from the flow restriction doesn't use fuel, so a turbocharged engine is more efficient. A Roots-type blower, on the other hand, will "windmill" under high-vacuum driving conditions, such as constant-speed cruising. In other words, when the engine is running with the throttle closed, or only slightly open, vacuum will be produced in the intake manifold rather than boost, and this vacuum will turn the supercharger rotors like a windmill. Under such circumstances, the blower will not be using up crankshaft horsepower. To prove this point, you can disconnect the drive belt from a Roots blower and watch the drive pulley spin by itself while the engine is running.

Finally, all superchargers raise the temperature of the intake charge as they pressurize it, because the temperature of any gas rises when it is compressed. The amount of intake-charge temperature increase will vary with the amount of boost being produced and the efficiency of the supercharger (which we will discuss more fully later). This increase in intake temperature can lead to detonation in the combustion chamber, and possible parts damage, if it isn't kept under control.

Types of Superchargers

There are many ways to pump things. Just think of the numerous types of water pumps or air fans you've seen. Most of the designs that have been used for superchargers over the years – including current styles – were actually intended for some other purpose originally. You may have heard the story that the Roots supercharger was initially used to pump fresh air into mine shafts. Actually, it was first used to blow air into forges, as were several varieties of centrifugal blowers, well before the internal combustion engine was even invented. Roots blowers have also been used for such varied purposes as pressurizing airplane cabins and pumping flour or molasses, just to name a couple.

You have undoubtedly also heard that the internal combustion engine is basically an air pump. Certainly it is. In fact, most air compressors use a similar valve and piston arrangement. Therefore, it isn't unthinkable to use a couple of the cylinders in an engine to supercharge the other cylinders, and a few early examples of such self-supercharging engines were actually designed and tested, but both the mechanical efficiency and the pumping rate of such a design were too low to be practical. A piston-and-valve air pump is good for high-pressure/low-volume work (such as an air compressor, which uses a large storage tank), while an engine supercharger needs to pump a large volume of air at a relatively low pressure.

Of course, there are other types of internal combustion engines besides the piston variety, which are also types of air pumps, and some of these have been used as superchargers. The Wankel rotary engine, for instance, was first designed as a supercharger and was used very successfully on some record-setting NSU motorcycles years ago. The jet engine, or radial fan, is also a type of blower, and this same principle was used in the Latham axial-flow supercharger made in the 1950s and 1960s.

Countless other varieties of pumps, compressors, blowers, and variations on each have existed in the past and may well appear in the future. But at present, three major types of blowers are the most commonly used designs for automotive supercharging, and those will be discussed in detail in subsequent chapters.

Positive Displacement Superchargers

The type of supercharger most readily associated with hot-rod engines is the Roots type. The famous GMC blowers are of this design, which is described as a bi-rotor, inter-meshing gear pump. A pair of rotors turns inside a closed housing (with an intake opening on one side and an outlet opening on the other) in opposite directions, meshing like a pair of gears. Most Roots blowers have two or three lobes per rotor (though they could have more). The open space between the lobes catches the air at the intake opening, carries it around as it rotates (sealed in by the wall of the case), and then pushes it out the opening at the bottom. The meshing of the rotors in the center of the blower seals that area so the air cannot escape back up the middle. A Roots blower is called a positive-displacement pump since it theoretically moves the same volume of air through it on each revolution (i.e., boost from a Roots blower is proportional to engine, and thus blower, RPM). The oil pump in most automotive engines works on exactly the same principle as the Roots blower.

Another type of positive displacement air pump that has been used for automotive supercharging is the vane type. There have been several variations on this design, but basically it consists of a cylindrical housing with a single cylindrical rotor that rotates on an offset axis. This rotor is slotted for any number of protruding vanes (usually two to four), which maintain light or near contact with the walls of the case at all times. Thus, as the rotor spins, the vanes sweep air into the pump through the inlet port, pushing it around between the rotor and the case. At the same time, as the offset rotor moves closer to the case while it spins, it compresses the air trapped between the vanes before pumping it out the outlet port. Several types of vane superchargers were made during the 1920s and 1930s, but they haven't been very common lately (the Judson and the Shorrock are two of the more recent, besides a Bendix blower that never reached production). The Wankel design is a variation on the vane type of pump.

Centrifugal Superchargers

The third common type of supercharger is known as the centrifugal blower. It moves air by means of a bladed fan that spins at high speed inside a spiral housing shaped sort of like a snail's shell. Air enters at the center of the fan (called an impeller), is picked up by the spinning blades, and is then rapidly accelerated by centrifugal force before being flung out the outlet port. The centrifugal supercharger is not a positive-displacement type; the delivery air volume increases as the square of the rotational speed of the impeller. Consequently, centrifugal superchargers must be turned at extremely high speeds to produce usable boost, and boost drops off significantly at lower engine speeds. Common centrifugal blowers were the types used on American high-performance cars of the 1920s and 1930s, such as the Duesenberg, Cord, and Graham. The McCulloch centrifugal blower, installed on Fords, Studebakers, and Packards of the mid 1950s, survives today as the Paxton supercharger. Other aftermarket centrifugal superchargers have been introduced by companies such as Vortech, ATI, and Powerdyne.

WHAT IS A TURBOCHARGER?

Of course, all of the common types of exhaust-driven turbochargers, which have received so much attention from racers and auto manufacturers, are centrifugal superchargers. The only difference is that they are operated by a turbine driven by the engine's exhaust, rather than by a belt connected to the engine's crankshaft. Besides that, the intake air moves through a turbocharger (and hence, boost is built) in the same manner as a centrifugal supercharger. Although we may make several comparisons between belt-driven superchargers and turbochargers later on, we'll provide some general guidance in the street use of turbos in this book. For more intense technical interests, the subject has been covered in detail elsewhere, and certainly it deserves separate study. However, I would point out that the intense recent interest in turbocharging has produced significant technical gains in that field, many of which have been and continue to be carried over into belt-driven supercharger technology.

Superchargers are relatively simple devices, to be sure, and we should keep

There are plenty of ways to blow or pump air. The lobster-like Latham axial-flow supercharger of the 1960s uses several sets of radial fans (much like a jet engine) to accelerate air/fuel mix into the manifold. This is a draw-through system, since the blower pulls air through the carbs.

The advent of electronic fuel injection (EFI) on new cars has created a whole new market for centrifugal superchargers, which employ a single, fan-like impeller inside a snail-like housing and are best suited to blow-through applications, where the supercharger blows dry air into the induction system. In moderate-boost EFI systems, the mass airflow sensor can read increased airflow and add proportional fuel. In high-boost applications, additional fuel flow, or even supplemental injectors, may be needed.

The only real problem with street super/turbocharging is that it's easy to get carried away. The temptation is always there to dial in a little more boost for more horsepower. This isn't what we'd call a street motor, but if it fits your definition, just be sure you have a strong bottom end for this level of excess.

them that way. Today's blower designs are still plenty short on efficiency (well, so are today's gasoline engines – that's nothing new). However, Detroit and Europe have been embracing positive displacement superchargers (Eaton and Lysholm designs) as a more practical and effective method of increasing overall power and efficiency – especially on smaller engines – in the street-driving RPM ranges. We're seeing some dramatic developments and refinements in the state of the art of supercharging – and we're here to take advantage of the new technology.

For ultimate power, you can't beat well-designed turbo motors. The Turbonetics-sponsored Celica piloted by Matt Scranton is fast and quick. The Pro RWD turbocharged Toyota has a best e.t. of 6.745 seconds with a best speed of 203.68 mph in NHRA competition.

When GMC blower rebuilders started making manifolds and drive kits with provisions for street accessories to fit a wide variety of engines, the street blower movement really took off. This is a lineup of Don Hampton 6-71s for Chevys, Fords, and Mopars.

Ford Racing Technology (FRT) unveiled the Focus FR200, a 304-horsepower, turbocharged version of the Ford Focus ZX3, at the 2000 SEMA show. Tom Kendall, four-time SCCA Trans-Am champion, right, and Dan Davis, director, Ford Racing Technology, drove the vehicle through a barrier at the debut. Kendall told the gathering, "This car drives like it is pissed off." (Joe Wilssens photo Courtesy of Ford)

Ford Europe built this World Rally Focus. The turbocharged engine develops incredible power. Notice how the air is ducted from a cold air source outside the engine bay to the inlet of the turbocharger. Even with the state-of-the-art supercharged/turbocharged engines, the colder and denser the air you start with, the cooler and denser the charge will be after being compressed. That means the engine can make more power.

Introduction to Superchargers and Turbochargers

This Street Glow Bullish Racing turbocharged Toyota Solara driven by George Loannou is a 200-mph drag racer. At the 2003 NOPI Nats, he ran a 6.810 @ 203.890 mph.

This turbocharged Mopar is an example of a full-race package that competes in Pro FWD drag-racing class. Driver Shaun Carlson and crew chief Rob Miller tuned their '03 Dodge SRT-4 to a best e.t. of 8.22 seconds with a best speed of 181.70 mph.

This is the Subaru 2004 WRX STi. Its turbocharged engine generates 300 horsepower — emissions legal — from 2.5 liters.

Vinny Ten drives this turbocharged Toyota Supra that has set the Modified e.t. record of 7.725 seconds, as well as the top speed of 178.45 mph in the NHRA sport-compact series. His best e.t. is 7.66 seconds, and his best speed is 177.18 mph.

Nelson Hoyos drives this 2.0-liter turbocharged, intercooled, Ecotec-powered Cavalier Pro FWD drag racer. This car has a best speed of 192.38 mph — the first FWD to go faster than 190 mph in the quarter mile.

Here's Lisa Kubo at the wheel of the Saturn Motorsports of San Diego Ion Coupe with a turbocharged 2.2-liter Ecotec engine. She has a best e.t. of 8.06 seconds and a best speed of 185.36 mph.

If you need proof of the soundness and reliability of the Eaton roots supercharger, all you have to do is check the latest factory supercharged engines. Factory supercharged engines have been developed to such an extent that they come with 100,000-mile warranties just like their naturally aspirated counterparts.

CHAPTER 2

SUPERCHARGING THEORY

THE IMPERFECT WORLD OF SUPERCHARGING AND TURBOCHARGING

One of the most basic tenets of the old-school hot rodder and today's tuner is a strong distrust, or downright disbelief, in theory as opposed to practical application. The modus operandi of hot-rod engineering is to look at what has worked the best in the past, figure out a few practical tricks to make it work a little better, and then bolt it on the car and give it a try. If it doesn't work better, you go back to what you know through experience will work.

Although the field of automotive performance modification is becoming more and more sophisticated these days, the ultimate test is what you can feel behind the wheel, or in what the time slip says at the drag strip. The manufacturers of speed parts these days rely on flow benches, dynamometers, and computers to design and test new products, but the average enthusiast – as well as most professional racers – still assert, "you can't drive a dyno."

Hot-rodders have known since the 1950s that superchargers work. You bolt one on an engine and it makes horsepower. Spin it faster, or bolt on a bigger one, and it'll make even more horsepower. Go too far and you'll blow head gaskets or melt pistons. Hot rodders have also learned that, although turbochargers make more peak horsepower than Roots blowers, they just don't deliver the same instant horsepower on the street.

Unfortunately, this mindset among hot rodders and the new generation of tuners can be both commendable and misleading. The new breed of tuners, like their hot-rodding predecessors, has done things with cars and engines that have left the theoretical engineers flabbergasted. These enthusiasts have often succeeded where a highly educated designer would never have attempted a project, just because they didn't know that it wasn't supposed to work. If a perpetual-motion machine or a perfectly efficient internal combustion engine could be built, it would be a dedicated gearhead that would figure out how through sheer perseverance and enthusiasm.

However, the harsh reality is that a perpetual-motion machine will remain an impossibility, and even the best internal combustion engine will be far from perfect. The laws of conservation of matter and energy are true: you cannot get more out of a system than you put into it. Second, and more important, a law called entropy applies: you can never even get as much out of a system as you put into it when you are converting matter to energy and energy to work as you are in an engine.

This is all very pertinent to supercharging, because a blower can increase the volumetric efficiency of an engine above 100 percent. And although a belt-driven blower uses up a certain percentage of the engine's horsepower in order to run, it produces much more power in the engine than it takes. These facts can fool us into thinking that a supercharger is some magical apparatus that can defy the laws of physics – but it can't.

The reason why a blower seems to work miracles on an internal combustion engine is that the engine is so inefficient to begin with. A good gasoline engine is lucky if it can convert 30 percent of the energy contained in the fuel into actual work. The addition of a supercharger, in most cases, actually lowers this figure (because it requires a greater percentage of fuel to make more power in the motor... we'll explain in a moment). And as I pointed out earlier, superchargers are similar to internal combustion engines in that they are both types of air pumps. All superchargers are themselves far from 100 percent efficient in terms of the amount of energy they consume compared to the amount of air they pump, and in terms of the mass (weight) of air they pump compared to the size of the blower and the volume of air it displaces.

We won't be able to fully explore the intricacies of supercharger design and efficiency here. In fact, a surprising-

Supercharging Theory

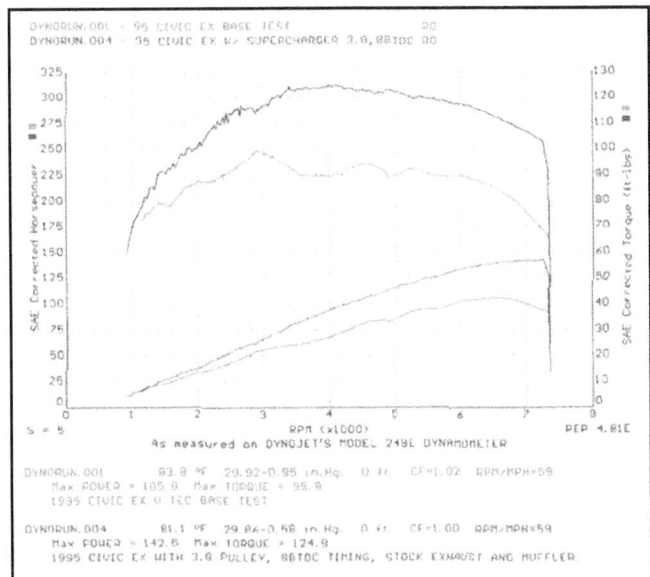

This dyno chart from Jackson Racing compares a '95 Honda Civic EX's power output before and after the installation of one of its superchargers. It shows just how effective supercharging really is.

ly small amount of research has actually been compiled on superchargers, especially Roots blowers, and the handful of existing books and the several engineers I consulted during this project either had few answers or openly contradicted each other. What I want to do in this chapter is give you just enough engineering background to understand what blowers can do and what they can't. I want to dispel some myths about superchargers, and to give you a more solid basis from which to choose the type of blower system that will be best for your vehicle and the way you drive it.

Density, Volume, and Pressure

Myth number one is that a blower's primary function is to increase the volume or the pressure of the air in the intake system of the engine. The real purpose of the supercharger is to increase the density of that air.

Density is the mass, or weight, of a substance in a given volume. For most solids and liquids, weight is nearly proportional to volume – increase the volume, and you increase the weight a proportional amount. In other words, the density of a given solid or liquid does not change very much under normal conditions. Consequently, we tend to think of an increase in volume of a substance as an increase in the amount (mass) of that substance.

However, such thinking is not correct, and it certainly does not apply to gases. The density of a gas such as air changes considerably as its temperature or pressure changes. Increase the temperature and the density of the gas decreases (if it's not in a closed container), because the gas expands. Increase the pressure, and the density will usually increase because a greater amount (mass) of the gas will be compressed into a smaller space (volume). I say "usually" because we are dealing with more than one variable at the same time when we are dealing with the state of a gas. If a gas is both compressed (which should increase its density) and heated (which should decrease its density) concurrently, the net result could be an increase, a decrease, or no change at all in the density of the gas.

These facts are extremely important to an understanding of supercharging, because a supercharger does in fact both compress and heat the air entering the engine, in addition to increasing the mass of air passing through the intake system.

The Gas Law

Before we go any further, let's take a quick look at the basic law that describes the relationship between the pressure, volume, weight, and temperature of a gas. Known as the Ideal Gas Equation, or just the Gas Law, it is usually stated by the equation:

$$PV = nRT$$

In this formula "P" is pressure, "V" is volume, "n" is the weight of the gas in moles, "R" is a constant (called the Molar Gas Constant, which has different values depending on the units used for the other quantities), and "T" is the temperature. It isn't within the scope of this book to fully explore how this equation can be used, or how gases act in general. What this equation should immediately show you, assuming you have a basic familiarity with algebra, is the relationship between the pressure, volume, temperature, and weight of a given gas.

If we're discussing a given amount of gas, in moles (that is, a certain weight of the gas, or a certain number of molecules of the gas), then both n and R in the Gas Law would be constant, and we could write the equation thus:

$$\frac{PV}{T} = \text{Constant}$$

What this tells us is that for a given amount (weight) of gas, increasing the pressure and keeping the volume the same will increase the temperature proportionally; increasing the temperature and keeping the volume the same will increase the pressure proportionally; increasing the volume and keeping the pressure the same increases the temperature, and so on.

In relation to supercharging, the significant things the Gas Law tells us is that increasing the pressure increases the temperature, and vice versa. It also shows us that a temperature rise at a given pressure will increase the volume, which means a decrease in density; and that both the pressure and the temperature could be increased without increasing the density.

The Problem of Heat

The thorn of supercharging is heat. Heat is a very common and easily manifested form of energy – a very easily wasted form of energy – that is a typical byproduct of work being done. In supercharging, heat is a multiple detriment. In the first place, the act of compressing air

Chapter 2

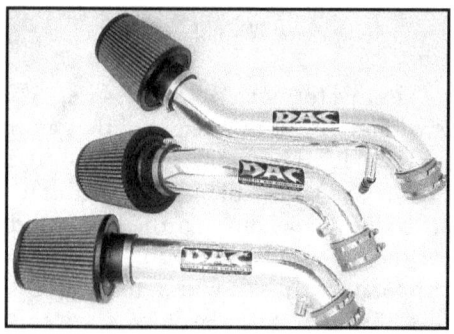

If the inlet on your blower draws air from inside a closed engine compartment, it can be drawing excessively heated — that is, less dense — air into the blower, which counteracts the supercharger's purpose (to make the air denser). The supercharger can only work with what you give it. Hypothetically, if you start with air at 180° Fahrenheit and the supercharger adds 100 degrees as it compresses the air, you'll get 280-degree charge air. If you started instead with 60-degree air, you'll get 160-degree charge air. The same relationship holds true for intercoolers; i.e., they only reduce temperatures a specific amount, so any way you look at it, starting with cool, dense air will offer the potential to make more power.

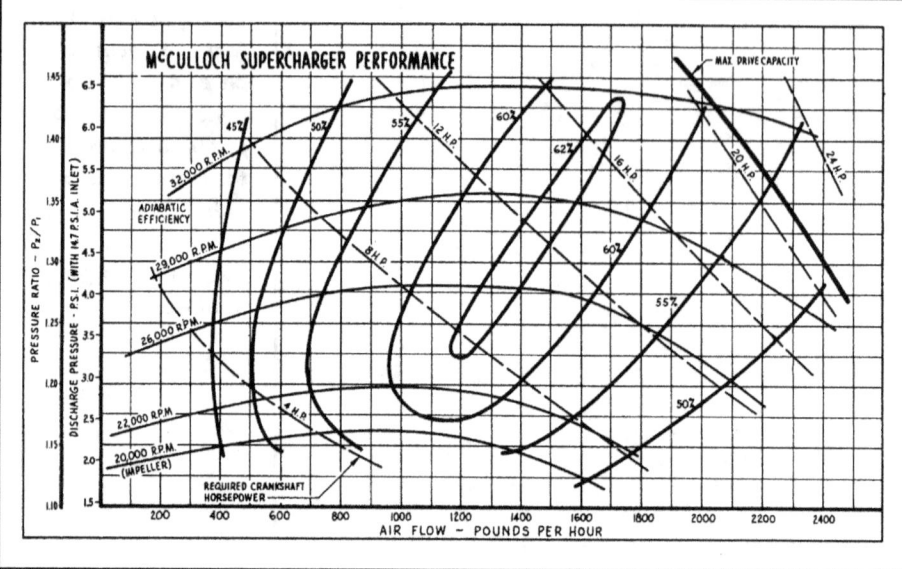

This compressor flow map for a Paxton/McCullough centrifugal supercharger shows adiabatic efficiency and horsepower required to drive the blower (mechanical efficiency). The ring near the center of the map — known as an "island" — indicates the range of this blower's maximum adiabatic efficiency; in this case, it's 62 percent.

heats it, as we saw above. Second, much of the engine horsepower used to turn the supercharger and compress the air eventually is converted to more heat, which is transferred to the air. Most blowers, especially Roots types, literally beat the air, which heats it considerably. In addition, friction between the air and stationary and moving surfaces, as well as the friction of air turbulence, all combine to heat the air further. The heat tends to expand the air (increase its volume), which raises the pressure, but does not increase the density.

To give you a practical example of what could be taking place in a supercharger, imagine a closed box full of air at room temperature and atmospheric pressure. Let's say the box measures one foot per side, so that its volume is one cubic foot. The volume of air in the box, one cubic foot, cannot change, since no air can get in or out. Likewise, the density of that air – the amount of weight of air, or the number of molecules of air, per cubic foot – cannot change. If we insert a pressure gauge through one of the walls of the box, it will read zero psi, since both the pressure and the temperature inside the box are the same as that outside. Most pressure gauges read in pounds per square inch above atmospheric. Thus, a 5-psi gauge reading is actually approximately 19.7 psi absolute, since atmospheric pressure is about 14.7 psi at sea level.

Now let's take our box of air and put it on the stove. As the air inside is heated it tries to expand, but it cannot because it is contained by the box. The result? The pressure increases. We'll actually see "boost" on the pressure gauge, even though the air isn't being compressed, and the density remains exactly the same. In other words, we see a boost reading on the gauge even though the amount of air in the box has not increased at all. The same thing can happen, in extreme cases, in the manifold of a supercharged engine. If a blower heats the air drastically, instead of pumping it efficiently, it could show a boost reading on the gauge – simply by expanding the air, without causing any increase in the volumetric efficiency – or power – of the engine.

To see how this could happen, we can use the Gas Law in its simplified form:

$$\frac{P_1 V_1}{T_1} = \frac{P_2 V_2}{T_2} = \text{Constant}$$

Knowing that the volume is constant in both cases, we can figure the pressure rise by using the proportion:

$$\frac{P_1}{T_1} = \frac{P_2}{T_2}$$

In this formula, the temperature must be figured in degrees Rankine (absolute temperature, which equals degrees Fahrenheit plus 460), and pressure in psi absolute. Using this simple equation, we find that if our box of air starts out at typical atmospheric temperature and pressure of 60° F and 0 psi (520R and 14.7 psi) and is then heated to 240° F, we will see a boost reading on the pressure gauge of 5.1 psi. Remember, we have neither compressed the air nor increased its density – we have simply heated it – and we have five pounds of boost on our gauge!

Now, although a blower manifold is not a closed box, nor is real air an ideal gas, the above example still gives a good approximation of what could happen in a supercharged engine. If you were getting a 200° F temperature rise in the manifold at 5 pounds of boost, your supercharger would be giving you no increase in charge density at all. Further, it would be robbing your engine of horsepower at the same time, since increasing intake temperature increases the likelihood of detonation. Most superchargers work considerably better than this example, but all sacrifice a good percentage of their potential benefit to heat.

BLOWER EFFICIENCY

Since machines such as engines and superchargers do not operate perfectly in the real world, we use the term efficiency to compare how well they do work to how well they theoretically could work in a world where perfection is possible. Blower manufacturers and blower salesmen often refer to a single "blower efficiency" figure, but this is very misleading. Like the internal combustion engine, which can be measured for volumetric, thermal, mechanical, and other efficiency ratings, the supercharger likewise must be examined for efficiency in terms of different functions.

Although the adiabatic, volumetric, and mechanical efficiency ratings of a supercharger influence one another to some degree, it isn't really practical to try to lump them all together into one comprehensive blower efficiency figure. One big problem is that the mechanical and volumetric efficiencies of a supercharger operating on a real engine are very difficult to measure practically or accurately. Consequently, and because it's the figure that has the greatest bearing on supercharger performance, the efficiency figure given for blowers is usually the adiabatic efficiency, which can be readily calculated. However, if someone gives you a blower efficiency figure for a given supercharger, you should always ask what sort of efficiency was measured and how the figure was determined.

Adiabatic Efficiency

If you are not familiar with thermodynamics, the term adiabatic efficiency may sound scary or complicated, but it's really quite simple. The problem is that many blower "experts" have used the term without fully understanding its meaning or its computation, and they have, therefore, spread some confusion about adiabatic blower efficiency. To the non-theoretical blower builder or user, the adiabatic efficiency of a blower is a measure of how much it heats the air that it's pumping. The less it heats the air, the more efficient it is.

As we have seen above, and will discuss further in a moment, the amount a blower heats the air charge has a large negative effect on the amount of power it'll produce in the engine. In addition, it's a good indicator of how well the blower is doing the job of pumping (that is, it reflects mechanical and volumetric efficiency losses), since extraneous work done on the air by the blower will be converted to heat.

The temperature rise across the blower (the difference between inlet air temperature and outlet, or manifold, air temperature) is easy to measure. Consequently, it's easy to compare the temperature rise with one blower at a given boost pressure on a given engine to that of a different blower at the same boost on the same engine. Such a comparison will certainly give us an approximation of the relative adiabatic efficiencies of the two blowers, but it won't give us a correct percentage figure.

One recent book on superchargers states that a blower that draws in air at 70° F, compresses it to 1.5 atmospheres (about seven pounds of boost), and discharges it at a temperature of 70° F would have 100 percent adiabatic efficiency. As we saw from the Gas Law, this is impossible unless we incorporate some very effective cooling device into the supercharger. The very act of compressing air heats it because we must do work on that air to compress it, and the air absorbs the energy of that work as heat.

If we could compress a gas by some physical means without adding any more heat to it than the heat generated by the act of compression, and we didn't let any of that heat escape, we would have perfect adiabatic compression, or 100 percent adiabatic efficiency. The term adiabatic simply means a thermodynamic process in which no heat is gained from, or lost to, sources outside the system. Although perfect adiabatic compression is impossible in the real world, we can calculate the heat of perfect adiabatic compression by the following formula:

$$T_2 = T_1 (P_2/P_1)^{.283}$$

In this formula, "T_1" is the inlet (or ambient) air temperature, "P_1" is the ambient air pressure, "P_2" is the outlet (or manifold) pressure, and "T_2" is the new temperature to which the act of compression will raise that air. Temperature is figured in degrees Rankine, and pressures are absolute. To get T_2 in degrees Fahrenheit, just subtract 460.

Raising a number to the .283rd power is a bit difficult, but the pressure ratio of (P_2/P_1), raised to this power, can be quickly figured from "Y-tables" for air in some thermo-dynamic textbooks or handbooks. Once you have figured the ratio of P_2/P_1, the Y-table will give you a value of Y for this amount. For instance, if P_2/P_1 is 1.5, or about 7.4 pounds boost, the value of Y is 0.12159. Then, using the simpler formula, you can figure the ideal temperature increase in degrees Fahrenheit for a compressor at 100 percent adiabatic efficiency.

$$T \text{ (ideal)} = T_1 \times Y$$

To show how the equation works, let's say that the ambient air temperature is 68° F; this is the blower inlet temperature, or T_1, which converts to 528° R. Ambient air pressure, P_1, is one atmosphere, or 14.7 psi absolute. Let's say that the blower is making 7.4 pounds boost in the manifold, so P_2 is 22.1 psi absolute. If our blower were a perfect compressor, the formula shows us that it would heat the air 63.36° F, or raise it to a T_2 of 131.36° F. If we raise blower boost to 14.7 psi (29.4 psi), T_2 would go up to 182.42° F. This would be the temperature rise in the manifold if the blower had 100 percent adiabatic efficiency. But, of course, no supercharger can have 100 percent adiabatic efficiency, because several other factors in a real mechanical pump contribute to

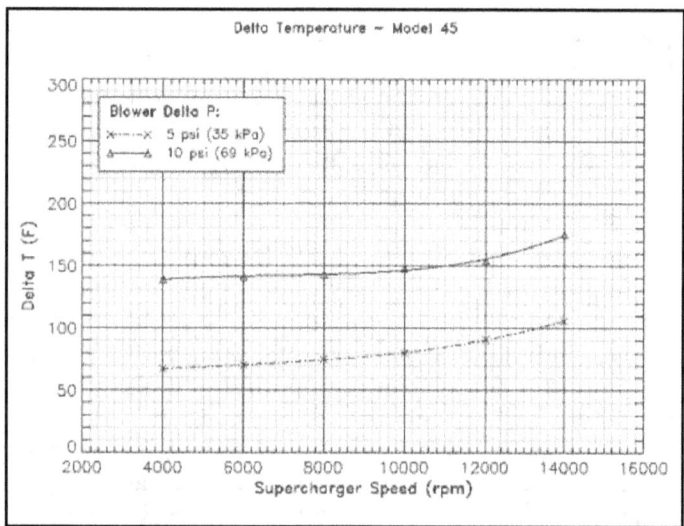
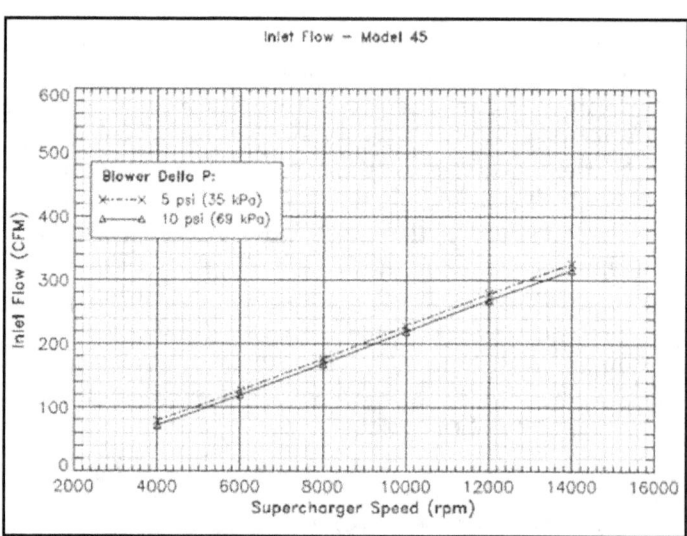
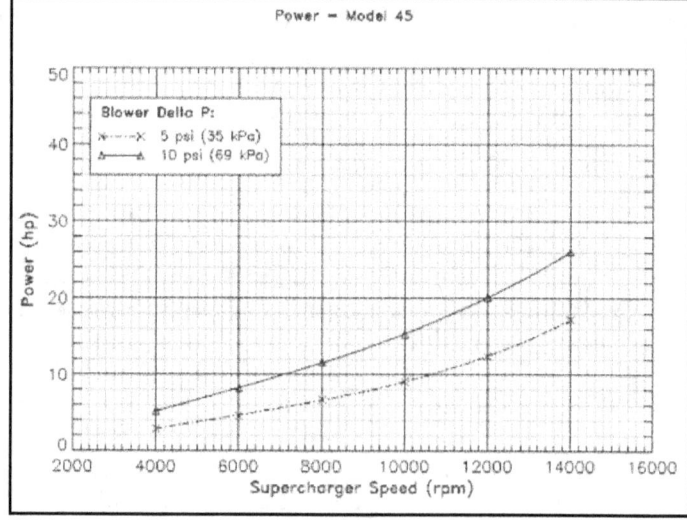

These three graphs plot airflow in cfm, temperature rise, and power required to drive a modern Eaton Roots-type blower. We don't know exactly how the tests were conducted or how the measurements were taken, but somehow blower outlet pressure was maintained at constant readings of both 5 psi and 10 psi throughout a wide RPM range. In actual use on an engine, most blowers will increase boost with increasing RPM. However, the general shape of these curves is indicative of typical supercharger performance. And it is particularly interesting to note the diminishing return in terms of airflow between a blower operating at 5 pounds boost and one at 10 pounds.

heating the air: friction of air against blower parts, friction of air against air, friction of mechanical parts, air leakage, and so on.

To figure the adiabatic efficiency of a given supercharger, use the equation:

$$\text{Adiabatic Efficiency} = \frac{(T2-T1)\ \text{Ideal}}{(T2-T1)\ \text{Actual}}$$

This is the ratio of the perfect (adiabatic) temperature increase figured from the previous equation, to the actual temperature increase observed across the supercharger. For instance, if we use the example above of the blower making 7.4 pounds boost with an inlet air temperature of 68° F, the ideal heat rise (T2 - T1) ideal, or the heat rise at 100 percent adiabatic efficiency, should be approximately 63° F. Let's say that the actual temperature in the manifold is 194° F. This would give us a (T2 - T1) actual of (194 - 68) or 126 degrees. Our adiabatic efficiency ratio would therefore be 63/126 or .50. Expressed in percentage, the adiabatic efficiency of this supercharger would be 50 percent. Given the same inlet temperature and manifold pressure, if the actual manifold temperature were 152° F, the blower's adiabatic efficiency would be 75 percent.

Hardly any superchargers have an adiabatic efficiency of 75 percent. In fact, most Roots-type blowers are doing well if they reach 50 percent adiabatic efficiency.

Mechanical Efficiency

In this section of the book we are dealing specifically with superchargers that are driven mechanically by the engine, as opposed to turbochargers that are driven by exhaust heat (which is engine energy normally wasted), or even superchargers driven by some other remote energy source (such as an electric motor – these have actually been advertised since the 1950s!). Consequently, all of the blowers we'll be discussing consume a certain percentage of the engine's power in order to make more power. If superchargers didn't make a lot more power than they consumed, we wouldn't use them; but you might be surprised to find out how much horsepower it takes to turn a big V-8 style 6-71 GMC blower making 15 to 20 pounds of boost.

The mechanical efficiency of a supercharger is a measure of the amount of engine horsepower the blower actually consumes to produce a certain amount of boost at a given speed, compared to the amount of power it would take to compress air at the same rate under ideal conditions.

From readily available thermodynamics equations, we could calculate the amount of horsepower it would take to turn a supercharger of a given displacement, at a certain RPM, to make a certain amount of boost under ideal conditions – that is, without any mechanical losses due to friction, turbulence, leakage, or other real-world conditions. The ratio of this figure to the actual horsepower a real supercharger consumes to produce the same amount of boost would give us the mechanical efficiency percentage of the supercharger.

However, a practical and reliable method for measuring the actual horsepower drag of a blower on a real running engine would be very difficult to devise. Since most of the mechanical losses in the blower show up in the form of heat, we could figure an approximation of the mechanical inefficiency of a blower by converting the measurable extra heat energy gain (above 100 percent adiabatic efficiency) into work energy units (horsepower). However, this would still be a rough approximation involving too many variables – and it shows that the adiabatic efficiency figure, which is easier to calculate, is more meaningful; doubly so, since it partially reflects mechanical efficiency as well. So we won't delve into the formulas for figuring mechanical blower efficiency here.

Volumetric Efficiency

A third measurement of blower performance, at least in positive displacement blowers, is volumetric efficiency. Blower volumetric efficiency is very similar to engine volumetric efficiency (remember, both engines and blowers are air pumps), and it's actually measured the same way. Specifically, the volumetric efficiency of a supercharger is the ratio of the actual volume of air it pumps per revolution, compared to its internal displacement per revolution.

In my opinion, supercharger volumetric efficiency is perhaps the least understood, or just the most difficult to pin down, of blower ratings. In the first place, the internal capacity of a positive-displacement blower, such as a Roots, is easy to calculate, since there is a measurable swept volume per revolution. In a Roots-type it's the volume contained between two rotor lobes and the case, times the number of lobes that "circulate" in one revolution. However, the static internal volume of non-positive displacement blowers such as centrifugal or axial flow types is nearly impossible to figure, especially for deriving a volumetric efficiency number.

For the sake of measurability, supercharger testers figure blower VE as the ratio of air volume drawn into the blower to blower displacement, rather than trying to measure the actual pumping volume on the outlet side. The volume of air being drawn into the blower inlet can be measured in cubic feet per minute with a manometer-type airflow gauge as used to measure air-flow through throttle bodies and mass-airflow meters.

Whether we measured the air going into the blower, or the air coming out, either way we could get figures to compare the pumping efficiency of a given blower under varying conditions, or of different blowers under the same conditions. But trying to determine a numerical volumetric efficiency for any one supercharger, especially compared to other types of superchargers, is difficult and usually misleading.

The problem is, once again, that we have several variables operating at the same time. Most textbooks, and some engineers involved with superchargers, contend that the volumetric efficiency of a Roots-type blower increases with its rotational speed. They base this assertion on the observation that air leakage around the rotors is the primary volumetric loss in the supercharger. Since the amount of air that can leak past clearances around the rotors is a function of time (it takes a certain amount of time for the air to leak through the clearances), the faster the rotors turn, the less leakage occurs per revolution. Consequently, the higher the blower RPM, the higher the volumetric efficiency.

On the other hand, with any type of supercharger, but especially with a Roots or other back-flow compressor, as manifold pressure increases with blower speed, volumetric efficiency will decrease because of backpressure, which causes increased leakage.

Since superchargers are air pumps similar to internal-combustion engines, it stands to reason that blowers would suffer the same volumetric deficiencies as engines. That is, any blower has a given size intake port and what we might call cylinders, or air pumping cavities. Although we have the supercharger to force-feed air to the engine, we still have only atmospheric pressure to feed air into the blower. As the rotors in a Roots blower, for instance, turn past the inlet port opening, there is only a given amount of time for the atmosphere to push air into the rotor cavity before it closes (turns past the opening to seal against the case). The faster the rotors turn, the less time they'll have to fill completely with air, and the lower the blower's volumetric efficiency will be.

The goal is to determine accurately, under actual operating conditions, which of the several factors affecting blower volumetric efficiency is predominant, or how they combine for a net VE under various conditions.

This is more important than it might seem at first. At least one new Roots-type blower has been designed primarily around the assumption that volumetric efficiency is the major design criterion, and that blower VE is predominantly a function of air leakage around rotor clearances – at least in street boost ranges up to 10 psi. Given this assumption, the conclusion is that as small a blower as possible should be used on an engine for two reasons: (1) because you want the blower to run as fast as possible to make a given boost (in this case, it's designed to be driven nearly twice as fast as the engine), and (2) since air leakage is not only a function of time, but also of total clearance surface area. Making the blower smaller, or just making the rotors shorter, will reduce the size of the air leakage path and therefore improve volumetric efficiency.

There is certainly logic behind this thinking; however, I think it fails to take into consideration enough of the vari-

Chapter 2

As we saw, performance auto designers were quick to learn the effectiveness of cooling the outlet charge of the supercharger, as evidenced by all the convection fins on early blowers and manifolds.

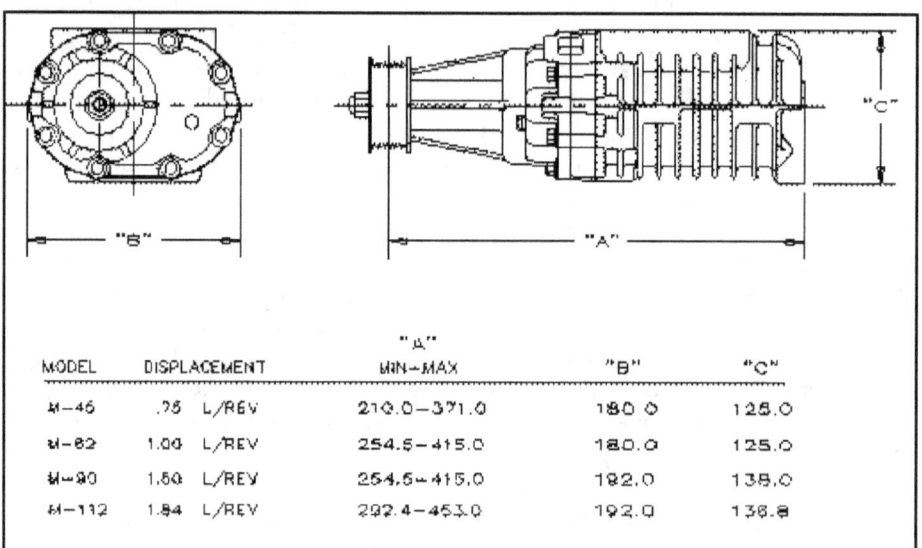

MODEL	DISPLACEMENT	"A" MIN–MAX	"B"	"C"
M-46	.75 L/REV	210.0–371.0	180.0	125.0
M-62	1.00 L/REV	254.5–415.0	180.0	125.0
M-90	1.50 L/REV	254.5–415.0	182.0	138.0
M-112	1.84 L/REV	292.4–453.0	192.0	138.8

What size blower do you use on what size engine? The question has more ramifications than are immediately apparent, but for positive-displacement blowers, the basic answer is logical — match blower displacement to engine displacement.

ables determining overall blower efficiency to make it the primary factor in sizing a blower and determining its overdrive ratio. There are logical reasons for stating that a larger blower, turned at a slower speed, with tighter rotor clearances, would be the better choice. The slower blower RPM would allow setting the rotor clearances closer, since there would be less rotor growth and, in GMCs, less rotor "untwist." If the blower turned more slowly relative to engine speed to make the same boost, it would be beating the air less, or doing less extraneous work on it, which would heat the air less (that is, raise the adiabatic efficiency). This is not only desirable in itself, but it would also heat the blower parts less, reducing expansion and allowing tighter clearances for better VE. Further, although tighter clearances will slightly increase the power needed to turn the blower, a longer blower turned at slower speed will produce more boost with the same, or less, drag from gears, pulleys, belt, and so on.

The purpose of the above illustration is two-fold. First, it demonstrates that the science of blower technology requires a close examination and evaluation of many variables before accurate assumptions can be made. Worse, because so many variables are involved, it's often difficult to determine exactly what change – or what side effect of a change – led to an observed increase or decrease in blower performance. Second, it indicates that a good formula or rule of thumb for choosing the proper-size supercharger for a given engine will be impossible to give.

I was hoping that I would be able to discover or devise some sort of table or equation that would immediately tell you how large the optimum blower should be for a given displacement engine. But once again, a broad array of variables has thwarted us. In a practical sense, the sizing of a supercharger to an engine is not as critical as one might think – certainly not as critical as the sizing of a turbocharger. For one thing, the mechanical drive of the blower can be stepped up or down easily to help regulate the output to the engine's needs. The sizing of a centrifugal supercharger is a bit more complicated because it involves different impeller designs in a given case, as well as different-sized cases and drive ratios. The correct sizing of a centrifugal blower to a given engine is more critical because boost increase is not linear with blower speed. Put too "big" a centrifugal blower on an engine, or drive it too fast, and you can get into parts-breakage boost in a hurry. However, the current supercharger manufacturers – centrifugal or positive displacement – have tested their units and designed kits for specific installations. They can usually tell you which blower will make what amount of boost, at what RPM, on a given engine.

The Air-Density Ratio

The biggest problem with using blower volumetric efficiency as a guide in designing or sizing a supercharger is the same problem we described earlier about confusing air volume with air density. Even if we could accurately measure the volume of air being pumped out of the blower, this isn't really an accurate measure of the increase in air the blower is supplying to the motor. Why? Because, as we saw earlier, air is elastic – differences in temperature or pressure will change the volume of a given amount of air; and this is exactly what happens on the outlet side of a supercharger.

It is not an increase in volume, but an increase in density of intake air, that increases power in an engine. We want to pack more molecules of air into the cylinders so that (1) we'll have more molecules of oxygen to combine with more molecules of fuel (to burn); and (2) we will have more molecules of matter per volume in the cylinder to expand and exert pressure on the piston after combustion. We measure the number of molecules of a gas in a given volume by the weight of the gas per volume, and this is called the density.

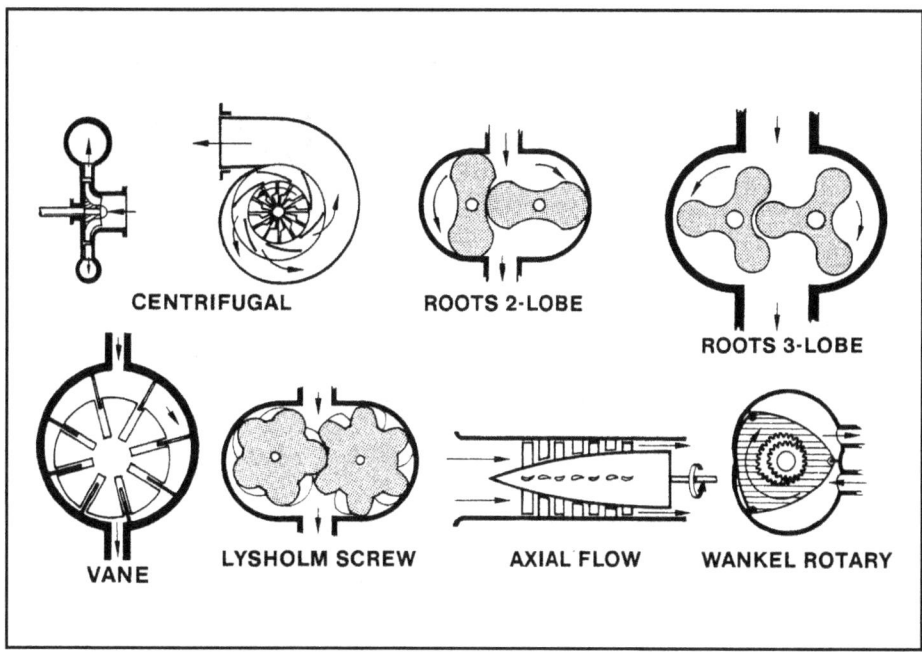

This line drawing illustrates the seven fundamental types of superchargers used for automotive supercharging.

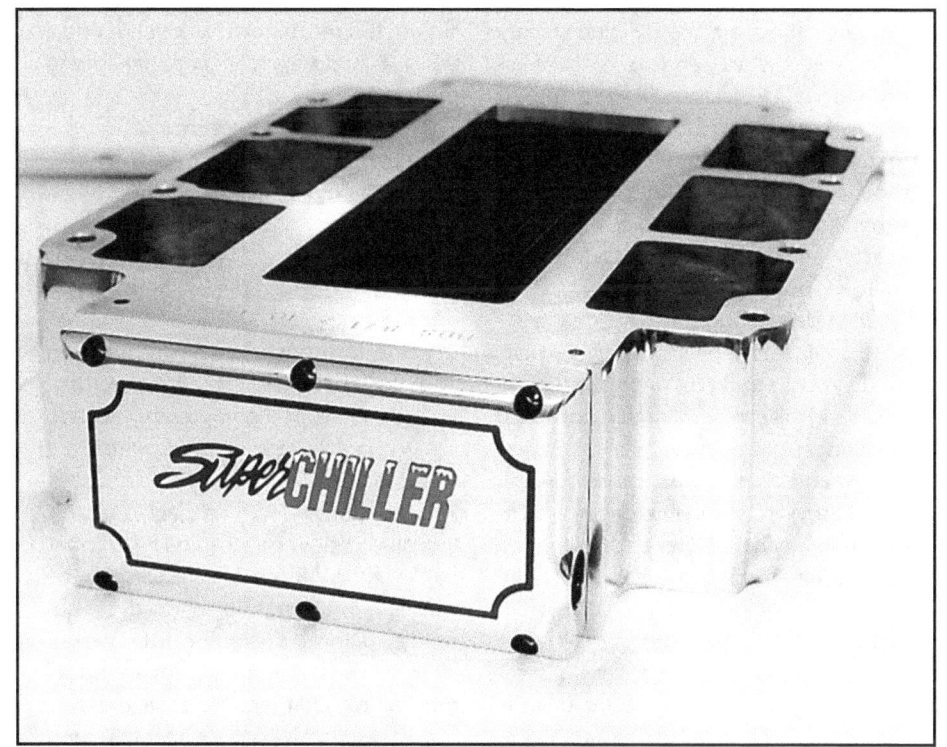

The SuperChiller is a water-to-air intercooler that bolts between a Roots-type blower and intake manifold. This type of intercooler requires a constant source of cold water to be pumped through its heat exchanger to effectively cool the compressed air/fuel mixture. If you have the room and the ability to fabricate, it should be reasonably easy to apply this tactic to a street setup. Vortech aftercooler systems have a water reservoir and separate water-to-air radiator, but they are used with centrifugal blowers. Spearco and Turbonetics are a good source of intercooler cores and advice on sizing and fabrication.

As we saw from the Gas Law, the density of a gas depends on both its pressure and its temperature. Since these are quantities we can readily measure for the intake charge, we can figure the actual air density increase being produced by the supercharger in the intake manifold. Although the air-density ratio is a term not often mentioned in relation to superchargers, I feel it is a much more meaningful (not to mention more easily calculated) measurement than the blower's adiabatic or volumetric efficiency. The formula for calculating the air density ratio is shown below. If we use the previous example of a supercharged engine operating at an ambient temperature of 68° F and standard atmospheric pressure (14.7 psi absolute), making 7.4 pounds of boost in the manifold, and recording a temperature in the manifold of 131° F, we can plug in these figures and find the density ratio:

$$\text{Density Ratio} = \frac{\text{inlet temp R}}{\text{outlet temp R}} \times \frac{\text{outlet pressure absolute}}{\text{inlet pressure absolute}}$$

$$\text{Density Ratio} = \frac{68 + 460}{131 + 460} \times \frac{7.4 + 14.7}{14.7}$$

$$\text{Density Ratio} = \frac{528}{591} \times \frac{22.1}{14.7}$$

$$\text{Density Ratio} = .8934 \times 1.5 = 1.34$$

The air density ratio measured across the supercharger for this engine is 1.34 to 1, or a 34-percent increase. The beauty of this equation is that it takes into consideration most of the real factors operating on the intake charge, such as the cooling effect of evaporating fuel in the air.

You can figure the air density ratio in your engine easily by installing a manifold boost pressure gauge and a manifold air temperature gauge in your car. No supercharged vehicle should be without these two instruments. These measurements are also available from your car's engine management system, so with the proper scan tools, you can check these parameters as well. To get accurate calculations, you should also know the ambient air temperature and pressure, for which you would need a thermometer and a barometer (if the blower intake is not routed to fresh air, you need to know the actual underhood temperature, but you should be drawing in fresh air to the blower). For rough calculations, you could certainly approximate outdoor temperature and figure ambient pressure at 14.5 to 14.7 psia.

Since engine power is roughly proportional to intake air density, the blower air density ratio will tell you how much increase in horsepower the supercharger is providing, minus the horsepower consumed by the blower to operate. For instance, if the engine above made 200 hp while unblown, the blower would increase horsepower 34 percent to 268 hp, minus, let's say 15 hp, to run the blower. This makes for a net horsepower

'03 Mercedes-Benz SLR McLaren

You can learn a lot about the proper way to build a boosted machine from this state-of-the-art supercharged supercar from Mercedes-Benz.

An abundance of power and high-tech features – these are the defining characteristics of the V-8 engine in the Mercedes-Benz SLR McLaren. Okay, so this isn't exactly a sport compact, but hey, you have to dream, don't you? Plus, let's face it: though there are many aftermarket supercharger kits available, there isn't exactly an abundance of OEM-supercharged sport compacts.

When developing the powerplant, the AMG engineers applied both the expertise they had acquired during their three-decade involvement in motorsports and the stringent standards of the Mercedes-Benz brand. After an extensive concept phase, they decided in favor of an 8-cylinder design with a 5.5-liter displacement, a cylinder angle of 90 degrees, a Lysholm screw-type compressor, and a crankshaft supported by five bearings.

The result is impressive: from a mere 1,500 rpm, the SLR powerplant delivers torque of over 440 ft-lbs, rising to 515 ft-lbs at 2,000 rpm. The maximum of 575 ft-lbs is available from 3,250 to 5,000 rpm. The supreme torque curve is coupled with the agile response of a sporty engine that never denies its high-performance character. Figures such as 626 hp at 6,500 rpm – an extraordinarily high engine speed for this displacement size – speak a powerful language.

As the figures indicate, the new SLR is endowed with what is currently one of the most powerful engines to be found in a series-produced road-going sports car.

An overview of the key data:
- Cylinder Arrangement: V-8
- Valves per Cylinder: 3
- Displacement: 5.439 liters (332 cubic inches)
- Bore/Stroke: 97/92 mm (3.82/3.62 inches)
- Cylinder Spacing: 106 mm (4.17 inches)
- Compression Ratio: 8.8:1
- Horsepower: 626 @ 6,500 rpm
- Torque: 575 ft-lbs from 3,250-5,000 rpm
- Engine Weight: 511 pounds

With this much power under the hood, the SLR's performance figures are among the best in its class:

0-62 mph:	3.8 seconds
0-124 mph:	10.6 seconds
0-186 mph:	28.8 seconds
Top Speed:	207.54 mph

Power from the Screw-Type Compressor

Since this book is about boosting engines, let's talk about the supercharger. The mechanical compressor has two screw-type aluminum rotors, which are Teflon-coated to reduce friction losses. The charger is so compact that it's installed between the two cylinder banks of the V-8 powerplant. Despite the space-saving design, its innovative technology allows a significantly higher charge pressure than conventional mechanical chargers because the two rotors achieve a top speed of around 23,000 rpm, making 0.9 bar (13.05 psi) of boost. This means the blower compresses around 30 percent more air than the figure achieved by other systems.

In order to ensure the greatest possible efficiency, the AMG engineers created an intelligent engine management system to regulate the operation of the

'03 Mercedes-Benz SLR McLaren
(continued)

The Lysholm-supercharged AMG V-8 engine is celebrating a crushing victory in the International Engine of the Year Awards after gaining a clear majority of votes from the 50-member jury in the newly created Best Performance Engine category. This conclusive result is in the face of competition from its rivals in Europe, Japan, and the USA.

screw-type compressor according to the engine speed and load. This means that the charger is only active when it is needed, but the system ensures that the maximum output is available as soon as the driver steps on the gas. When this occurs, the electronics of the engine management system trigger an electromagnetic coupling that immediately activates the compressor, which is powered by a separate poly V belt. Because the charger delivers its output in fractions of a second, even the most perceptive driver will not notice the phases without charger support. The charger system's air recirculating flap, opened under partial load, helps reduce fuel consumption.

Air-Charge Coolers

In addition to the compressor, the electronics also ensure optimum control of the water circuit for the air-charge cooling system, as efficient air-charge cooling is essential where high output is concerned.

In the Mercedes-Benz SLR McLaren's V-8 engine, two separate charge-air coolers are responsible for this key task – one per cylinder bank.

The highly effective air-charge coolers operate along the lines of an air/water heat exchanger (intercooler): The air, compressed and hence warmed by the compressor, is cooled via a separate water circuit, making the process independent of the temperature outside. This means that the engine can deliver its maximum output and torque at any time.

The high-performance figures of the engine, however, not only demand good cooling of the combustion air, but also require greater engine cooling. The engineers met this need by incorporating generous cool-air inlets and outlets and a powerful 850-watt suction-type fan.

High-Pressure In-Tank Pumps

The SLR's high-performance engine draws its fuel from two interconnected aluminum tanks. They're installed at a relatively low level to keep the center of gravity as low as possible to further enhance dynamic handling. The tanks, which have an overall capacity of 25.8 gallons (including a 3.2-gallon reserve), are equipped with two integral high-pressure fuel pumps. These are controlled by the engine management system to ensure that the fuel supply matches the engine speed and load. It's interesting to note that one pump operates constantly, while the second is only activated as required. At high output, they can pump a combined total of up to 310 liters of fuel an hour (81.9 gallons per hour).

The reason for this technical look at the SLR is to offer you a model on which to judge your combination. This is the cutting edge of reliable high-performance automotive technology. The combination of components is carefully chosen and designed to increase power output from the engine reliably over many years of service.

of 253, or a net power gain of 26.5 percent. These figures were not taken from any real engine, remember; they're simply examples to show how the calculations work. On the other hand, they're not very far off from typical street-blown engines. The point is, although anybody can tell you a blower will double or triple your horsepower, you don't know what it's really doing unless you put the engine on a dyno – or much more simply – install boost and temp gauges and figure the above calculations.

THE LIMITS OF SUPERCHARGING

What the blower density ratio tells us is that you can pump more horsepower into your engine in direct proportion to the increased air/fuel charge you pump into it. That's the undeniable beauty of supercharging – it overcomes the natural limits imposed by a naturally aspirated engine's volumetric efficiency. But there are obviously limits to the amount of power we can pump into a motor with a blower.

There are three basic limits to supercharging. First is the point of diminishing returns of the blower itself, which is determined by its overall efficiency. At some point, the blower will not be able to make any more boost because of pumping losses, or it will heat the air more than it compresses it, or it might even reach the point of consuming more engine horsepower than it is providing. Some of these problems become factors in blown competition engines, but they rarely affect street supercharging where boost levels will normally be less than 10 pounds. The only exception would be trying to supercharge an engine with much too small of a blower.

Second, the amount of boost you can pump into the engine, and the resulting increase in cylinder pressure, will be limited by the physical strengths of engine components. It does no good to raise boost beyond the point where you blow gaskets, burn pistons, or break cylinder walls. In a competition engine, you can increase the strengths of these components to a point where they will withstand greater pressures or temperatures. But, again, most street supercharging applications do not reach the physical limits of even stock engine components.

For street supercharging, the practical limit to horsepower gain is detonation. Once an engine begins to detonate (knock), its horsepower curve stops climbing. And not only does the detonation point of an engine limit power output beyond that point, but serious detonation in the cylinders will also quickly destroy engine components such as pistons, rings, and spark plugs.

Two primary factors determine the point at which an engine will detonate: the effective compression ratio (or peak cylinder pressure) and the octane rating of fuel used. In a street-supercharged engine, the fuel will be pump gasoline, which comes in dismal octane levels these days. The octane number of a fuel is simply and literally a measure of the point at which it begins to detonate in a special test engine with a variable compression ratio – the higher the number, the higher the compression before it knocks. Since part of the reason for adding a supercharger to a motor is to increase the effective compression ratio, and since the blower will also raise the temperature of the charge in the cylinder (which also abets detonation), other means will have to be taken to control detonation.

First of all, naturally, you will want to use the highest-octane gasoline available. While there have been limited instances of regular filling stations serving 100-octane race gas at the pump, these days you are pretty much limited to 92-octane unleaded. If your supercharged vehicle is a weekend toy, you could consider using octane boosters available in a can at your speed shop, using high-octane racing gas (if it's available in your area), or even running the car on alcohol (just remember, you use twice as much alky as gas). But none of these solutions is practical if the vehicle is driven a lot, or for long distances.

Other tricks that help control detonation in street engines include richening the fuel mixture (to cool the intake charge), retarding the ignition, or injecting water into the intake airstream. Each of these methods is practical and effective on a blown streeter, but you should realize that each is a compromise. With any of the above "Band-Aids" you will be getting more power than you could if the engine goes into detonation – but not as much as you would if the engine didn't otherwise detonate at that point (for instance, if the fuel octane rating were higher, or the intake air temperature were cooler).

The point is that on a blown street motor running on gasoline (as opposed to race motors running on much "colder" fuels like alcohol or nitromethane), the primary factor limiting the amount of boost you can pump in with the supercharger will be the octane rating of available gas, rather than the melting or breaking points of engine parts.

In fact, one seldom-mentioned benefit of supercharging pointed out by British author L.J.K. Setright in his book on turbocharging and supercharging is that the mean effective pressure (MEP) in the cylinder of a supercharged engine is considerably higher than that of an unblown motor. The pressure has to be higher for the engine to make more power, since engine power is a function of MEP, but the peak cylinder pressure allowable in either engine cannot exceed the physical strength limits of the engine parts (or the detonation limit of the fuel). This first of all demonstrates why a supercharged engine can make more power than a naturally aspirated engine of the same effective compression ratio. In other words, this is why it is better to lower the static compression ratio and add a blower rather than to use high-compression pistons to achieve the same effective compression in the cylinder. Doing so allows the supercharged motor to produce more pressure in the cylinder throughout the power stroke, whereas the high-compression piston produces a high initial (peak) pressure above the piston at combustion, but proportionally less pressure as the piston travels down the bore.

Setright's point is that the higher continuous pressure in the cylinder of a blown engine produces a more constant loading on the piston, rod, and crank during the power stroke than that in an unblown engine. The same is true during the intake stroke when the blower, by pressurizing the intake tract, forces air into the cylinder, actually helping to reduce mechanical stresses on engine parts by cushioning inertia loads. The most stress a rod bolt sees is at top dead center with both valves open. Pressurizing the intake acts like an air spring for the piston and connecting rod components at this point of its travel. Further, since the blower makes more power at given RPM levels, this means that a blown engine doesn't have to spin as fast to make the same power as an unblown motor, thus further reducing stress on engine parts.

EXPANSION RATIO AND THERMAL EFFICIENCY

A negative effect of the lowered static compression ratio necessary in a supercharged engine is a consequent lowering of the expansion ratio and thermal efficiency of the engine. The expansion ratio in a cylinder is a measure of how much the compressed air/fuel mixture in the combustion chamber can expand (and therefore exert pressure on the piston) before the exhaust valve opens somewhere near bottom dead center (BDC) on the power stroke and blows down the cylinder. It's the expansion of the heated gases in the cylinder that does the work to run the engine, so the expansion ratio obviously has a direct bearing on engine power.

If valve timing remains the same, the expansion ratio in an engine is proportional to the geometric (static) compression ratio. By lowering the compression ratio in a supercharged motor (that is, by enlarging the combustion chamber volume), we can get a larger quantity of air and fuel into the cylinder, which will expand with a proportionally greater force once it is burned (heated). However, considering that the cylinder is still the same size, this heated charge of gas will still have only the same distance to push the piston, and the same piston top area to push on. In other words, although we have greatly increased the force pushing on the piston for the entire length of its power stroke, the piston reaches the bottom of that stroke well before the power of the expanding gas has been used up.

Remember that the temperature of a gas drops as that gas expands in volume. In an engine cylinder, the heat that makes the gas expand in the first place comes from the energy content of the fuel (energy that can be converted to heat and can be measured in BTUs). The thermal efficiency of an engine is a measure of the percentage of potential heat energy in the fuel that is actually converted to work in the cylinders. Without going into a lengthy explanation of all these processes, I hope you begin to understand how the static compression ratio, expansion ratio, thermal efficiency and, ultimately, the fuel economy of an engine are all closely related. In terms of supercharging, the results are that, for a large increase in power, we must waste some of the potential power available, which means wasting some fuel, and this wasted power will show up as an increase in exhaust heat and/or water temperatures.

In a street-supercharged engine, the expansion ratio can be increased somewhat by retarding the exhaust valve opening timing and reducing intake and exhaust valve-timing overlap. The extra pressure (heat) of the burned gases in the supercharged engine at the end of the power stroke will help push the exhaust through the valve and out the port.

Horsepower-Rich Tuning Tips

The reason we've spent so much time discussing blower and engine theory is to answer, or at least begin to answer, some questions for those of you who need to know what makes things tick and why. Such questions are far too seldom asked about superchargers, and supercharging and turbocharging theory in general has progressed very little since the 1930s. We'd also like to dispel certain misconceptions about blowers. But in this book, and in super tuning in general, we are much more interested in practical application than we are in detached theory.

We know from practical experience that blowers and turbos work. We have given several reasons why they aren't perfect, and we have shown some ways in which they can be improved, but these are usually relatively minor faults. In most applications, the blower gives much more than it takes. In typical installations, a supercharger gives more power per cubic inch, more power per RPM, and more power per dollar than all the standard unblown engine modifications. On the other hand, don't expect a blower to give you better gas mileage from equal-sized engines.

We've seen that the major problem associated with a street boost is heat. When the charger is making boost, it'll be making more heat in the engine, and this means that you have to increase the capacity of the cooling system to carry away this heat before it damages engine parts. The heat carried away by coolant, or blown out the exhaust, is power wasted. Likewise, the more the blower heats the air in the intake manifold, the less efficient it is, the less potential power it'll be pumping into the engine, and the more power it'll be taking from the engine to operate.

Therefore, the most important and effective thing you can do to improve blower performance and efficiency is to keep the intake charge as cool as possible. This means drawing in cool air to the blower, using as efficient a blower as possible to keep manifold temperature down, and thereby lowering combustion temperature so that more of the power of the expanding gases can be extracted in the cylinder. Since we cannot very well raise the operating temperature of the engine (especially on a street motor), this means that the only way we can maximize engine power and efficiency, from the thermodynamic standpoint, is to lower the temperatures of all processes down the line ahead of the exhaust stroke. Lowering the intake and combustion temperatures will also lessen the tendency of the engine to knock on available gasoline.

In order to determine exactly how well the supercharger is working, or how much you are cutting down on intake heat, I strongly recommend installing both temperature and pressure sensors in the intake manifold. Without a good boost gauge and manifold temperature gauge in your boosted car, you're driving blind.

Finally, we should realize that the big difference between supercharging for street cars and competition supercharging is that a street machine is driven at part throttle the vast majority of the time. A gasoline engine is terribly inefficient in the first place, but it's considerably worse at anything less than wide-open throttle. At part throttle, the blower is basically a parasite on the engine. However, since it won't be making boost, or pumping "thick" air, a blower will take much less horsepower to operate at part throttle than it will at full throttle; plus manifold vacuum will actually spin a Roots-type blower like a windmill. But at part throttle a supercharger will very likely be taking more power than it is giving – not much, but some.

But most of us who want to bolt a blower onto our street motors aren't very worried about fuel economy in the first place, nor about part-throttle operation. In most of the literature that has been written about blowers either in magazines or in books, much has been made of the drawbacks of blower noise and size. It is my opinion and observation that the majority of today's blower buyers do not intend to hide the fact that their vehicle is supercharged, nor do they want a blower that nobody can hear. A big part of the appeal of supercharging is the sight and sound of the total package – added to the sudden kick in the pants only a supercharger can give the instant you mash the throttle.

Chapter 3

Roots Blowers for Sport Compacts

Numerous large OEM suppliers, including Bendix, Allied Signal, Holley, and others, have designed a variety of unusual superchargers in hopes of securing a large-volume deal with one of the Detroit manufacturers for an OEM application. The only company to actually do it so far is Eaton, and it did it by refining the basic Roots blower design.

The first production vehicles to use the Eaton blower were 3.8-liter V-6 Ford Thunderbird (and Mercury Cougar XR7) Super Coupes beginning in 1989. I spoke with Ford engineers working on this program in the mid 1980s, and they were impressed by the Roots blower's simplicity and reliability. But for a factory application, especially considering CAFE and EPA standards, this blower's parasitic pumping losses, heating of the intake charge, noise levels, and overall efficiencies all had to be improved. Eaton began working on the project in 1982 and is continuing to improve this blower, which was in its fourth generation as of this writing. Study this blower carefully if you want to learn the state of the art in Roots blower technology.

As of this writing, more than 300,000 cars roll off the assembly line with Eaton blowers. Consider that in 1992, Buick switched from an intercooled turbocharger to a non-intercooled Eaton M90 supercharger for its 3.8-liter V-6. That should tell you something. Eaton blowers of various sizes have been used in OEM applications on the '89-'95 Ford T-Bird and XR7; '92-up Buicks and other GM V-6s; the '95-up Mercedes C-Class and the SLK roadster; the '95-up Jaguar XJR, XJ8, and XK8; the Aston Martin Vantage and DB-7; and the '03 and '04 Ford SVT Cobra and Lightning pickup.

As of this writing, Eaton blowers are available in four sizes: 45, 62, 90, and 112 cubic inches. T-Birds used the 90, while '92-'95 Buicks used the 62, and then switched to the 90 in 1996. The '89-'93 Eatons were Stage I models, while 1994-95s were Stage II models with revised inlet and outlet for higher airflow and an acrylic powder coating on the rotors.

Keys to the Eaton blower are: the uniquely shaped, 60-degree helix, tri-lobe rotors; the unique, computer-designed and tested rear inlet and front outlet optimized for adiabatic and volumetric efficiency and noise reduction; and its bypass valve.

The bypass is especially important. We tend to forget that in normal driving the engine is very seldom in full-power, wide-open throttle (WOT). In a supercharged engine, this is the only time the blower is actually being used. The rest of the time, at part-throttle cruise, idle, or deceleration, even a supercharged engine has vacuum in the intake manifold. This vacuum is used to open the bypass valve to open a passage between the throttle and the manifold (bypassing the supercharger). This equalizes vacuum in the entire system so that pumping losses in the blower are minimized. Factory tests have shown that an Eaton M90, with this valve, produces only a 1/3-hp parasitic loss while cruising at 60 mph. As a result, the V-6 factory applications with this blower average about 30 miles per gallon.

In addition, the helix-angled rotors, along with specially designed inlet and outlet port geometry, also reduce pressure variations, resulting in a smooth discharge flow and a lower level of noise during operation. The associated ducting and mounting used in installing the supercharger can play a major role in reducing the extra noise.

The reliability of the Eaton supercharger was the first criteria, which was addressed during early design development. Dedicated engineers with backgrounds in compressors, gearing, tribology, and metallurgy, as well as thermal and structural analysis, enabled Eaton to find solutions to many reliability concerns. In addition, strict customer durability test criteria have been achieved. Successful comple-

With more than 500,000 units in the field, Eaton superchargers come in a variety of shapes, sizes, and applications. This lineup includes (left to right): an M45 (45 cubic inches) used on sport compacts by Jackson Racing, an M62 used on '92-'95 Buick 3.8-liter V-6s, an M90 used on '92-'95 Thunderbird V-6 Super Coupes, and an M112 made by Magnuson Products for special projects on 4.6-liter Ford engines.

The GM 3800 V-6 used a 62-ci Eaton in 1992-95 (right), but it switched to a 90-ci Eaton (left) in 1997. Note the vacuum canister at the rear of each, which opens a small bypass valve under high-vacuum conditions (idle, cruise), equalizing vacuum throughout the intake system (in the blower and manifold), greatly reducing blower parasitic drag. In GM's case, this reduced the drag to 1/3 hp at a 60-mph cruise. All this technology is available in aftermarket Roots blowers for sport compacts.

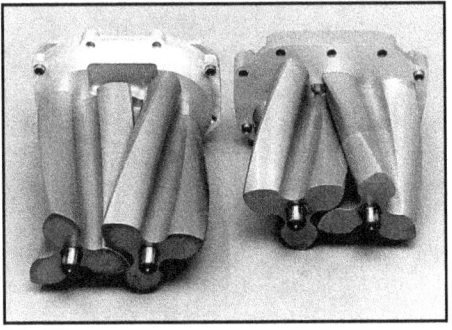

This is the fourth-generation design of the involute, three-lobe Eaton rotor, which has a 60-degree twist and a special acrylic coating.

It's not a pretty sight, especially installed on the engine, but this M112 incorporating the EFI induction tract, available from Ford Motorsport SVO or Roush Racing, adds a much-needed torque and power boost to the 4.6-liter, 2-valve, SOHC Ford V-8. Though I'm not aware of any sport compact kits with this arrangement, it looks like a viable approach to a V-6 supercharger manifold.

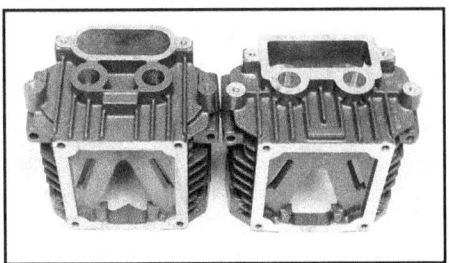

Most Eaton cases have a rear inlet and a bottom outlet, and the cases have gone through several design generations. The oval-port 90 ci (left) was used on 1989-'93 T-Birds; the one on the right with a larger, rectangular (more importantly, lowered) inlet was used on 1992-'95 T-Birds and is four percent more efficient. Note the triangular, forward-placed outlet; the slots next to it allow a small percentage of backflow, which reduces blower noise.

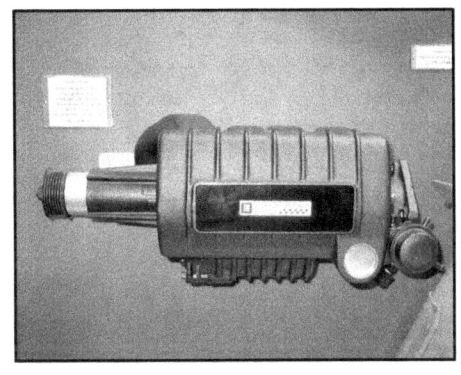

The GM Performance Parts 2.4-liter Twin Cam Supercharger is said to bring your 2.4-liter up to 190 horsepower and add over 40 ft-lbs of torque. This blower met GM engineering standards by undergoing extensive testing and tuning, so you can bet it's factory reliable.

tion of numerous 500-hour durability tests established a firm grasp on achieving a reliable product. In addition, numerous vehicles have successfully completed 100,000-mile OEM (original equipment manufacturer) vehicle durability tests. Improvements in bearing and seal designs also contributed to a final product that meets all OEM durability criteria.

With the continued interest in performance, and the desire to maintain fuel economy, supercharging could be the ideal performance improvement. Using an Eaton supercharger to increase power on a smaller-displacement engine, in turn achieving the performance of a larger engine but not compromising fuel economy, seems too good to be true – but that is what an Eaton supercharger provides. Current annual OEM usage is 300,000 superchargers.

Eaton in Aftermarket Supercharger Kits

The majority of Eaton supercharger applications have been designed for specific OEM applications. This is due to the fact that each engine application has unique hardware installation requirements, and the design criteria of the supercharger is matched to the specific engine. Recent interest has, however, been shown in this market and has resulted in aftermarket applications being sourced through Magnuson Products. The sole factory rebuilder and aftermarket distributor of Eaton superchargers and parts for North America is Magnuson Products, operated by Jerry Magnuson, the former maker of Magna Chargers. Jerry has also been refining the Eaton design and offers styles not available as OEM.

The following is a buyer's guide of sport compact kits using Eaton Roots-type superchargers.

GM Performance Parts 2.4-liter Twin Cam Supercharger

Applications:

- 2000-02 Chevrolet Cavalier 2.4 liter (RPO-LD9) with manual transaxle (RPO-M86)
- 2000-02 Chevrolet Cavalier 2.4 liter (RPO-LD9) with manual transaxle (RPO-M94)
- 2000-02 Pontiac Sunfire 2.4 liter (RPO-LD9) with manual transaxle (RPO-M86)
- 2000-02 Pontiac Sunfire 2.4 liter (RPO-LD9) with Manual Transaxle (RPO-M94)

This integral Roots-type supercharger and manifold design was developed to maximize both engine horsepower and torque without sacrificing durability. Plus the integral design gives the supercharger a clean, factory look. Getting the Vehicle Control Module (VCM) calibration is a key factor in both performance and driveability. The supercharger kit for the 2.4-liter has undergone more extensive testing and tuning than any other power-adding device. If your goal is to make a reliable 190 hp and add over 40 ft-lbs of torque to your 2.4-liter-powered J-body, this is a great way to go. The result is a reliable, compact powertrain that has more power than many V-6 engines.

The kit includes:

- All mounting brackets and all mounting fasteners required for installation.
- All air ducts and adapters, including new PCV hoses, baffle, and tubes required for installation.
- Gen II MAP sensor, four spark plugs, accessory drive belt required for installation.
- Recalibration of the vehicle control module (VCM) is also included in the kit.

Only regular hand tools are required to install this supercharger kit, but recalibration of the onboard vehicle control module must be done at an authorized GM dealership. A skilled mechanic could easily complete a full installation in a single day.

The 2.4-liter Twin Cam Supercharger Kit carries a warranty covering the complete kit for defects in material and workmanship for a period of 12 months or 12,000 miles from date of installation. In addition to the product warranty, this supercharger kit will cover the powertrain (internally lubricated engine and transmission components) for the length of the original factory powertrain warranty. For specific details, contact your local GM Performance Parts dealer.

Jackson Racing

Civic Si Kit

Jackson Racing, having successfully tuned its supercharged RSX-S, eagerly anticipated the delivery of the '02 Civic Si. Honda's new K20A3 engine offered a strong torque curve from throttle input all the way to redline. Large valves and a square bore and stroke (86 mm x 86 mm) were ideal for making power. However, the K20A3 engine didn't have a high-speed cam, thus its 6,500-rpm redline, which could prove to be a challenge to making big power gains.

Jackson Racing built the Si Supercharger system around its new Gen IV JR62 Supercharger. Using the latest

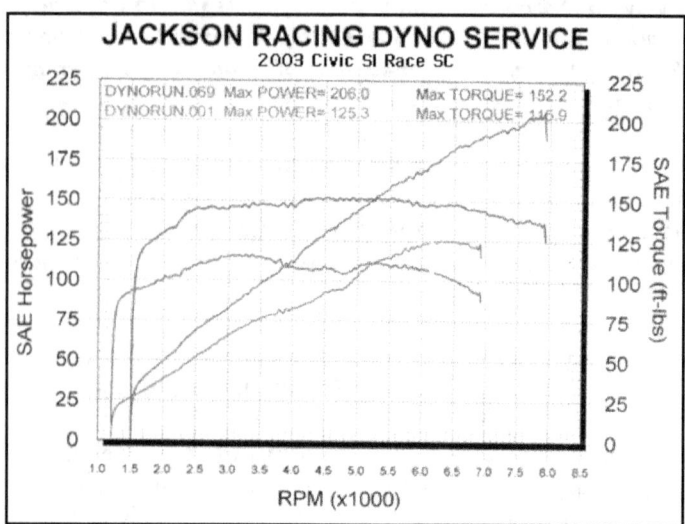
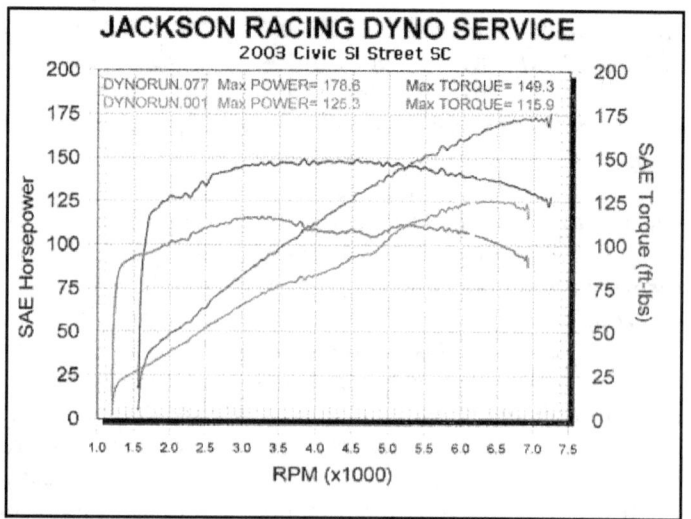

This pair of dyno charts shows the power output of the Jackson Racing race- and street-tuned supercharger kits for late-model Honda Civics. The race-tuned kit doesn't make a bunch more torque, but it's calibrated to work at a higher RPM, allowing the motor to make power all the way to 8,000 rpm.

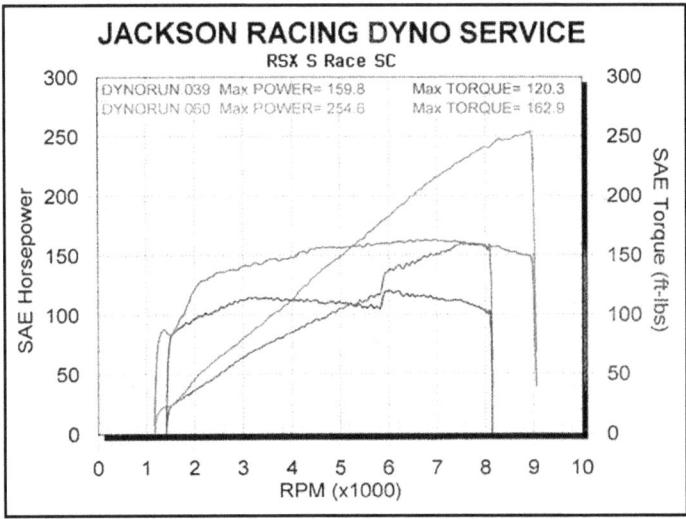
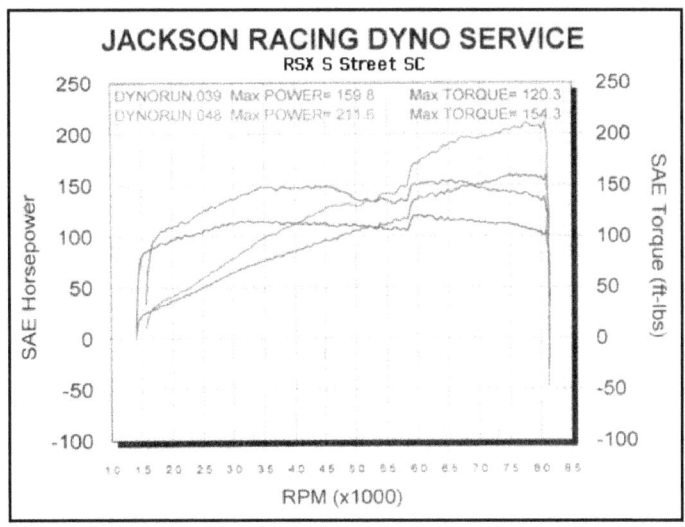

Acura's big new RSX motor has a lot of potential buried in it, as this pair of dyno charts makes abundantly clear. The totally emissions-legal street supercharger kit rips it up pretty good; but check out the screaming power curves of the race kit. Flat torque to 9,000 rpm. What a rush that'd be to drive.

fourth-generation Eaton Rotor Groups, Jackson Racing designed and developed a proprietary supercharger housing with improved intake and discharge port timing. The result is a highly efficient supercharger that creates boost more quickly while also reducing discharge temperatures.

The next point of business was fuel management. Jackson's Digital Tuning Technology was originally employed on the SVT Focus, with amazing results. The Jackson Powercard takes full control of the injectors under boost to keep things running right. Its plug-and-play system installs in minutes and offers full self-diagnostics.

The resulting supercharger systems were truly impressive. The Civic Si Race System increased horsepower by 64 percent to 206.0 hp and 152.2 ft-lbs of torque. The Street system, which carries CARB EO #D-344-10, made 178.6 hp (up 42 percent) and 149.3 ft-lbs of torque compared to a baseline of 125.3 hp and 115.9 ft-lbs of torque.

RSX-S Kit

Jackson Racing had a serious challenge on its hands when it set out to create a supercharger system for the Acura RSX Type-S. A more stringent emissions package, restrictive intake and exhaust systems, dead-head fuel system, and an 11:1 compression ratio presented

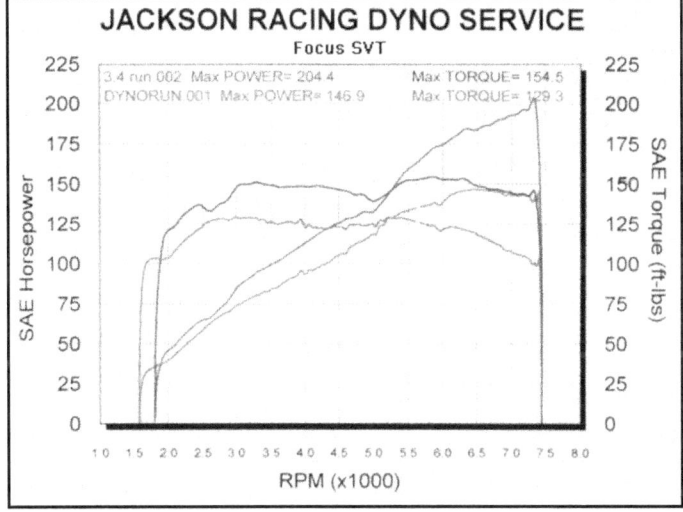

This Jackson Racing-Equipped Ford Focus SVT unleashes over 200 horsepower — over 50 ponies more than the standard supercharged Focus.

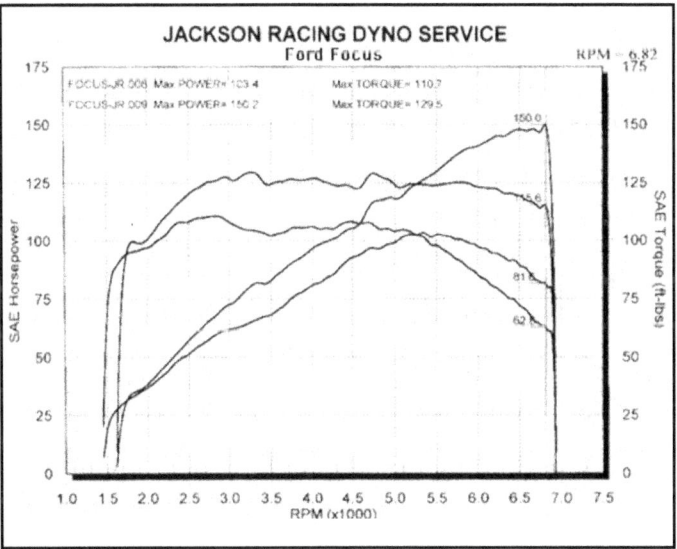

The Jackson Racing supercharger kit produces impressive power gains, as demonstrated in this dyno test on a 2000 Ford Focus.

Chapter 3

The Focus SVT engine bay is, as most FWDs are, cramped — attractively styled, but cramped. The compact size of the Eaton supercharger unit makes packaging the Jackson Racing supercharger kit possible.

Jackson Racing's Focus SVT supercharger kit installs as if it were a factory part.

huge roadblocks to building a powerful yet fully streetable supercharger system. But the I-VTEC system and huge intake and exhaust valves found in the K20 engine provided the potential for incredible power gains and could not be overlooked.

At the heart of this completely new system is Jackson Racing's Gen IV JR62 supercharger. This setup uses the same fourth-generation Eaton Rotor Groups and supercharger housing with improved intake and discharge port timing as mentioned above.

Another significant advance is JR's Digital Tuning Technology. The days of sensor manipulation are gone; JR's new electronics take complete control of the fuel injectors while under boost. This new plug-and-play system installs in minutes and offers full self-diagnostic capability. After countless hours of development and hundreds of dyno runs, Jackson Racing has achieved astonishing results.

This Jackson Racing RSX Type-S supercharger system is available in two configurations. The first is a CARB-approved street system running 5 psi of boost. The second is the Race system, which also runs 5 psi of boost but uses 440-cc injectors and a JR-tuned/Hondata-flashed ECU program. By flashing the ECU, JR and Hondata were able to adjust cam phasing and ignition timing and raise the rev limiter. All this results in another 40+ hp to the wheels. The Race system is not CARB exempt.

Focus SVT Kit

The Ford Focus SVT doesn't just look racier than its non-SVT sibling; its performance is on a completely different level. SVT engineers used all the good stuff: beefy brakes, special suspension, low-profile tires, a dual-mass flywheel, and even a Getrag 6-speed manual transaxle. The Focus SVT pretty much comes with everything but a supercharger to take full advantage of the engine's excellent breathing characteristics.

That's where Jackson Racing's supercharger for the '02-'03 Ford Focus SVT comes in. Jackson selected the 62-cubic-inch Eaton supercharger for boost duties based on the SVT's free-flowing throttle body and variable-timing intake camshaft. The improvements, with only six psi of boost, result in an extra 26.4 ft-lbs of torque and an additional 55.8 horsepower at the wheels. Even better, a large portion of that power is available right from 2,000 rpm and continues to build all the way to the redline, offering seductively smooth driveability and seamless acceleration. All this power doesn't come at the expense of fuel economy however, as the innovative bypass system allows the supercharger to freewheel under light throttle, reducing loads on the engine and optimizing mileage. Jackson Racing's blowers are 50-state emissions legal and offer OEM-caliber reliability as a result of attention to proper tuning and engine management. The entire system is 100 percent bolt on and only takes about six hours to install.

Jackson Racing Powercard – Digital Tuning Technology

Necessity is the mother of all invention. No truer words could describe the genesis of the Jackson Racing Powercard with Digital Tuning Technology.

Stringent emissions standards, ultra fast ECUs, and dead-head fuel systems left previous tuning solutions in the dust. For two years, Jackson Racing experimented with various methods of fuel management with little success. The future of fuel management would come from the computer industry, using a super-fast microprocessor that could react in milliseconds. The Powerercard also features self-diagnostics, so it not only knows when something is wrong, it will also tell you how to fix it!

The Powercard easily installs in between the factory ECU and the injectors. During idle, mild acceleration, or cruise, your car reacts just as the manufacturer intended. Mash the throttle and Powercard responds with added fuel in milliseconds. When this is coupled with instantaneous boost, power is delivered as fast as your right foot can work the accelerator pedal. The result is a smooth transition to boost and seamless driveability – in a completely emissions-legal package.

Installation of the Powercard couldn't be easier. Just hook up the vacuum/boost hose and six wire connections. It should only take about 20 minutes. Jackson Racing has one of the most complete supercharger lines, covering most of the popular sport compacts.

Applications:
Honda
- 1995 Civic EX
- 1996 Civic EX
- 1999 CRV, Civic CX, DX, LX
- 1999 Civic EX
- 1999 Civic Si
- 1989 CRX
- 1999 Prelude
- 1999 Prelude with VPAC

Acura
- Integra GS/LS/RS
- Integra GSR
- Type R

Miata
- 1991 Miata
- 1994 Miata
- 1999 Miata

Ford
- 2000-02 Ford Focus with the 2.0-liter Zetec (ZX3)
- 2002-03 Ford Focus with the 2.0-liter SVT

STILLEN SUPERCHARGERS

Stillen 350Z/G35 Roots/Intercooled Supercharger Kits

Stillen stepped up to the supercharging plate this year with fourth-generation rotors in Eaton charger units for the Nissan 350Z and Infinity G35. The kits are also designed to work with automatic or manual transmissions.

Stillen's Stage 2 and Stage 3 kits have CARB approval, so they're legal for street use in all 50 states. Stillen says their engineering team worked intensively on this project for nearly a year before the first unit was sold. The end result is a supercharger kit that optimizes air flow and fuel distribution for efficient and effective power production. It also provides for the intercooler.

The units also come to you or your installer fully tuned. Fuel is supplied via a seventh injector that is mounted in the inlet tube. It is regulated via an electronic unit, factory set for your vehicle, that modifies the timing map to optimize it for the supercharged engine.

You will need to add hood clearance in order to fit the supercharger. Stillen offers a paintable fiberglass, as well as a carbon fiber, replacement hood. Paintable fiberglass or carbon fiber hood cowls (350Z and G35 Coupe) are also available. The FX35 uses the stock hood. They also have a high-boost pulley available.

Stage Details, Warranty, Options

Stages 1 and 2 are available with an optional 3-year/36,000-mile engine warranty, Stages 2 and 3 are intercooled. The supercharger is covered by its own 12-month warranty. Each of the kits is upgradable, and the superchargers are now also available in polished finish!

Applications:
- 407350: 2003 350Z Stage 1
- 407350IC: 2003 350Z Stage 2 (intercooled)
- 407350IC3: 2003 350Z Stage 3 (intercooled)

Stillen Maxima Supercharger Kit

Motor Trend magazine tested a supercharged SMX Maxima (December 1998) and got the following results: 0-60 mph in 5.9 seconds (stock was 7.4). The 1/4-mile time dropped to 14.4 seconds @ 98.8 mph from 15.5 seconds @ 90 mph stock. *Motor Trend*'s conclusion: "...a roomy...four-door that humbles prestigious sport sedans costing double, triple, or quadruple (as much)." Driving a Maxima equipped with a Stillen supercharger is awesome. The car starts and idles normally with just a hint of a whine being the only initial clue of what is to come. As the gas pedal is applied, the whine vanishes and car pulls normally to about 3,500 rpm. Above 3,500, it just flat takes off and pulls hard to redline.

For the '95-'99 Maxima kit, Stillen says horsepower at the flywheel is increased from the stock 190 to approximately 275. It also makes a kit for the 2000 Maxima.

The Stillen Maxima supercharger kit is complete and consists of a vane-type supercharger, engine mounting bracket, new drive belt, intake plumbing, air cleaner, additional fuel management module, fuel pump and wiring, relocation hardware for the windshield washer reservoir, and more. Installation should be done by a trained and experienced professional. The kit must be used with good quality 92+ octane fuel and is not to be combined with any other engine or engine control unit (ECU) modifications. There is a one-year warranty on the supercharger and most components of the kit. Electrical components carry a 30-day warranty only. Vehicle components including engine and drive train are not covered.

Applications:
- PN 407000: 1995-99 Nissan Maxima (All Models)
- PN 407000: 1996-99 Infinity i30
- PN 407500: 2000 Nissan Maxima

The after-production supercharging kit from Toyota Racing Development (TRD) for 3.4-liter V-6s (T-100, 4Runner, Tacoma) uses an Eaton M62 with this special inlet/outlet housing. It gives a 62-percent power gain (from 142 to 216 rear-wheel horsepower) at 6 psi of boost.

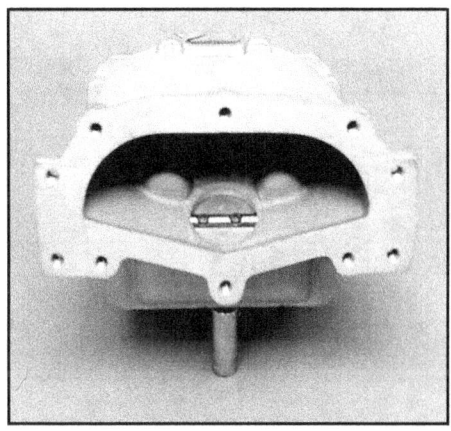

This is the enlarged inlet side of a special M112 housing made by Magnuson, which incorporates the bypass valve. Magnuson also offers "S" models of various Eaton blowers with case openings "massaged" for greater flow and efficiency.

TOYOTA RACING DEVELOPMENT

All TRD superchargers are installed and tested to ensure the durability of the supercharger system and the engine families on which they are used. Lengthy full-throttle dynamometer test sessions are conducted on supercharged engines, which are then disassembled and inspected for any sign of accelerated wear. Likewise, supercharger-equipped vehicles are run through closed-course proving

Sizing an Eaton Blower for a Custom Application

Eaton provides several sizes to accommodate various engine sizes and mass flows. The charts for each model indicate the airflow in CFM, power required to provide two boost levels, and air temperature rise at two boost levels at various supercharger speeds. Use these to choose the model unit that best fits your engine combination. For example, if you're spinning your 2-liter engine to 10,000 rpm to move roughly 650 cfm naturally aspirated you can see that the normal sizing isn't going to cut it. The M45 is normally recommended for a 2- to 3-liter engine, but tops out at 325 cfm. That means you'll have to upsize.

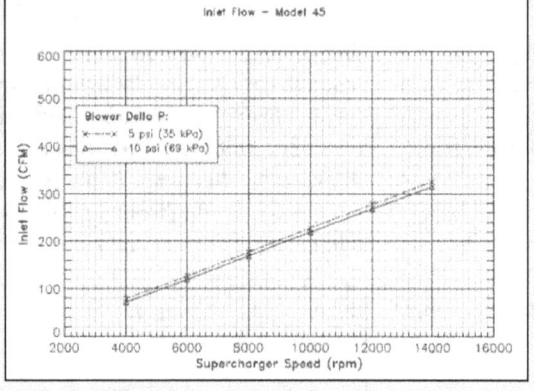
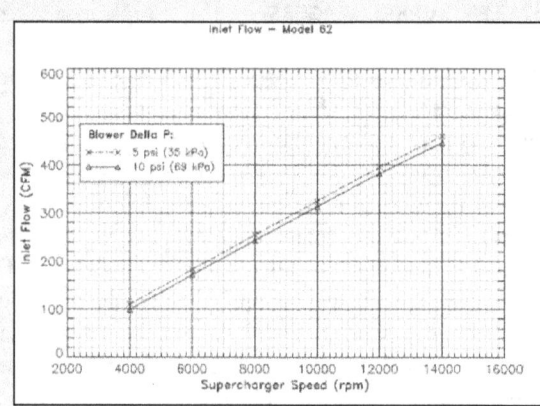
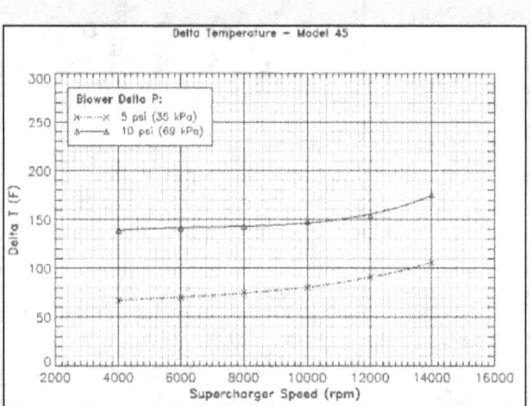
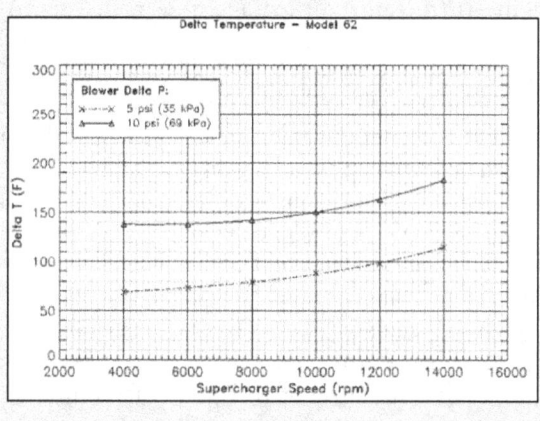
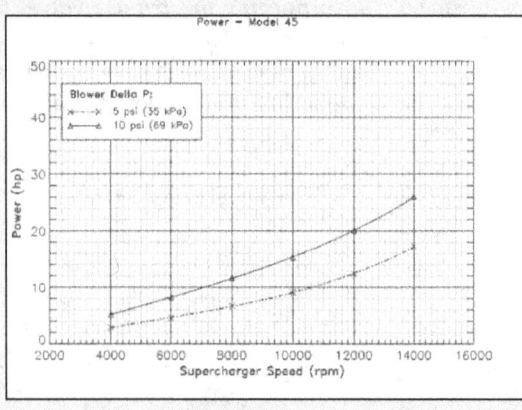
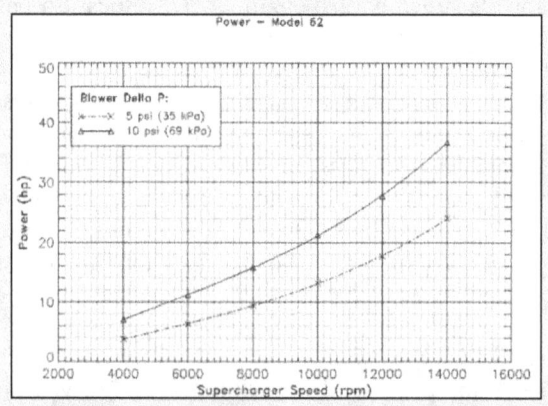

The Eaton Supercharger Model 45 is designed for 2.0- to 3.0-liter passenger car and light-truck engines, but may also be suitable for other engine sizes, depending on total system performance requirements.

Eaton recommends the Model 62 for 2.5- to 4.0-liter passenger car and light-truck engines. However, this blower could easily become necessary in a sport compact application.

Sizing an Eaton Blower for a Custom Application (continued)

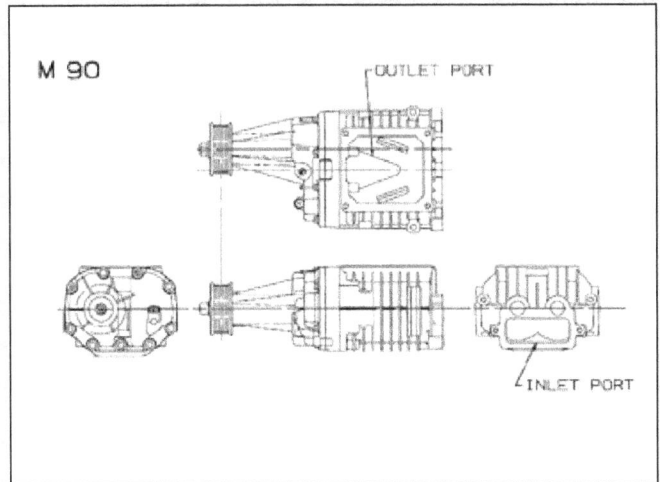
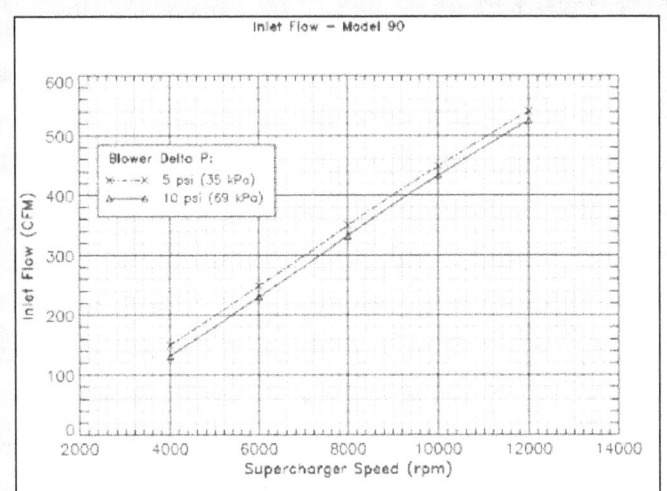
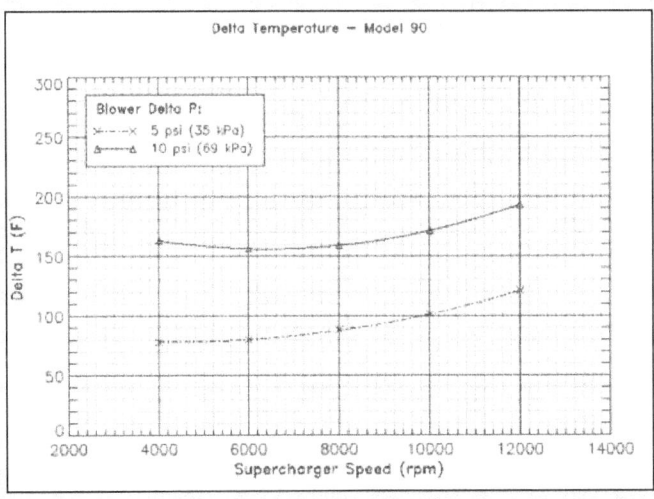
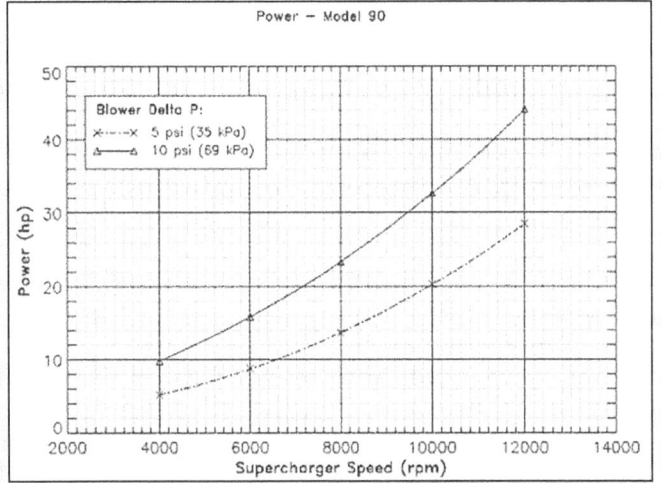

The Model 90 is designed for 3.0- to 5.0-liter passenger car and light-truck engines. Since even the Model 62 is an upgrade for most aftermarket sport-compact supercharger kits, the Model 90 is usually reserved for custom race applications.

ground-test sessions designed to simulate thousands of miles of severe use to ensure that powertrain and engine durability is not diminished.

Keep Your Warranty

When installed by a Toyota dealer, the TRD supercharger warranty works seamlessly with your Toyota new vehicle warranty. If installed by a Toyota dealer on a vehicle with any of its new vehicle powertrain warranty remaining, you'll receive either 12 months, unlimited mileage from the date of installation, or the remainder of the new vehicle powertrain warranty, whichever is longer. Units installed by do-it-yourselfers have a 12-month, unlimited mileage warranty. All warranties require that the system is not modified, abused, used in any type of motorsports activity, or installed in any application for which it is not intended. These Toyota superchargers can be purchased and installed from any Toyota dealer, nationwide.

3.0-liter V-6 (1MZFE) Supercharger Applications:

- 00602-17620-301: 1999-02 Solara (Manual Trans)
- 00602-17620-302: 1999-03 Solara (Auto Trans)
- 00602-17620-303: 1997-01 Camry (Auto Trans)
- 00602-17620-304: 1997-01 Camry (Manual Trans)
- 00602-17620-305: 1998-00 Sienna (Auto Trans)

The TRD supercharged 3.0 V-6 engine produces more torque down at 2,000 rpm than the naturally aspirated engine does at its torque peak of 4,400 rpm.

1.8-Liter Supercharger

Power Specifications:
- Peak torque is 145 ft-lb @ 4,000 rpm (supercharged) vs. 125 ft-lbs at 4,200 rpm (stock).
- Peak horsepower is 166 @ 6,800 rpm (supercharged) vs. 130 hp @ 6,000 rpm (stock).
- Maximum horsepower gain: 40 hp @ 6,750 rpm
- Maximum torque gain: 36 ft-lbs @ 4,000 rpm

Applications:
- 00602-17620-101: 2003 Matrix (XR, Base), 2003 Corolla (Auto Trans)
- 00602-17620-102: 2004 Matrix (XR, Base), 2003 Corolla (Manual Trans)

Exclusive TRD Engine Management System

Supplemental TRD ECU provides recalibrated engine management for optimum supercharger performance. Systems include supplemental injectors that create an intercooling effect, permitting higher boost levels for increased efficiency and enhanced power and torque.

THE LYSHOLM SCREW-TYPE COMPRESSOR

As we said earlier, there are any number of ways to pump, accelerate, or blow air. Another type of supercharger design we have not yet discussed is the Lysholm screw-type compressor. This type of compressor was designed and patented in Sweden in the 1930s by Svenska Rotor Maskiner AB (SRM), whose chief engineer was a Mr. A. Lysholm. This company still holds the patents on these screw compressors.

For years, because of the exceptionally high cost of machining the two mismatching, convoluted rotors, screw compressors were used primarily on large stationary engines, examples being the Elliot-Lysholm and the Broom-Wade, and in special applications requiring a highly reliable source of oil-free air, such as in airplane or submarine cabin pressurizing. Over the years, SRM created hundreds of designs and sizes of screw compressors and licensed them to dozens of companies in many countries for various industrial, aeronautic, refrigeration, and other applications.

Between 1986 and 1988, Norm Drazy painstakingly developed a large screw-type supercharger, using a four-lobe male rotor and a six-lobe female rotor (turning 30 percent more slowly), called the PSI, hoping to introduce it to Top Fuel drag racing. In dyno testing, the 385-ci prototype PSI made the same horsepower (1260 on alcohol) at 28 pounds of boost as a 14-71 (552-ci) Roots blower at 36 psi; plus the outlet temperature of the PSI was 85 degrees compared to 150 for the 14-71. Unfortunately, the PSI was banned from Top Fuel by the NHRA, but the PSI and the newer large Whipple screw compressor have become the standards in Top Alcohol drag racing, not only because of their high efficiency, but because they don't need to be "re-stripped" with Teflon after every round.

In his book *Street Supercharging*, Pat Ganahl stated that we would probably never see small versions of screw superchargers for automotive use because the cost of making them was prohibitive compared to other superchargers already available. Well, the wonders of CNC machining and CAD-CAM proved him wrong, and SRM's parent company in Sweden, Opcon AB, formed a new company called Autorotor to develop screw compressors for the automotive market. It has already made several sizes of screw blowers for street and race automotive applications in at least a couple of design generations. Until 1995, Whipple Industries of Fresno, California, was the sole distributor for these blowers under its Whipple Charger brand. As this book was being written, Whipple Industries is now importing Lysholm superchargers made by Lyshom Technologies in Sweden that formed in 1995. The Autorotor units, still manufactured by Opcon AB, also in Sweden, are now imported by Kenne Bell.

The Lysholm is designed somewhat like a GMC Roots-type blower in that it has two counter-rotating, spiral-cut, meshing rotors. However, the principle on which the Lysholm operates is nearly the opposite of the Roots. In fact, the compression process in the Lysholm is more like that in the eccentric-vane supercharger.

The rotors in the Lysholm are different, one having convex lobes and the other having larger concave cavities. Unlike a Roots blower, which carries air around the outside of the case in the rotor cavities, the Lysholm draws air in at one end of the case, pumps it through the case longitudinally between the rotors, and then expels it from the other end of the case. The air is not only pumped, or moved, from one end of the case to the other by the intermeshing screw action of the rotors, but it is also squeezed between the rotors to compress it.

The beauty of the Lysholm screw-type compressor is that it combines the advantages of the Roots blower with the advantages of the vane compressor, without incurring the disadvantages of either. That is, it's a positive-displacement pump; it has no contacting parts or friction drag other than the rotor gears; it therefore needs no internal lubrication; and it's perfectly balanced like a Roots blower. Still, it affords internal compression like a vane supercharger, which greatly increases the Lysholm's adiabatic and volumetric efficiency over the Roots, especially at boost levels above 15-20 psi. In fact, Lysholm screw superchargers tend to see adiabatic efficiencies in the 60 to 65 percent range compared to about 50 percent for a good Roots blower. It's definitely a good design, it doesn't wear out, and it's efficient in all respects under boost (in a vehicle) or in constant-pressure industrial applications. The only drawback to a screw compressor in a vehicle – and it's relatively minor – is that the act of compressing air in the

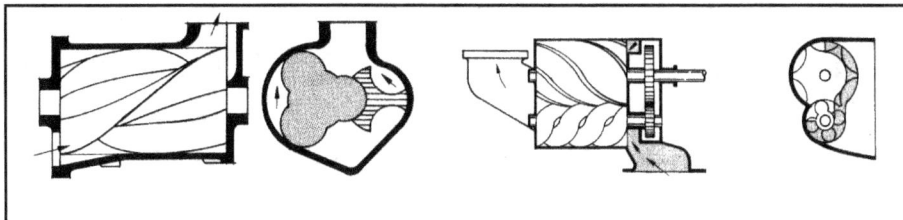

These diagrams portray two variations of Lysholm screw-type supercharger designs. The Lysholm is very efficient and effective, being a positive-displacement blower with internal compression. However, until the advent of modern computerized machining, it was too costly to produce.

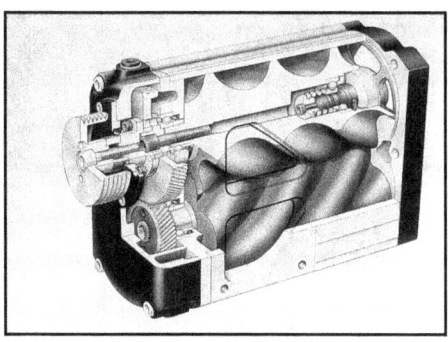

This cutaway illustration of the Autorotor screw compressor shows the male (bottom) and female twisted rotors and bevel gears that turn them in a 5:7 ratio. In this view, the inlet is at the rear and the two triangle-shaped outlets are in front.

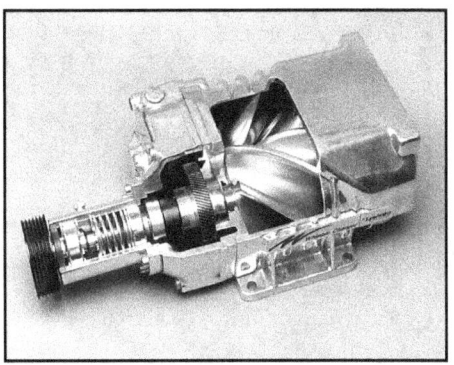

Another style of Lysholm screw-type supercharger is made by Whipple Industries, as demonstrated by this polished cutaway. This one is a rear inlet, but it also comes in a top inlet style.

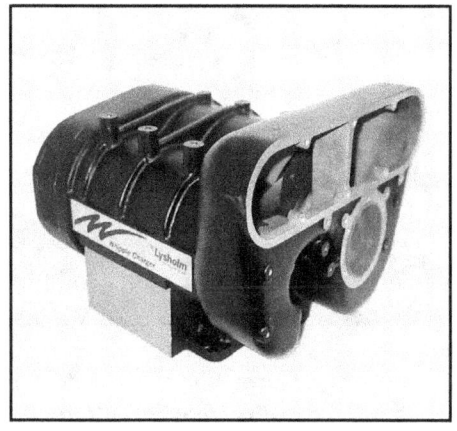

This huge 9.8-liter Whipple Charger used on alcohol dragsters and funny cars incorporates the fuel injector into the inlet housing.

Kenne Bell uses the Autorotor Twin Screw Charger, which comes black powder coated or polished. This lineup, seen from the outlet side, includes (left to right) the original 1.5 liter; a new rotor design and revised case that pumps 2.2 liters from the same size blower; and a 1-inch shorter new-design 1.8 liter.

blower gives it a bit more parasitic drag during the majority of street-driving time when the blower is not in boost mode. However, most of the engineering firms marketing Lysholm-based supercharger kits are incorporating a bypass valve to reduce drag and improve mileage.

Whipple Industries

Former drag-racing crew chief Art Whipple first began looking into the use of a screw-type supercharger for drag racing sometime before 1990. He first imported a 1.2-liter Sprintex screw compressor from Australia, but this unit was far too small for his purposes, and the costs of developing a larger unit with Sprintex were prohibitive. Also about this time, Norm Drazy debuted his big PSI screw blower, and the NHRA banned it from Top Fuel.

About 1990, Whipple acquired a screw compressor from Opcon Autorotor in Sweden. Although it was the right size for automotive use, it needed a few changes to be optimized. Whipple suggested these changes, which Autorotor made, and Whipple secured the rights to be the exclusive distributor for the supercharger, which he calls the Whipple Charger. This supercharger uses an extruded billet aluminum case, which can be cut to different lengths to vary blower displacement. The initial blower displacements were 1.3 and 1.5 liters. Later, Autorotor redesigned its rotors – being the first redesign of a screw compressor specifically for automotive internal-combustion engine use – and increased the output of these two blowers to 1.8 and 2.2 liter, respectively (using the same cases).

In about 1995, SRM split from Opcon and decided to release its own screw compressor for automotive applications, giving it its original name, the Lysholm. This unit uses rotors similar to the first-design Autorotor, but has a cast aluminum case with distinctive fins. This blower comes in 1.6- and 2.1-liter sizes, and both the Autorotor and Lysholm blowers come in rear

Lysholm-Supercharged Ford GT

Ford is using a Lysholm supercharger unit in its new supercar, the GT. The Lysholm seems to be gaining favor with carmakers, because it's more efficient and able to extract more power and performance from the factory's "Halo" performance cars. The new Lysholm blowers are also manufactured by Eaton, so they're reliable enough to be installed on very expensive, high-performance cars that carry a particular manufacturer's reputation.

Here's a quick run down on the engine combination that Ford selected to work with the supercharger. You can learn a lot by paying attention to what the factories do.

Specs: V-8, aluminum block, aluminum four-valve heads, H-beam connecting rods, forged aluminum pistons
Bore x Stroke: 90.2 mm x 105.8 mm (3.54 x 4.17 inches)
Displacement: 5.4 liters (5,409 cc/ 330 ci)
Compression Ratio: 8.4:1
Horsepower: 500 @ 6,000 rpm
Torque: 500 lb-ft @ 4,500 rpm
Specific Output: 92.6 hp/L
Redline: 6,500 rpm
Valvetrain: double overhead camshafts, four valves per cylinder
Intake Valves: two per cylinder, 37 mm each
Exhaust Valves: two per cylinder, 32 mm each
Ignition System: electronic distributorless, coil-on-plug
Fuel System: sequential multi-port electronic fuel injection (SEFI) with dual injectors per cylinder
Supercharger: Eaton model 2300 screw-type
Throttle Body: twin 70 mm
Exhaust System: cast-iron manifolds, low restriction dual exhaust with active mufflers

The Ford GT uses a Lysholm-type supercharger instead of the refined Roots-style Eaton found on the Ford Lightning pickup, Mustangs, and Thunderbirds. The GT had to be special and cutting edge, with a top speed above 200 mph. To get there, Ford needed a compressor with more efficiency.

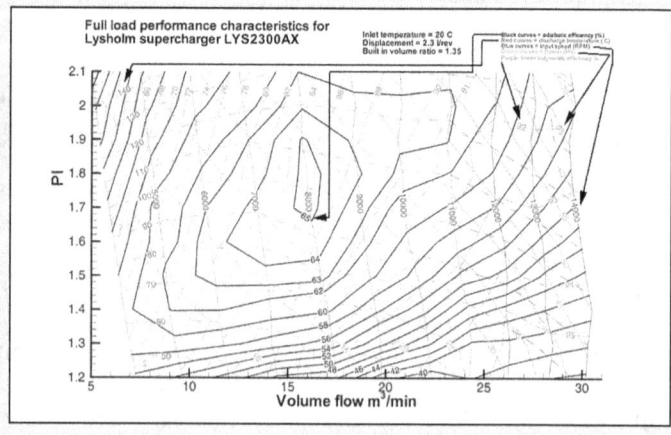

The Eaton-built Lysholm supercharger is easily identified by the distinctive webbed cast-aluminum case. This Eaton model 2300 Lysholm supercharger draws air through a pair of 70-mm throttle bodies. This supercharger also uses a bypass valve to route intake air so that the supercharger freewheels while cruising to improve efficiency and mileage.

Looking at the compressor map for the model 2300 Eaton-built Lysholm supercharger, we can see this unit has very desirable qualities. It has a very efficient sweet spot right around 8,000 compressor rpm. At this point, it can make seven psi of boost with 212-degree-Fahrenheit outlet temps. The compressor's adiabatic efficiency is right at 65 percent, its volumetric efficiency is at 85 percent, and it's taking less than 33.5 horsepower (25 kw) to do all this work.

Roots Blowers for Sport Compacts

This view compares the revised inlet of the newer style (right) to the original. The Autorotor Chargers used by Kenne Bell are all rear-inlet style.

(radial) inlet, or top (axial) inlet configurations, can be ordered in black finish or fully polished, and use self-lubricating bearings so no oil hook-up or reservoir is needed.

Currently, Whipple only markets charger kits for most late-model GM small- or big-block V-8 applications. However, the company does advertise a Lysholm-based kit for the Acura NSX designed, tuned, and marketed through Comptech.

Comptech

Comptech Sport has designed a supercharger package exclusively for the NSX. The kit provides a substantial increase in horsepower that begins building at 2,000 rpm and continues all the way to redline. This combination helps provide almost instant boost to increase and broaden the torque curve substantially, while the bypass system allows the system to cut boost at cruise and idle. The kit comes mostly assembled with Comptech manufactured manifold and all parts required to make it a bolt-on installation, and the efficient design of the supercharger means you don't need to use an intercooler. These Comptech supercharger packages are 50-state legal and all components have been tested to ensure factory reliability and fit.

Comptech also manufactures headers, a cat-back exhaust system, and a carbon-fiber cold air box assembly.

Application:
- 1991-94 NSX Coupe
- 1995-96 NSX Targa*
- 1997-02 NSX Targa*
- 1997-02 NSX Coupe
- 1991-01 Supercharger Belt NSX

*Targa kits come with a Comptech Sport Billet Strut Bar and a new engine cover assembly that will accommodate the targa top.

Kenne Bell

Kenne Bell (KB) Performance Products in Rancho Cucamonga, California – founded by Jim Bell in 1968 and named partly after Buick drag-racing legend Pop Kennedy – used to specialize strictly in Buick performance products. In the 1990s, however, Bell decided that supercharging was the way to go (just like Buick did), and he made an agreement with Art Whipple to use his imported screw-chargers and to devise installation kits for non-GM applications.

The only sport compact kit in the KB portfolio is one for the Mazda Miata. KB claims that combining the most efficient supercharger and the firm's Laminova finned tube air-to-air intercooler results in the ultimate Miata kit. The firm says these kits put up to 10 more horsepower at the flywheel compared to the available Roots-based kits because it takes 10 less horsepower to drive the Twin Screw Lysholm-design, Autorotor-built supercharger. In addition, they highlight the fact that the charge temperature is up to 46 degrees cooler. Remember, cooler and denser charge makes more power. KB includes four new high-capacity fuel injectors and a pre-tuned Optimizer to re-tune fuel ratios and ignition timing, which is mandatory for '99 and later supercharged Miatas. According to KB, no additional tuning or tweaking is required.

Highlight of the Miata kits begin with an advertised 65 to 115 percent increase in power. The Miata kit is also available with or without the intercooler, in 6-, 9-, and 12-psi boost levels.

It also comes with a bypass system standard and allows you to retain the stock strut brace in the engine compartment. It's available in satin/black or polished and comes with all necessary parts. One thing to consider is that the Kenne Bell supercharger and intercooler are billet-aluminum, as opposed to a less-expensive cast-aluminum unit.

Applications:
- TS8000-6: 2001-up Miata 1.8-liter, 6 psi
- TS8000-9: 2001-up Miata 1.8-liter, 9 psi with intercooler
- TS8000-12: 2001-up Miata 1.8-liter, 12 psi with intercooler

CHAPTER 4

CENTRIFUGAL BLOWERS FOR SPORT COMPACTS

The only similarity between a Roots-type blower and a centrifugal supercharger is the result they produce, and even in this respect, they are significantly different. In the first place, a Roots is literally a pump, whereas the centrifugal is more like a fan, or a literal blower. The Roots traps and moves a given volume of air through it with each revolution of the rotors (not accounting for leakage); consequently, it's known as a positive-displacement pump. Its pumping output (again, not counting inefficiency) is directly proportional to the speed at which it is being turned.

A centrifugal blower, however, is an inertial compressor. Its one primary moving part is a fixed-blade fan called an impeller, which actually looks like a disk with fan blades protruding on one side. Whereas the Roots blower is similar to a typical engine oil pump, a centrifugal blower is similar to a typical engine water pump.

The impeller is enclosed in a housing shaped more or less like a snail's shell, with an inlet hole above the center of the impeller, and an outlet at the end of the chamber of the "shell." Air enters the blower axially (along the rotating axis of the impeller), being sucked in by the low pressure created by the "fan," which is blowing air out of the housing. As soon as the air enters the blades of the impeller, however, it is rapidly accelerated radially toward the outer tips of the fan blades by centrifugal force.

Here's how one source describes the action of a centrifugal blower: "The air-moving element is a form of bucket wheel that hurls air outward from a central inlet against a collector housing called a volute. As the heavy air is hurled outward from the center of the impeller, the partial vacuum thus creat-

This shot of the ProCharger 350Z kit shows off the packaging advantage of centrifugal superchargers. A centrifugal blower can be mounted most anywhere on the engine (within reach of a drive belt). That helps in packaging a blower in today's small and crowded engine bays. Also, since centrifugals are best for blow-through applications, they are excellent for plumbing dry, pressurized air directly into today's self-contained, self-programming electronic fuel injection systems.

ed at the center pulls more air into the inlet. It's a centrifugal pump."

To get a better idea of the principle on which a centrifugal blower works, think of a merry-go-round found in a schoolyard or city park. One or more children push the merry-go-round, while the rest hang on and spin around on it. If you are sitting near the center of the merry-go-round, you won't be spinning very fast. But the farther toward the outside you move, the faster you go, even though the merry-go-round itself is still turning at the same speed (that is, the same RPM). Furthermore, as you may remember from your childhood, the spinning motion of the merry-go-round tends to force your body towards the outside edge (that is, radially), and, if you don't hang on tightly enough as it picks up speed, it'll hurl you off the edge with considerable velocity. The children's game of crack the whip operates on the same principle.

The tendency of a rotating body to want to fling objects on it, or contained by it, toward the edges is called centrifugal force. It is a demonstration of the laws of inertia, which can be used in the case of the centrifugal blower like an energy multiplier. For instance, let's say you and a friend are playing on a merry-go-round. You are pushing, and your friend is riding. If your friend is sitting on the outside edge, it will be hard for you to get the merry-go-round going (a body at rest tends to remain at rest), because you will have to accelerate his weight at the speed of the outer perimeter of the merry-go-round. However, if he moves in toward the middle, it will be much easier to get the thing going because you are pushing rapidly at the outside edge, but his weight is moving slowly in the center. This is the same basic principle as reduction gearing: using a low gear to get an automobile moving, for instance, and then shifting to higher gears once it's under way. So, since you are an intelligent kid, you have your friend sit in the middle while you get the merry-go-round under way. As your friend moves outward, it will be a little harder to keep it going at a constant speed, but nowhere near as hard as it would have

The several machined discs in the foreground represent the tedious trial-and-error process of reproducing an impeller for a 1920s Miller supercharger at the Briggs Cunningham auto museum. In the background is the Miller blower housing, which has a definite nautilus shape.

An interior view of the Miller blower shows the relationship of rotor to housing. This blower uses a straight-blade impeller but also has a diffuser ring that extends beyond the impeller tips. It can be plainly seen in this photo.

This Miller centrifugal blower impeller used forward-curved-tip blades as early as the 1930s. However, the tips, which were bent in a jig after the blades were machined, tended to break off under high boost pressures, so the design was not used extensively.

Centrifugal blowers were not only used on several production automobiles in America before World War II, they dominated Indy-type racing, usually on Miller or Duesenberg engines. This supercharger is actually a Miller copy (a 1927 Cooper), which uses a straight-bladed rotor and a slightly snail-shaped housing. The inlet is in the center.

This view of a Paxton supercharger clearly shows the snail shape of its housing. The fan blades pull air into the inlet, and the hole at the right side is the outlet port.

The primary operating component in a centrifugal supercharger is its simple, small (only about four inches across), cast-aluminum impeller. The straight-blade design of this particular impeller is not very sophisticated, but it's certainly adequate and reliable for street applications.

been to get it going with him out there. As Newton put it, a body in motion tends to remain in motion.

The reason a body tends to be flung off a rotating object is that inertia (the fact that the moving mass wants to remain in motion) is linear – that is, the body wants to keep moving in a straight line. But the rotating object moves it in a curving line. If the body is firmly attached to the rotating object, its mass will tend to keep the object rotating, but part of its inertial energy (also called kinetic energy, or the energy "contained" in a moving body) will be lost.

To illustrate this principle, again think of yourself on the merry-go-round. If you are sitting on the outside edge and your friend is pushing at a good speed, the weight of your body will keep the merry-go-round spinning for quite a while after he stops pushing. This is the effect of inertia, or kinetic energy – work continues to be done although no apparent energy is being put into the system. But, in this case, it is only part of the energy available. If you are sitting on the outside perimeter of the merry-go-round, you're going to have to hang on with lots of your own energy to stay in place – an amount of energy equal, but opposite, to the amount of kinetic energy that would propel your body in a straight line (tangentially) off the merry-go-round as soon as you let go.

Perhaps we're overdoing the explanation of how a centrifugal blower works, but it does illustrate why a centrifugal blower is much more efficient than a Roots or other type of positive-displacement pump, which simply pushes the air with direct force. By using the energy multiplying effect of centrifugal force (the inertia of the mass of the air molecules) to help compress the air, the mechanical efficiency of a centrifugal blower is, consequently, much higher than other types, meaning that it requires less horsepower from the engine to make good boost. The spinning blades of the impeller in a centrifugal blower rapidly accelerate the air molecules, greatly increasing their velocity, which gives them a considerable amount of kinetic energy.

How this velocity is transformed into pressure is a bit more difficult to understand. If you look at a cross-section of an impeller and its housing, you will notice that most (though not all) types decrease in cross-sectional area from the center to the tip of the blades. That is, the cavity is enclosed by a pair of blades and the housing is wedge-shaped, tapering toward the outer edge. It would appear, therefore, that air would be compressed in this cavity as it is "squeezed" outward into the smaller area near the impeller tip. But such is not the case, for two reasons.

First, although the cross-section (or the width) of the blade decreases toward the tip, the distance between two adjacent fan blades, since they are radial, increases from the center to the edge, thus increasing the enclosed volume. The combined effect might be a constant-area cross-section, but in fact, many centrifugal housing designs (as used in turbochargers) actually have parallel walls. Second, and much more significant, as the air is accelerated along the impeller blade, two things happen to it. It tends to stack up against the face of the blade, which would compress the air. But at the same time, as the blade accelerates the air molecules radially, they will stretch out as their velocity is increased. This latter condition is similar to the effect of a carburetor venturi, which, as you know, decreases the density and the pressure of the air by increasing its volume (the air molecules are stretched farther apart).

All of this may be a little confusing, but don't worry too much about exactly what is going on inside the centrifugal blower housing. The one point we want to make here is that it's nearly impossible to compute a volumetric efficiency figure for a centrifugal-type blower, since it's not a positive-displacement pump. We don't speak of the internal displacement of a centrifugal blower, as we do of a Roots or a vane-type blower. In fact, the shape of the impeller blades and the housing have nearly as much effect on the output of a centrifugal blower as does its physical size.

The adiabatic efficiency of the centrifugal supercharger is very significant, however. Remember, the energy imparted to the air by the blower (ultimately by the engine) is minimal in a centrifugal unit because of its good mechanical efficiency. That is, there is comparatively little work done on the air – since we're actually using the weight of the air molecules to provide much of the energy – and therefore the centrifugal supercharger doesn't heat the air nearly as much as a Roots blower. Also, the centrifugal blower doesn't beat the air, so the flow of air through the blower is much smoother than in a Roots.

Second, the compression process itself is much more efficient in the centrifugal supercharger. After the air molecules are accelerated along the impeller blades, they are flung off the ends at a velocity approximately equal to that of the tips of the blades. As this high-velocity air is hurled into the scroll housing, it literally piles up against the air already packed into the housing and the manifold, which means that the air actually compresses itself with its own momentum. The kinetic energy imparted to the air molecules by the impeller in the form of velocity is immediately, and efficiently, converted into static energy in the form of pressure. Some heat is certainly generated by this process, since the volume of the air is reduced as it "stacks up" (thus increasing the density of the air at the same time that it increases the pressure, which is what we want from a supercharger), but the heat gain in a good centrifugal blower can be so low as to approach 100 percent adiabatic efficiency. Even the less sophisticated types used for automobile superchargers are capable of 70 percent to 80 percent adiabatic efficiency.

Another advantage of the centrifugal supercharger is the extreme mechanical simplicity of the impeller and housing, which involve only one basic moving part. There is very little stress on the impeller, it's very lightweight, and it doesn't mesh with, or come in close contact with, any other moving parts. Therefore, there is little need for strengthening, clearancing, or ever having to rebuild these components. Also, there is no pulsing of the output airflow from a centrifugal blower, as there is in most other types, nor are there any eccentric moving parts to cause vibration or wear, as in a vane-type, Wankel, or piston pump. And finally, a centrifugal blower can produce significantly strong boost pressures from a relatively small and lightweight unit, which can be mounted in a variety of convenient locations on the engine.

Is this beginning to sound too good to be true? As you might expect, there are a couple of flies in the ointment – otherwise every car would run a centrifugal blower, and that would be that.

The major problem is that not only is the centrifugal blower not a positive displacement pump, but the kinetic energy imparted to the air molecules by the spinning impeller increases roughly as the square of the tip speed of the blades. This might sound like another asset at first – if you get 10 pounds of boost at a given blower RPM, doubling the blower speed will give you four times as much boost, and tripling blower RPM will give you nine times more boost.

But think of it in reverse: Your engine can only handle a given amount of boost on the street; therefore, the maximum boost level is set. Let's say you want 10 pounds of boost at 6,000 engine RPM, and you gear the blower accordingly. No problem. But, at 3,000 engine RPM, the blower speed will be cut in half (since the blower is geared in direct proportion to the crank regardless of the overdrive ratio), and the boost level will be reduced by four times, to only 2.5 pounds. If the centrifugal blower makes seven pounds boost at 6,000 rpm (which is typical for a street setup), it will only make 1.75 pounds at 3,000 rpm.

Thus, the centrifugal blower is very peaky, or speed-sensitive. It will give good, efficient boost at higher RPM, but very little boost or torque, at lower engine speeds. As a result, a centrifugal blower is excellent for top-end speed contests, such as Bonneville, or sustained high-RPM racing such as on a long oval track (i.e., Indianapolis). But a centrifugal blower doesn't work nearly as well as a positive-displacement type for road racing, drag racing, or any type of driving that covers a wide engine RPM range – and street driving would have to fall into this category.

On the other hand, we are comparing centrifugal blowers to Roots blowers (primarily) here, and this "low-end response" argument against centrifugal blowers usually refers to racing situations. On the street, you don't want gobs of horsepower until you put your foot into the throttle. The centrifugal blower might not pin you to the seat immediately like a Roots will, but it'll come on like gangbusters at the top end. More important, it'll be far less of a parasite on your engine when you're not in need of extra power. Moreover, it's much lighter and more compact to carry around under your hood (a major consideration for street driving); and it'll be much more efficient when it's making boost.

Another drawback to the way the centrifugal blower makes boost is that the impeller must be driven at extremely high rotational speeds to get usable boost pressures. Impeller speeds in the neighborhood of 50,000 rpm are not uncommon. Consequently, centrifugal blowers, like turbos, require very high-quality shaft bearings and a good oiling system to maintain bearing life at these high shaft speeds. However, the fact that the impeller shaft is not subjected to extreme heat levels, as it is in an exhaust-driven turbocharger, simplifies the situation.

To attain the high impeller speed obviously requires some sort of wide-ratio step up gearing between the crankshaft and the impeller shaft beyond that feasible with overdrive belt pulleys. Using simple spur gears inside the blower housing to overdrive the impeller shaft has been the typical procedure in the past, and this works fine over a moderate RPM range. However, if the engine is rapidly revved up or down, the blower's impeller and shaft would undergo severe rates of acceleration and deceleration. Early centrifugal blowers, which used relatively large and heavy impellers, would strip the teeth off the drive gears under such conditions. Today's automotive centrifugal blowers use small, lightweight impellers, as well as sophisticated drive mechanisms and shaft oiling systems, to eliminate this problem. Nonetheless, this impeller size limitation – as well as a maximum RPM limit – obviously restricts the ultimate boost levels available from these blowers.

Consequently, you need to be careful not to over rev a centrifugal blower on a street engine for two reasons. First, the blower itself has a definite "redline" in terms of rotor and gear RPM speeds. Since the boost output from a centrifugal blower increases roughly as the square of engine RPM, winding the motor an extra grand could shoot blower boost unexpectedly to a dangerous level, possibly resulting in engine damage. However, some superchargers and most turbochargers often use a wastegate or other mechanical device to monitor the boost level and protect against excessive boost.

Speaking of turbochargers, these are simply another form of centrifugal supercharger, which you may have fig-

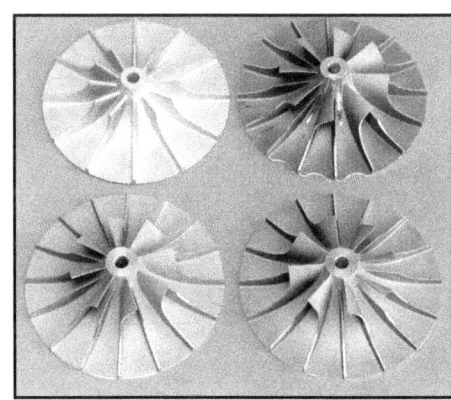

While lower-boost applications don't need a sophisticated impeller design, as seen in the straight-fin, B-trim Vortech at upper left, today's centrifugal blowers employ more aggressive impeller design to increase boost levels. Vortech's standard S-trim, in clockwise and counter-clockwise versions (bottom left and right), employ curved blades at the blower inlet, as does the high-boost T-trim (upper right), which uses a larger housing inlet. All of these designs are made of investment-cast aluminum. Lucky sport-compact enthusiasts get to enjoy all the technology that Vortech originally developed for its V-8 blowers.

Chapter 4

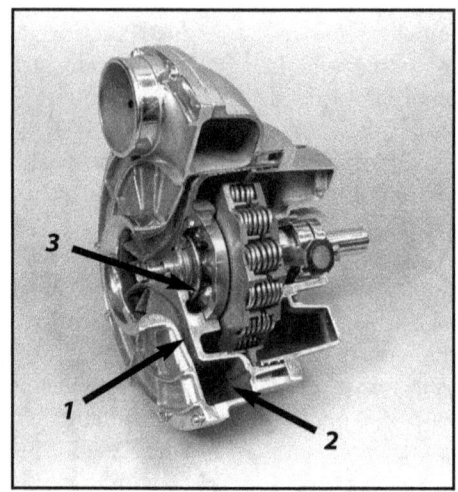

A cutaway of a Paxton blower graphically shows the relationship between the impeller cavity (1) and the pressure housing (2). All of the mechanisms to the right of (behind) the impeller are simply drive components, and the large steel balls that step up rotational speed of the impeller are clearly visible in their race (3).

The oil in the reservoir of ball-drive centrifugal blowers can get quite hot, especially in high-boost units. To combat this scenario, Paxton makes a recirculating cooler that can drop the oil temp by 150 degrees and has a pickup that inserts in the dipstick hole.

A big asset of most centrifugal blowers is that they're relatively small and surprisingly light. Most models can be mounted anywhere on the engine as long as the oil and pickup tube are towards the bottom.

Even a high-output impeller for the ball-drive Paxton SN 2000 looks pretty simple (left), but the standard impeller for the new Novi blowers shows a much more modern design (right). Both are investment castings.

The biggest refinement over the years in the ball-drive Paxton blowers has been closer tolerances between the drive balls and races. Luckily, there was plenty of research and development time before these blowers made their way onto any modern sport compacts.

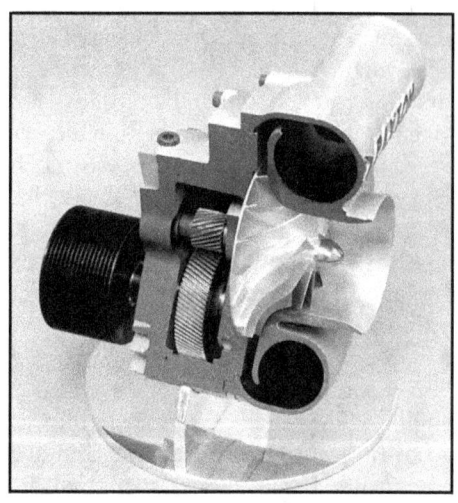

The Paxton Novi 2000, released in the latter 1990s, is the first new Paxton design in 40-some years. It uses a pair of helical cut 3.54:1 step-up gears held in place by high-grade roller bearings, turning a lightweight aluminum impeller. This view also gives you a good look at the relationship of the impeller, the narrow diffuser passages, and the increasing diameter of the scroll housing.

ured out by the design similarities. We'll discuss turbos in the following chapter.

VORTECH

Of several new supercharger companies to emerge in the 1990s, Vortech Engineering of Moorpark, California, has been one of the more aggressive. Not only does it offer complete supercharger packages for the latest sport compact cars, all of which are 49- or 50-state smog-legal, but it also offers several larger or more powerful centrifugal superchargers for higher performance or all-out racing.

Currently, the Vortech line of centrifugal blowers includes the V-1 with an S (standard street) or R (race) trim impeller in clockwise and counter-clockwise versions, and either side or rear outlet housings; the larger V-3 in R trim or higher-performance J trim; the giant (more than 11 inches in diameter) V-4 for all-out racing; and a small V-5 for engines in the 1.6- to 4-liter range. The V-3 in J trim is claimed to produce as much as 1,100 hp, while the V-4 can make 1,300 hp.

Though Vortech's early supercharger kits didn't include intercoolers, in the latter 1990s, it began employing intercoolers (which Vortech calls aftercoolers)

Centrifugal Blowers For Sport Compacts

With straight (side), front, and rear discharge housings for centrifugal blowers, plumbing can be pretty simple. Also note that this installation includes a bypass valve between the blower inlet and outlet tubes to reduce unwanted boost during deceleration and cruise modes.

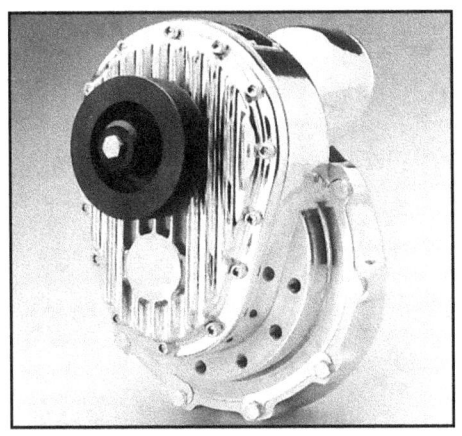

The Powerdyne supercharger is a good-looking unit with a finned housing that is available polished (shown), or in a satin finish. Powerdyne is developing a six- to eight-psi kit for the 1995-98 V-Tech Honda Civic without A/C.

The unique feature of the Powerdyne blower is its cogged belt drive for impeller step-up gearing. This makes the unit quieter and eliminates the need for an oil bath.

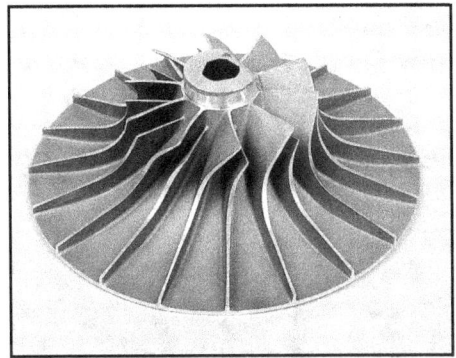

The Hyperdyne impeller is of an advanced design with curved blades at the inlet. The impeller is computer-matched to the scroll housing shape.

more vigorously, usually of the air-to-water configuration. This system includes the water-cooled aftercooler in the pressurized ducting between the supercharger and the EFI inlet, a small water tank and electric pump, a radiator to cool the water, and the necessary hoses to connect them. Besides street and moderate racing versions, Vortech also makes a huge Mondo Cooler capable of passing 2,500 cfm for power in the reported 1,700-hp range, primarily for drag racing.

Vortech also offers several accessories such as race or street bypass valves to reduce blower surging on rapid deceleration and a variety of ignition and fuel system accessories (pumps, larger injectors, supplementary injector units, larger mass airflow sensors, and fuel management units that increase fuel pressure relative to boost) all specifically for multi-point EFI systems.

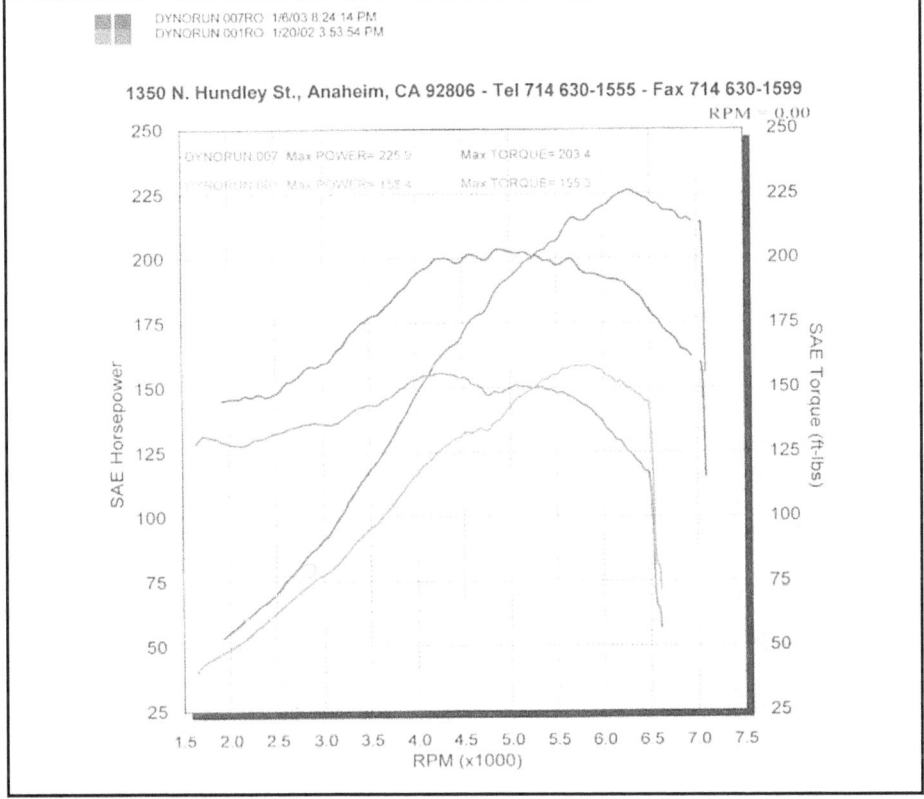

The dyno chart for the VF-Engineering VW Golf supercharger kit shows incredible horsepower gains. These kits are OBD I OBD II compliant and feature an RPM limiter increased to 7,000 rpm with soft rev limiters completely removed. It also has increased SC pulley belt wrap, so that an idler bracket and pulley are not required. A Bosch pressure relief bypass system bleeds off pressure when decelerating to facilitate smooth, reliable operation under all driving conditions.

Vortech Engineering's newest system is a high-output system for the

2000-2003 Ford Focus ZX3 with the 2.0-liter Zetec engine. The addition of the V-5 F-Trim supercharger at 8 psi is said to increase horsepower from 130 to 195 and torque from 135 to 170 ft-lbs at the flywheel.

The system includes an integrated dual-pass air/water charge aftercooler, which features a closed-loop water-cooling system with a stand-alone pump, tank, and front-mounted heat exchanger. Vortech's patented extended supercharger drive technology allows remote placement of the supercharger on the driver's side of the engine compartment. All components needed to bolt the system to a stock vehicle, such as billet aluminum mounting brackets, supercharger oil feed and drain, compressor bypass valve, fuel system upgrade including high-flow replacement injectors, and all required fasteners are included. The installation also allows you to retain all your factory accessories, including A/C and power steering. This system is CARB legal under E.O. #D-213-20, and you can get it in satin or polished finish.

Vortech employs one of the most sophisticated research and development departments in the blower business, including a blower dyno, flowbench, and other computerized data acquisition equipment. We will undoubtedly see further refinement and innovation from Vortech in the future.

Applications:

Acura:

- 1994-01 Acura Integra GSR w/1.8-liter DOHC, V-5 SQ G-Trim (7 psi - polished), counterclockwise rotation
- 1994-01 Acura Integra GSR w/1.8-liter DOHC, V-5 SQ G-Trim and Aftercooler (8-9 psi - polished), counterclockwise
- 1994-01 Acura Integra GSR w/1.8-liter DOHC, V-5 SQ G-Trim (7 psi - satin), counterclockwise
- 1994-01 Acura Integra GSR w/1.8-liter DOHC, V-5 SQ G-Trim and Aftercooler (8-9 psi - satin), counterclockwise
- 1996-01 Acura Integra LS w/1.8-liter DOHC, V-5 SQ G-Trim (7 psi - satin or polished), counterclockwise
- 1996-01 Acura Integra LS w/1.8-liter DOHC, V-5 SQ G-Trim and Aftercooler (8-9 psi - satin or polished), counterclockwise

Ford Focus:

- 2000-03 Ford Focus SVT 2.0-liter Zetec, V-5 F-Trim (polished or satin)
- 2000-03 Ford Focus 2.0-liter SVT, V-5 F-Trim and Aftercooler (polished or satin)
- 2000-03 Ford Focus ZX3 2.0-liter Zetec, V-5 F-Trim (polished or satin)
- 2000-03 Ford Focus ZX3 2.0-liter Zetec, V-5 F-Trim and Aftercooler (polished or satin)

Honda:

- 1999-00 Honda Civic Si w/1.6-liter DOHC, V-5 SQ G-Trim (6 psi - satin or polished), counterclockwise
- 1999-00 Honda Civic Si w/1.6-liter DOHC, V-5 SQ G-Trim and Aftercooler (8-9 psi - satin or polished), counterclockwise
- 2000-03 Honda S2000, V-2 SQ SC-Trim and Maxflow Aftercooler (satin or polished)
- 2003 Nissan 350Z/Infinity G35, Supercharger Kit and air-to-air intercooler (8 psi - satin or polished)

VF-ENGINEERING

The VF-Engineering management and engineering team evolved supercharging modern sports cars such as the Lotus, VW, BMW, and Opel. Joint projects and partnerships with firms in the UK and Switzerland have given VF-Engineering the opportunity to market in Europe and obtain the latest information on newly released vehicles. VF uses the Vortech supercharger in the company's supercharger kits.

Since a lot of VF-Engineering's portfolio is directed at the VW Golf, we'll take a close look at a couple of these kits. They also make kits for the Mazda Miata.

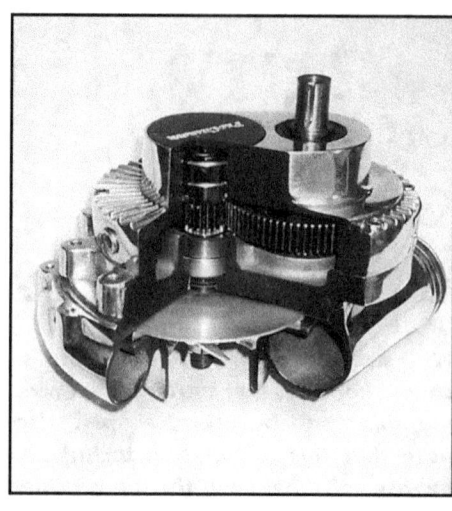

The ATI ProChargers mix and match drive pulley size, step-up transmission size, scroll-housing size, and impeller size and design for a broad range of boost levels. This cutaway shows the larger D-series blower with 4.44:1 square-cut gears with twin Duplex bearings on the shafts, and a billet helix impeller.

The vast majority of ATI blowers use 7075 T-6 machined billet impellers with helix blades, such as this 6.25-inch-diameter example used in the P1200 and D-1 superchargers. Billet impellers allow higher boost from a smaller blower through increased RPM.

The VF-Engineering Stage 1 Supercharger Kit for 2002-up VW Golf/Jetta MK4 with the 2.8-liter VR6 24-valve (6 psi - satin) is designed using the infamous "bullet proof" Vortech Engineering supercharger unit. The key to the design of this supercharger kit is how easy it is to bolt on. The kit is supplied with every part needed to get your car up and running supercharged on the same day.

Centrifugal Blowers For Sport Compacts

The Vortech supercharging system for the 2002-2003 Ford Focus SVT will impress you with the obvious attention to detail and fully integrated appearance. Increase your horsepower from 170 to 276 and torque from 145 to 204 ft-lbs. It's available in satin or polished finishes and uses the V-5 SQ F-Trim compressor, air-to-water intercooler, and blow-off valve.

Vortech does its research and development on a heavily instrumented blower dyno that includes a flow bench. This adds up to a system that's better suited to your needs.

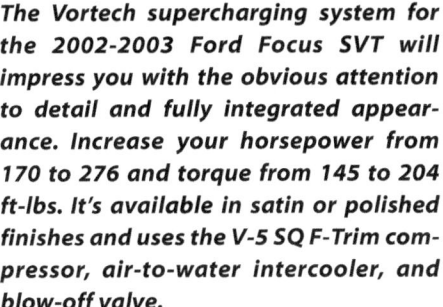

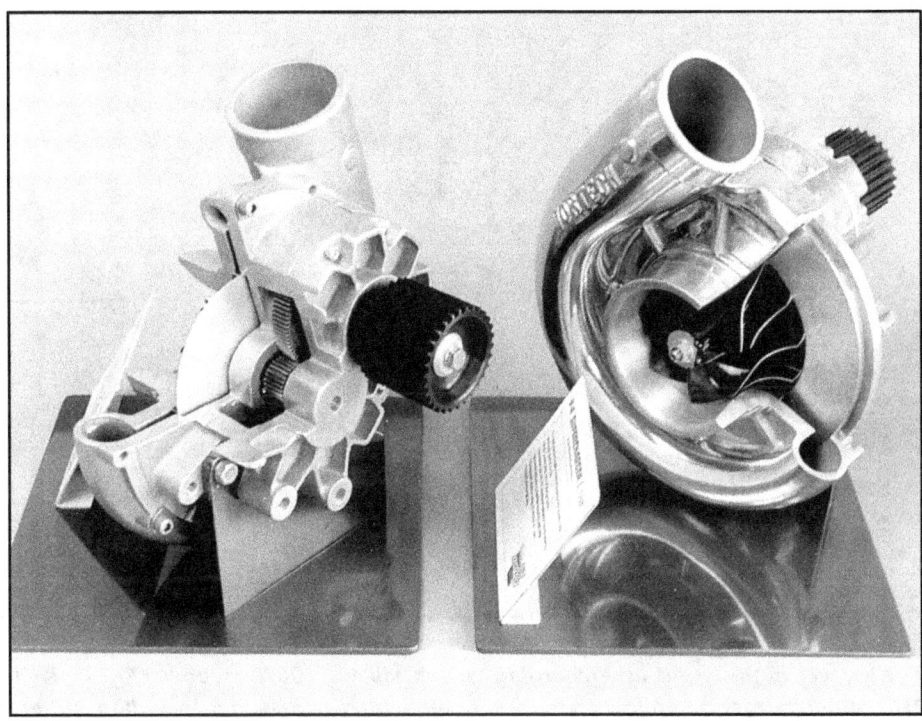

ATI also heavily stresses the use of air-to-air intercoolers in most applications, especially those blowing into electronic fuel-injection systems, or those involving constant load (i.e., trailer-towing trucks). For marine applications, they use air-to-water coolers.

The Vortech superchargers use straight or helical cut step-up gears, with a variety of impeller designs to vary output. They also have clockwise or counterclockwise rotation impellers, allowing housings with left or right, front or back outlets. On the left is the most common V-1 Vortech, while the huge V-4, at right, measures more than 11 inches in diameter. These are probably a little larger than what Vortech would recommend for the average sport compact.

The history of the VR6 supercharger kit dates back to 1995, when Z-Engineering was the first to make the Vortech supercharger kit for the VR6 Golf. The company marketed this kit in Europe and the UK and it was very well received. Now Z-Engineering has revisited the MK3 VR6 supercharger kit with more experience and a new approach to kit design. The mass-airflow sensor has been relocated and a boost-overrun valve (pressure relief system) is incorporated with all stages of this kit. The kit is also fully compatible with OBD I and OBD II computer systems. Even with this supercharger setup, the VR6 idles and accelerates as it should – smoothly and relentlessly.

The VF-Engineering kit is set up in three stages to give you an increasing amount of horsepower and torque. Each stage is a bolt-on kit and can be added on to the previous stage. Performance, reliability, and stock feel were major factors in the extensive research and development carried out in California. Custom proprietary GIAC software is supplied with this kit to safely realign all fuelling and engine management parameters.

The unique advantage of all VF-Engineering products is the 3-year unlimited mileage warranty, coupled with lifetime software support and world-renowned customer service.

Chapter 4

The Vortech high-output supercharging system will add 108 horsepower @ 7-8 psig to the Honda S-2000. It features a V-2 SQ SC-Trim supercharger and allows retention of all factory accessories including A/C and power steering. The integrated dual-pass air/water Maxflow Power Cooler charge cooler system allows for effective street operation using a closed-loop, water-cooling system with a stand-alone pump, tank, and front-mounted heat exchanger. All components needed to bolt the system to a stock vehicle, such as mounting plates, fuel pump, supercharger oil feed and drain assemblies, electronic timing controller, and compressor bypass valve are included. A three-year limited warranty is provided on the supercharger. Satin or polished finish components are available.

Applications:

Mazda:
- 1999-02 Mazda Miata MX5, Stage 1 Kit (6 psi)
- 1999-00 Mazda Miata MX5, Stage 2 Kit (8 psi)

Volkswagen:
- 1991-99 VW Golf/Jetta/Passat/Vento MK3 w/2.8-liter VR6 12-valve, Stage 1 Kit (6 psi)
- 1991-99 VW Golf/Jetta/Passat/Vento MK3 w/2.8-liter VR6 12-valve, Stage 2 Kit (8 psi)
- 1991-99 VW Golf/Jetta/Passat/Vento MK3 w/2.8-liter VR6 12-valve, Stage 3 Kit (9.5 psi)
- 1999-02 VW Golf/Jetta MK4 w/2.8-liter VR6 12-valve, Stage 1 Kit (6psi)
- 1999-02 VW Golf/Jetta MK4 w/2.8-liter VR6 12-valve, Stage 2 Kit (8psi)
- 1999-02 VW Golf/Jetta MK4 w/2.8-liter VR6 12-valve, Stage 3 Kit (9.5psi)

PROCHARGER

Accessible Technologies, Inc., (ATI) of Lenexa, Kansas, began producing the ProCharger centrifugal supercharger in 1993. ATI offers a variety of boost levels for street/strip applications by varying drive pulley ratios, or by using different impellers. The P-series blower features a 9-inch diameter housing and 3.5:1, square-cut, step-up gearing, which is lubricated by engine oil. The P600 has a cast, straight-fin impeller; the most popular P600B has a CNC-machined straight-fin billet impeller; and the P1200BR has a taller, curved-fin (helix) billet impeller.

The P-series ProChargers are used in a wide variety of installation kits to produce a number of different boost levels (between 6 and 17 psi) in 5- to 6-liter engines. Most of these kits incorporate an air-to-air intercooler for higher-boost applications (9 to 17 psi). The majority of these applications are 50-state EPA legal. Non-intercooled, blow-through kits for the P600 or the P600B are also available for carbureted engines of the size specified above. ATI strongly recommends intercooling for street and strip installations to allow the use of pump gas at higher boost levels. They use a fuel-enrichment system, rather than ignition retard, to help curb detonation.

To give an indication of the positive effects of intercooling, ATI claims its 9-psi intercooled kit for a 5.0L push rod V-8, using the P600 blower, gives a 60 to 70 percent horsepower increase, while its non-intercooled 9-psi kit, using a P600B blower, gives only a 35 to 45 percent increase.

Next, ATI introduced its D-series competition ProChargers. These blowers employ an extra heavy-duty step-up gear "transmission" featuring 4.44:1, square-cut gears, a thicker case that is line-bored for shaft bearings, and dual Duplex bearings on the impeller shaft. The D-1 uses this transmission unit with the 9-inch scroll housing and the 6-inch helix billet impeller used in the P1200BR. The D-2 uses a giant 12-inch scroll housing with a 6.25-inch helix billet impeller. The enormous D-3 uses a 12-inch housing with a 5-inch diameter inlet and 8-inch diameter billet impeller. Because of its size, the D-3 can produce more boost at higher efficiency because of lower impeller speed, and it has produced as much as 1,800 hp in dyno tests.

For the sport compact market, the crew at ProCharger tuned the firm's new C-1 ProCharger compressor to keep with the flow rates of sport-compact engines. The C-1 ProCharger is the first and only gear-driven centrifugal sport compact supercharger to feature self-lubrication, and it contains the industry's most advanced technology. The C-1 shares many of the design elements that deliver the record-setting durability and performance of ProCharger competition superchargers, and it is also street legal.

The patented SC design eliminates the need for oil lines and punching a hole in the oil pan. Additionally, instead of being forced to use heated engine oil or the grease in sealed bearings, SC ProChargers are lubricated with an extremely high-quality synthetic oil, which is specifically engineered for high-speed use, and produces the least frictional heat and parasitic load. The self-contained design not only eliminates the heat that is transferred to a supercharger by engine oil in oil-fed applications, but it also avoids the risk of clogged supercharger oil lines, oil drainage problems, or engine oil leakage. By combining an advanced multi-patented supercharger transmission design with the highest quality oil, SC ProChargers produce a larger net power gain because they run cooler and consume less power than comparable oil-fed designs. This is also the only supercharger technology proven to repeatedly produce full-out race turbo levels of power.

Complete intercooled ProCharger systems are currently available for the Nissan 350Z, Infiniti G35, Civic Si, the 1.8-liter Integra, and will soon be available for the Ford Focus. For all other sport compact applications, a universal sport-compact kit is being offered (fabrication and tuning required). The universal kit contains the C-1 ProCharger, a compact 2-core sheetmetal intercooler, a universal tubing kit, a right-hand or left-hand universal supercharger bracket, a Bosch surge/bypass system, and an air filter. Optional items include ProPump fuel-pump assembly, FMU (fuel management unit) assembly, and a compact 3-core sheetmetal intercooler.

Applications:
- 2003 Nissan 350Z, 7 psi with C-2 and 3-core intercooler, 55-60% horsepower gain
- 2003 Infiniti G35, 6 psi with C-2 and 3-core intercooler, 45-50% horsepower gain
- 2003 Infiniti FX35, 6 psi with C-2 and 3-core intercooler, 45-50% horsepower gain
- 1999-00 Honda Civic Si, 8 psi with C-1a and 2-core intercooler, 70-75% horsepower gain
- 1994-01 Acura Integra GS-R and Type R, 8 psi with C-1a and 2-core intercooler, 70-75% horsepower gain
- Universal Sport Compact Kit, with C-1 and 2-core intercooler, horsepower gain varies

HKS Rotrex Supercharger Kits

The HKS Rotrex supercharger kits are the latest in forced induction systems. The centrifugal type supercharger features a unique traction drive with a closed oil circulation system. The traction drive uses fixed-ratio planetary rollers that are more efficient than traditional gear wheels. Because the planetary rollers do not have teeth like traditional gear wheels, noise is decreased and reliability is increased. The closed oil circulation system cycles a specially formulated Traction Oil that lubricates and cools the supercharger, dramatically increasing longevity and reliability. The Traction Oil is cooled through a liquid-to-air oil cooler included with each kit.

All HKS Rotrex supercharger kits are developed as complete bolt-on systems. For certain applications, HKS will include a front-mount air-to-air intercooler, Super Mega Flow intake, bypass valve, additional injectors, upgraded fuel pump, and/or an upgraded fuel computer. Also included with each kit is a high-performance cast-aluminum bracket, which has been precisely engineered to reduce noise and vibration.

Applications:
- 12001-XN001 2003-2004 Nissan 350Z

Chapter 5

Turbocharging Theory

Since a turbocharger is essentially an exhaust-driven supercharger, and because we've spent so much of this book explaining how superchargers work, the best way to transition into talking about turbos is to compare and contrast them with centrifugal superchargers. In an ultimate power shootout, turbochargers always win. There is a reason F1 cars were turbocharged. Perhaps the best example is the most powerful F1 engine ever created – the 1,500-cc BMW turbocharged engine powering the Brabham car in the mid 1980s. It developed over 1,500 horsepower in qualifying tune. That's over one-horsepower per cubic centimeter of displacement!

Getting back to turbo theory, the compressor section of a turbo is exactly the same as a centrifugal supercharger; the difference is that the turbo uses another impeller and scroll housing, through which hot exhaust gas travels to drive the unit. Thus the turbo takes no crankshaft horsepower from the engine to run. Instead, it recovers some of the heat and mass-flow energy normally wasted by the engine in the exhaust to do the work of compressing the intake charge. Combustion heats the exhaust, causing it to expand; so the exhaust is already pressurized. The drive portion of the turbo works in the reverse of the compressor side – it "absorbs" the pressure of the exhaust gas to spin an impeller. The exhaust enters the impeller radially at the blade tips and leaves axially from the center. The impeller of the turbo driven by the exhaust is connected directly, by a common shaft, to the impeller that compresses the intake charge.

If the above is slightly confusing, let's unpack the process by focusing on a few fundamentals. Remember that the internal combustion engine is an air-

The twin-turbocharged Toyota iForce V-8 that powers the Turbonetics Celica is a masterwork of modern turbocharger technology. The roller bearing turbos spool quickly and feed into a huge air-to-water intercooler. This car was the first import racer to run an NHRA sanctioned 200-mph quarter-mile speed.

Layout and Explanation of a

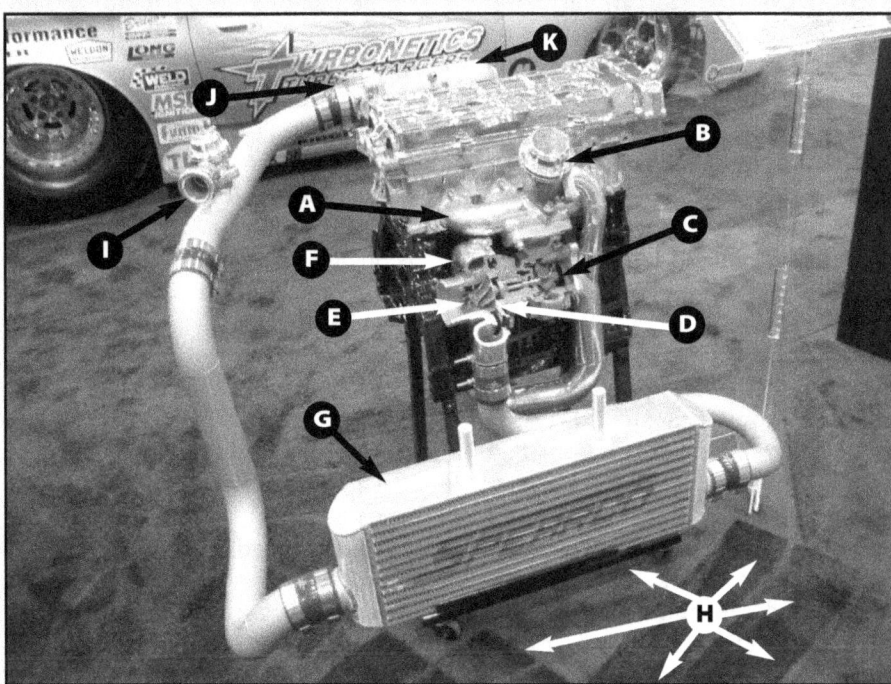

This is a picture of a turbocharger unit as installed on a typical four-cylinder, front-drive, sport compact. Of course, this may vary depending on the orientation of your engine within the engine bay. The exhaust gas exits the engine through the exhaust manifold (**A**) and passes the wastegate (**B**), which regulates the boost level, on its way to the turbo. The exhaust gases drive the turbine (**C**), which spins the compressor (**D**). The compressor draws air in from the center of the housing (**E**) and accelerates it into the scroll (**F**) where it is compressed. As the air is compressed, it heats up. It also absorbs some of the heat from the turbine section. The heated air travels through the intercooler (**G**), where as much heat as possible is transferred to the atmosphere (**H**), preferably with the least amount of pressure drop. The intake charge then travels past the blowoff valve (**I**), through the throttle body (**J**), into the intake manifold (**K**), and into the engine. In the combustion chamber, fuel is added, the mixture is compressed, and then it is ignited. As the mixture expands, it forces the piston down the bore. The piston comes back up, forcing the exhaust out of the engine through the exhaust manifold, and the cycle begins anew.

Here is a closer look at the turbo itself. The turbine component is a centripetal, radial, or mixed-inflow device in that the exhaust gas flows inward, past the wheel blades, and exits at the center of the turbine housing's diameter. The expanded exhaust gas is directed through the exhaust manifold into the turbine housing. The exhaust gas pressure and the heat energy extracted from the gas causes the turbine wheel to rotate, which drives the compressor wheel.

The compressor side is a centrifugal, or radial-outflow device in that the air flows outward, past the wheel blades, and exits at the outer diameter of the housing. The rotating compressor wheel draws ambient air through the engine's air filtration system (not shown). Its blades accelerate and expel the air into the compressor housing where it is compressed and directed through the intercooler, throttle body, intake manifold, and into the engine.

The exhaust control devices – swing valves, poppet valves, and wastegates – help control turbine speed (which in turn helps to control boost) by releasing excess exhaust pressure from the turbine housing. They can be an integral part of the turbine housing and/or mounted remotely (in this photo, the wastegate is mounted to the exhaust manifold). They are activated either by diaphragms or cylinders and pistons filled with air or oil. When opened, excess exhaust pressure is released from the turbine housing, directed to the exhaust system, and expelled into the atmosphere.

consuming machine (burns air and fuel). A turbocharger is an air pump that operates on the normally wasted energy in the exhaust gas. These gases drive the turbine wheel, which is coupled to the compressor wheel. The turbine spins the compressor wheel at very high RPM, and in doing so, increases the pressure and density of the air in the intake tract. As a result of the increased mass of compressed air, more fuel can be burned to produce more heat and pressure – and thus horsepower – from a given engine size.

To better understand turbocharging, you need to understand engine operation. Basically, it's all about pressure differentials and mass flow through the engine's four-cycle process. To get any useful force transferred to the crankshaft, you need to get very high pressure developed in the cylinders. Near the end of the power stroke, even though most of the useful pressure has been captured as work, cylinder pressures can still be quite high. At this point, the exhaust valve opens and the high pressure releases its energy into the exhaust manifold.

The amount of energy released as waste into the exhaust is directly proportional to the power level the engine is producing. For example, little energy is left over to exit into the exhaust manifold at part throttle or at idle. On the other hand, at full throttle, full load, significant amounts of energy in the form of high-temperature, high-pressure air is wasted in the exhaust system. The turbocharger captures some of this energy and uses it to provide denser air back into the engine. The force-fed cylinder develops more pressure and power at the crank, and so produces more energy to drive the turbocharger – and the cycle begins anew.

However, the process isn't infinite, and at some point the capacities of the turbocharger, the intake and exhaust ports and manifolds, and of course ever-increasing friction, prevents further power increase. Intuitively, it's the physical limits of the engine, i.e., how much pressure it can contain, which comes first. The engine is also limited by the ability of the fuel to resist deto-

Turbo Lag

Rick Squire of Squire Turbo Systems has a unique approach to turbocharger systems: remote mounting. I mean like way in the back. Most of the systems he has developed are for American muscle cars and full-size trucks, as well as the Toyota Tundra and Tacoma, but it's only a matter of time before he applies this technique to a sport compact. The advantages of this setup are many, one being how much less space this type of system would take up in the typically crowded sport compact engine compartment. Rick's take on turbo lag is interesting because he's spent a lot of time figuring out how to make the turbocharger work at reduced temps in the remote mounted location. Check out the STS website: www.ststurbo.com.

Turbo lag is a term used to describe the time that it takes from when you push the accelerator to full throttle to when the turbocharger comes onto boost. Since turbochargers are designed and sized to operate at specific RPM ranges and airflow conditions, some turbo lag is inherent in the system. Turbos can be sized for specific applications to perform best at low, mid, or high RPM. However, just like any performance add-on, such as cams, manifolds, heads, etc., you can't have peak performance in all RPM ranges.

To fully understand turbo lag, you must first understand the operation principles behind what causes a turbo to make boost. Like most forced induction systems, boost is not made by RPM alone. There is a big difference in the airflow through an engine at 6,000 rpm in neutral, 6,000 rpm in first gear at part throttle, and 6,000 rpm in high gear at full throttle. Turbochargers are even more affected by these airflow differences – and especially load differences – than most other devices. This is why you may be able to see a small amount of boost with a positive displacement supercharger at WOT in neutral, but you will seldom see any at WOT in neutral with a turbocharger.

Since turbochargers are so sensitive to airflow and especially loads, you'll get very different turbo lag characteristics on the same vehicle during different conditions. For example, the loads placed on the system in lower gears are not as high as the loads placed on the system in the higher gears. This applies to first, second, third gear, etc., as well as to rear-end gears and tire sizes. Short tires with lower gears such as 4.88:1s will not produce engine loading like a taller tire with 3.08:1 gears. The weight of the vehicle also contributes to the load: more weight, more load.

A given turbocharged vehicle may produce full boost in first gear by 3,500 rpm. This same vehicle may produce full boost in fourth gear by 2,300 rpm. The same vehicle, when pulling a steep hill, may produce full boost by 1,800 rpm even in first gear. These conditions are more specific to manual transmission vehicles as the boost has to rebuild in each gear after the throttle is closed during the shift. Automatic transmission vehicles operate differently as they can be loaded by stalling up the converter and placing enough load to build boost before the vehicle even moves. Also, with an automatic transmission, the throttle is not shut during shifts. This can cause the boost to spike during a shift because the turbo is supplying enough airflow to feed the boosted engine at high RPM, and suddenly the RPM is drastically cut down by the shift, which also adds increased load on the system. This can cause an engine that is accelerating in first gear with low boost to instantly go to full boost upon shifting into second gear.

Since the STS turbos are mounted several feet from the engine, people always ask if the turbo lag is going to be exaggerated, since the exhaust gas is cooling

Turbo Lag (continued)

down. When you think about it, putting a torch to your turbo and getting it hot doesn't produce boost. What produces boost is airflow across the turbine, which causes it to spin. If turbochargers required very high temperatures to produce boost, diesel trucks and methanol racecars wouldn't be able to run turbos. However, each of these vehicles with extremely low exhaust temperatures works very well with turbochargers when (like any turbo application) the turbocharger is sized correctly.

The reasoning is as follows: In a conventional, exhaust-manifold mounted turbocharger system, the extra heat causes the air molecules to separate and the gas becomes thinner because of the extra space between the molecules. This extra space increases the volume of the air but it doesn't increase the mass. Because the volume is higher, the velocity of the gas has to be higher to get it out in the same amount of time.

By mounting the turbo further downstream, the gases do lose heat energy and velocity; however, there is just as much mass (the amount of air) coming out of the tailpipe as there is coming out of the heads. Therefore, you're driving the turbine with a denser gas charge. The same number of molecules per second are striking the turbine and flowing across the turbine at 1,200° F as there is at 1,700° F.

It's important to point out that the heat of the exhaust doesn't cause its velocity – heat creates volume. If you look at any of the physics laws for gases, you'll find that pressure, volume, and heat are related. $PV = nRT$ is a very useful formula, and the V isn't for velocity, it's for volume. The turbine housing has a big influence on the velocity. The scrolling design reduces the volume of the exhaust chamber as it scrolls around, so the gases speed up to maintain the same flow rate.

Hotter gases have more volume, thus requiring a higher A/R, which in effect means that it starts at, say, three inches, and scrolls down to approximately one inch. Lower-temperature gases are denser and have less volume, so they require a lower A/R housing that would start at the same 3-inch size, as the turbine housings use standard flanges, and scroll down to, say, 3/4 inch. If you were to reverse the housings in this example, the conventional turbo would spool up extremely quickly, perhaps starting at 1,500 rpm. However, it would cause too much backpressure at higher RPM because the higher volume of gas couldn't squeeze through the 3/4-inch hole without requiring a lot of pressure to force it through. On the reverse side, the remote mounted turbo, with its cooler, denser gases, wouldn't spool up till, say, around 4,000 rpms, but once spooled up it would make efficient power because it doesn't require much backpressure to push the lower volume of gas through the larger 1-inch hole.

Turbochargers are exactly the same as centrifugal superchargers in terms of basic impeller and housing design, and the way that they create boost. The only difference is that a turbo uses a second impeller and scroll unit attached in reverse fashion to the exhaust system (instead of a pulley for the drive belt) to drive the blower portion.

the exhaust stroke, causing a loss of power at the crankshaft.

In a race motor, an engine builder can optimize the RPM or power level at which this occurs by choosing different combinations of turbine housing, tuned exhaust, head porting, and cam choice, as well as compressor housing and impeller choices. For example, as a general rule, if you want to build a low-RPM power combo, use a smaller A/R turbo, as it'll reach crossover at a lower RPM than a high-RPM power combo with a larger A/R.

We've already discussed the differences between turbos and crank-driven blowers in general. However, some contrasts between turbos and belt-driven, centrifugal blowers – which seem, at first, to operate in identical fashion – are very interesting.

Let's first look at some of the less desirable features of turbochargers.

THE CASE AGAINST TURBOCHARGERS

To begin with, the transfer of heat from the exhaust turbine to the intake impeller along the common shaft is a real problem for a turbo. The problem arises not so much from the effect on bearing and oil life, but because of the

nation. There is also a limit in turbocharged engine combinations that tuners call "crossover."

In a properly designed and operating turbo engine, the backpressure should be lower than the boost pressure until it reaches crossover. Crossover is the point at which the backpressure equals the boost pressure. For example, with 10-psi boost in the intake, it'll have 10 psi of backpressure. In this condition, the intake pressure pushing on the piston when the intake valve is open equals the exhaust backpressure pushing on the piston when the exhaust valve is open, so the forces cancel. As the engine makes more RPM, the backpressure increases above the pressure on the intake, so the force acting on the piston when the exhaust valve is open is greater than the force acting through the intake. This resists the piston moving up the bore on

Chapter 5

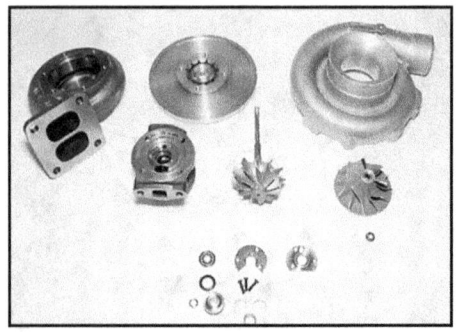

In short, turbochargers are composed of an exhaust-gas-driven turbine and a radial air compressor mounted at opposite ends of a common shaft and enclosed in cast housings. The shaft itself is enclosed and supported by a center housing, to which the compressor and turbine housings are attached. Note the twin-scroll turbine housing (on the left). This design is more effective than single-entry designs. Single-entry scrolls can cause cylinder dilution depending on the firing order of the engine and the type of exhaust manifold leading into the turbine. (Courtesy Garrett Turbo)

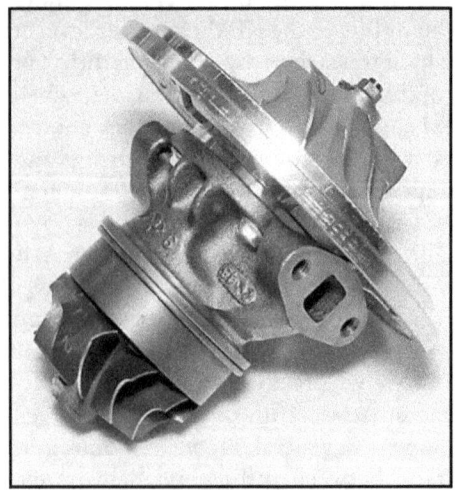

A turbocharger without the compressor and turbine housing attached is called a center housing and rotating assembly (CHRA). The typical turbocharger can rotate at speeds of 100,000 rpm and up. (Courtesy Garrett Turbo)

considerable amount of heat transferred to the intake air charge by the impeller, which reduces the adiabatic efficiency of the turbo. The belt-driven centrifugal blower doesn't have this problem. In fact, the centrifugal blow-

The turbine section is composed of a cast turbine wheel, a wheel heat shroud, and a turbine housing, with the inlet at the outer diameter of the turbine housing. (Courtesy Garrett Turbo)

er has the highest adiabatic efficiency of all types.

Also of concern is the control of power output and driveability issues of turbos compared to crankshaft-driven centrifugal superchargers. And although the belt-driven centrifugal blower is peakier in boost delivery than a Roots-type, it's not as peaky as a turbo. In a crank-driven centrifugal blower, regardless of the percentage of overdrive, the impeller rotation speed is directly proportional to engine speed – even though the amount of boost produced by the blower isn't. In a turbo, however, the peakiness is compounded since the rotational speed of the blower impeller depends on the rotational speed produced by the exhaust passing through the turbine portion, rather than being on a direct link to the engine. Thus, the sizing of the turbo relative to the engine, and matching the turbine size and design to impeller size and design, is very critical in a turbo application.

Even though a turbo puts no extra drag on the engine's crankshaft, it will inevitably be a restriction in terms of exhaust flow. On the other hand, a belt-driven centrifugal blower takes less engine horsepower to drive because of its high efficiency compared to a Roots-type blower, and it requires no changes to the exhaust system.

Though direct-port electronic fuel injection has made both centrifugal supercharging and turbocharging considerably more attractive (no need for an airbox over the carburetor), turbo systems are still more difficult to package than either type of supercharger. The centrifugal blower can be mounted in a variety of locations in cramped sport-compact engine compartments, and then plumbed directly into the mouth of the throttle body. Of course, with a turbo setup, the exhaust tubing will need to pass close by the intake tubing, since they both pass through the turbo. The extra tubing can further clutter up the engine compartment, especially if the system requires an intercooler, which is more likely with a turbo because of the extra heat.

THE CASE FOR TURBOCHARGERS

Even though all the above is true, it doesn't get around the brutal fact that a properly designed and tuned turbocharged engine allows an engine to make more power for a given amount of fuel. In other words, a properly tuned turbocharged engine is more efficient. In addition to their efficiency, turbochargers can be easily tuned to adjust power output at a wide variety of engine speeds and loads. True, turbochargers are more complicated to install. You have to make provisions to manage the heat produced in the engine compartment, intercoolers are pretty much mandatory, and you have to lubricate the turbocharger bearings. But the increased power output and efficiency is worth it.

Here's why a turbocharger is much more efficient than crankshaft-driven superchargers, even centrifugal units.

As we explained above, a turbo is powered by exhaust mass airflow. When the exhaust valve opens in an engine, there is still substantial pressure in the cylinder. The cam will typically open the valve at some point before BDC in order to use that pressure to allow the piston to blow down as the pressure is released. That pressure accelerates the exhaust gas out of the cylinder at a very high velocity. The turbocharger uses the energy of the high-speed exhaust mass to spin the

Turbocharging Theory

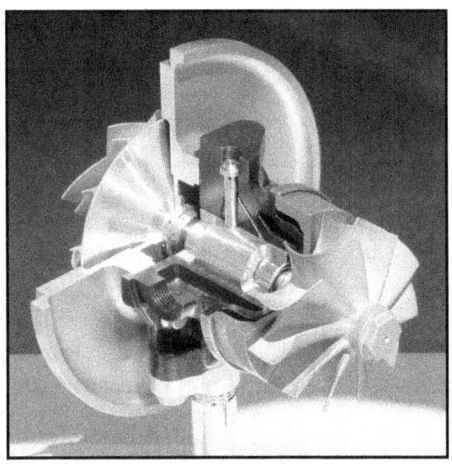

The compressor section is composed of a cast compressor wheel, a back plate, and a compressor housing, with the inlet at the center of the compressor housing diameter. (Courtesy Garrett Turbo)

In the case of center housing and rotating assembly (CHRA), the center housing (bearing housing) supports the compressor and turbine wheel shaft in a carefully designed bearing system. The bearing system, designed for high speed, does not see heavy loading as with crankshaft bearings. It must delicately position the wheels as closely as possible to the contour of the end housings. Key to the positioning is the oil filling the clearances between the center housing bore, bearings, and shaft. This oil-filled clearance is vital to a turbocharger's efficiency and longevity. (Courtesy Garrett Turbo)

Seal systems separate the center housing from both the turbine and compressor stage. The seals restrict the oil from entering the compressor and turbine areas and reduce the flow of gases from those areas into the center housing. These systems may include piston ring seals, carbon and O-ring seals, oil slingers, and labyrinth (threaded) seals to accomplish the task. The oil seals are activated when the shaft rotates and housing pressure develops. Various retaining rings and bolts secure the rotating components. Thrust components maintain axial integrity. A shaft nut or threaded wheel is used to join the compressor wheel and the turbine wheel. The turbine and compressor housing are attached to the center housing and rotating assembly by bolts, V-band clamps and/or clamp plates, lock plates, and bolts. (Courtesy Garrett Turbo)

turbine, which spins the compressor to, well, compress or pressurize the intake charge.

Turbochargers raise the pressure in the exhaust system because they are an exhaust restriction. If you're thinking in terms of a naturally aspirated engine, this restriction costs power. In a sense, that's correct, but since the turbo captures the energy that would otherwise be wasted, the turbo is able to move a sufficient quantity of mass with less effort and fuel than a belt-driven supercharger. In other words, the turbo pressurizes the intake by pressurizing the exhaust. The trick is where and when in the RPM range these pressure differentials occur.

Turbo Sizing: How to Get a Turbo That Fits Your Performance Needs

Before we get into discussing how to match a turbo for your combination, we first need to make sure you're up to speed on some turbocharging basics. You'll need to know how to read a compressor map, which means you need to understand the surge line, choke line, wheel trim, and the pressure ratio. You'll also need to understand what a turbine A/R (aspect ratio) is and how it influences the behavior of your system. All of these terms are explained in this chapter, so I won't be redundant and explain them here. But do scan a few pages to get familiar with the terms before reading this section. It'll make a lot more sense.

Achieving the pressure differentials we discussed above is a matter of sizing the turbocharger correctly. How do you do that? Well, that depends on what else you've done to your engine and where in the RPM range you want, or need, to make the most power.

To get you the inside story on matching a turbo to an engine, we went to one of the major sources of turbocharged power – Turbonetics. Rick Head, then with Turbonetics but now a principle of Innovative Turbo Systems, gave us the lowdown on turbo applications for this book.

When designing a turbo system you have to look at the application. Is it a street car, a mostly drag-racing car with some street driving, or mostly a streeter with an occasional full-boost blast down the quarter-mile? All that makes a big difference in your choice of turbocharger, because it tells the turbo tuner the RPM range in which the engine will need to make the most power. For example, Rick says that most racers that do well use turbos sized larger than what the books call for. Typically, a race engine is designed to make the most power at high RPM, so it'll need a turbo that delivers air differently from that needed by the street guy who can use a smaller turbo to get better low-RPM response during everyday driving. Of course, such a turbo combination won't provide a lot of mass flow at high RPM for high-horsepower like a bigger turbo would, but, then again, it drives much better around town.

The best way to size a turbo is to work backward from your horsepower goal. Choose your target horsepower. (It pays to be realistic here; try to stay within the principles of physics.) Once you know that, work backwards and it's

Turbocharger Terms
(Courtesy of Garrett Turbochargers)

Area/Radius Ratio

A/R (area/radius) describes a geometric property of all compressor and turbine housings. It's the ratio of the turbine scroll divided by the square area of the opening at the end of the scroll. Changing turbine A/R has many effects. Increasing compressor A/R optimizes the performance for low-boost applications by increasing boost response. By going to a larger-turbine A/R, the turbo comes up on boost at a higher engine speed (more lag), the flow capacity of the turbine is increased, and less flow is wastegated. Also, there will be less engine backpressure and engine volumetric efficiency will be increased, resulting in more overall power.

CHRA

The CHRA (center housing rotating assembly) includes a complete turbocharger minus the compressor and turbine housings. You may hear this term when choosing a compressor or discussing turbine A/R specs.

Clipped Turbine Wheels

When an angle is machined on the turbine wheel exducer (outlet side), the wheel is clipped. Clipping causes a minor increase in the wheel's flow capability; however, it dramatically lowers the turbo efficiency. This reduction causes the turbo to come up on boost at a later engine speed (increased turbo lag). High-performance applications should never use a clipped turbine wheel.

Free-Float

A free-floating turbocharger has no wastegate device. This turbocharger can't control its own boost levels. For performance applications, the user must install an external wastegate to monitor and control boost levels.

On-Center Turbine Housings

On-center turbine housings refer to an outdated style of turbine housing with a centered turbine inlet pad. The inlet pad is centered on the turbo's axis of rotation instead of being tangentially located. Using an on-center housing will significantly lower the turbine's efficiency. This results in increased turbo lag, more backpressure, lower engine volumetric efficiency, and less overall engine power.

Trim

Trim is an area ratio used to describe both turbine and compressor wheels. Trim is calculated using the inducer and exducer diameters. As trim is increased, the wheel can support more air/gas flow.

Wastegate

A wastegated turbocharger includes an integral device to limit turbo boost. This consists of a pneumatic actuator connected to a valve assembly mounted inside the turbine housing. By connecting the pneumatic actuator to boost pressure, the turbo is able to limit its maximum boost output. The net result is increased durability, quicker time to boost, and boost adjustability.

Twin-Scroll Turbine Housing

Originally developed for commercial diesel applications, turbochargers with a twin-scroll turbine housing have now been successfully adapted for use with passenger car engines (both gas and diesel). By using dual openings, or volutes, into the turbocharger's turbine housing, exhaust energy is optimized, resulting in better engine performance at low speeds, decreased backpressure at high speeds, and significant gains in fuel economy.

Traditionally, passenger car turbochargers have had only one volute leading to the turbine housing. Unfortunately, this single-entry design can sometimes lead to combustion inefficiencies, since some cylinders are expelling burnt gases while others are inhaling fresh air for combustion. What happens is that the hot, dense exhaust gases from the first set of cylinders are drawn into the second set of cylinders, diluting the combustion charge of the second set of cylinders, and thus reducing power output.

Several wastegate solutions were considered to counter this problem, with a twin-scroll design ultimately providing the best solution. A twin-scroll, or twin-entry, housing allows each set of cylinders to release its exhaust gases into a dedicated volute. That way, it doesn't interfere with the other set of cylinders that is taking in fresh air at that same time. As this technology is further developed, even smaller passenger car engines will be able to experience the benefits of the twin-scroll turbine housing design – including those fueled by natural gas.

---

real easy to size the turbo. For example, you know how big your motor is and how fast you're going to spin it. Now, if we know what kind of horsepower you desire, we simply calculate that figure into airflow. That way, we know what compressor to use without having to do a bunch of complicated math.

Now you can think about the other variables. Are you going to use an intercooler? What kind of fuel will you use? What are the average atmospheric conditions the car will operate in? What's the volumetric efficiency curve of the engine? All that information is important, and if we quantify it, a good turbo tuner can run through a computer program that does the math to get a spreadsheet showing RPM, boost, and the airflow in pounds per minute at points throughout the RPM range. From there, we go to the compressor maps and choose a compressor that's best suited for the application.

Garrett Variable Nozzle Turbine

This is a Garrett Variable Nozzle Turbine (VNT) turbocharger. It adjusts the gas cross section at the inlet of the turbine wheel in order to optimize turbine power with the required load. At low engine speed and small gas flow, the VNT turbocharger reduces the cross section, increasing turbine power and boost pressure. At full engine speed/load and high gas flow, the VNT turbocharger increases cross section, avoiding turbocharger overrev and keeping the boost pressure required by engine level. Cross-section modulation can be controlled directly by the compressor pressure through the use of a pressure actuator, or by the engine management system, using a vacuum actuator. To modify the cross section, the VNT Multivane models use a mobile multivane system composed of a number of vanes that pivot on their axis, while VNT Slidevane models employ a mobile nozzle piston system.

An engine with a Garrett VNT turbocharger responds more quickly, produces higher power and torque, consumes less fuel, and creates fewer pollutants than a traditional bypass turbocharged engine. Due to quicker response time and uniform acceleration, vehicle behavior and driveability are also improved. In comparison with a bypass turbocharger, a VNT turbocharger has better efficiency with a larger flow range.

In addition to VNT technology, Garrett is working on electric motor assist to help the turbo spool up at a lower RPM, thus enabling the use of a less restrictive turbine for top-end performance.

Airflow Power Equivalent

2.2 liters = 134 cubic inches

Airflow @ 100% Volumetric Efficiency

RPM	cfm	lb/min	Horsepower	Torque
11,000	426.50	31.13	304.65	
10,000	387.73	28.30	276.95	
9,000	348.96	25.47	249.26	
8,000	310.19	22.64	221.56	
7,000	271.41	19.81	193.87	217.13
6,000	232.64	16.98	166.17	186.11
5,000	193.87	14.15		155.09
4,000	155.09	11.32		124.07
3,000	116.32	8.49		93.06
2,000	77.55	5.66		62.04
1,000	38.77	2.83		
500	19.39	1.42		

Airflow @ 168% Volumetric Efficiency (10 psi boost)

RPM	cfm	lb/min	Horsepower	Torque
11,000	716.53	52.31	511.81	
10,000	651.39	47.55	465.28	
9,000	586.25	42.80	418.75	
8,000	521.11	38.04	372.22	
7,000	455.97	33.29	325.69	364.78
6,000	390.83	28.53	279.17	312.67
5,000	325.69	23.78	232.64	260.56
4,000	260.56	19.02	186.11	208.44
3,000	195.42	14.27	139.58	156.33
2,000	130.28	9.51	93.06	104.22

Airflow @ 134% Volumetric Efficiency (5 psi boost)

RPM	cfm	lb/min	Horsepower	Torque
11,000	571.52	41.72	408.23	
10,000	519.56	37.93	371.11	
9,000	467.60	34.14	334.00	
8,000	415.65	30.34	296.89	
7,000	363.69	26.55	259.78	290.95
6,000	311.74	22.76	222.67	249.39
5,000	259.78	18.96	185.56	207.82
4,000	207.82	15.17	148.45	166.26
3,000	155.87	11.38	111.33	124.69
2,000	103.91	7.59	74.22	83.13

Airflow @ 200% Volumetric Efficiency (14.7 psi boost)

RPM	cfm	lb/min	Horsepower	Torque
11,000	853.01	62.27	609.29	
10,000	775.46	56.61	553.90	
9,000	697.92	50.95	498.51	
8,000	620.37	45.29	443.12	
7,000	542.82	39.63	387.73	434.26
6,000	465.28	33.97	332.34	372.22
5,000	387.73	28.30	276.95	310.19
4,000	310.19	22.64	221.56	248.15
3,000	232.64	16.98	166.17	186.11
2,000	155.09	11.32	110.78	124.07

Chapter 5

ENGINE DISPLACEMENT (CID)	=	110	4 CYCLE ENGINE
VOLUMETRIC EFFICIENCY	=	1 (100%)	FLOW IS LB/MIN CORRECTED FOR GARRETT MAPS 28.4 in. HgA & 545 R**
COMPRESSOR EFFICIENCY	=	.7	
COMPRESSOR INLET TEMP	=	80° F	PR = PRESSURE RATIO*
COMPRESSOR INLET PRESS	=	29.9 in HgA	DR = DENSITY RATIO
INTERCOOLER EFFECTIVENESS	=	.8	
INTERCOOLER PRESSURE DROP	=	1 PSI	T2 = COMPRESSOR OUTLET TEMP, IC OUT = INTERCOOLER OUTLET TEMP
INTERCOOLER COOLANT TEMP	=	80° F	*Pressure ratio equals boost plus 14.7 divided by 14.7
			**To convert lb/min to cfm divide by .07. (40.6 / .07=580 cfm)

BOOST RPM X 1000>

v	1000	2000	3000	4000	5000	6000	7000	8000	PR	DR	T2	IC OUT
0.00	2.10	4.10	6.20	8.20	10.30	12.40	14.40	16.50	1.00	0.93	80.00	80.00
1.00	2.20	4.40	6.60	8.80	11.00	13.20	15.40	17.60	1.07	0.99	94.00	82.00
2.00	2.30	4.70	7.00	9.30	11.70	14.00	16.40	18.70	1.14	1.06	108.00	85.00
3.00	2.50	4.90	7.40	9.90	12.40	14.80	17.30	19.80	1.20	1.12	122.00	88.00
4.00	2.60	5.20	7.80	10.40	13.00	15.70	18.30	20.90	1.27	1.18	134.00	90.00
5.00	2.70	5.50	8.20	11.00	13.70	16.50	19.20	22.00	1.34	1.24	147.00	93.00
6.00	2.90	5.80	8.60	11.50	14.40	17.30	20.10	23.00	1.41	1.30	158.00	95.00
7.00	3.00	6.00	9.00	12.00	15.10	18.10	21.10	24.10	1.48	1.36	170.00	97.00
8.00	3.10	6.30	9.40	12.60	15.70	18.90	22.00	25.20	1.54	1.42	181.00	100.00
9.00	3.30	6.60	9.80	13.10	16.40	19.70	22.90	26.20	1.61	1.48	191.00	102.00
10.00	3.40	6.80	10.20	13.60	17.00	20.50	23.90	27.30	1.68	1.54	202.00	104.00
11.00	3.50	7.10	10.60	14.20	17.70	21.20	24.80	28.30	1.75	1.60	212.00	106.00
12.00	3.70	7.30	11.00	14.70	18.30	22.00	25.70	29.40	1.81	1.66	222.00	108.00
13.00	3.80	7.60	11.40	15.20	19.00	22.80	26.60	30.40	1.88	1.72	231.00	110.00
14.00	3.90	7.90	11.80	15.70	19.60	23.60	27.50	31.40	1.95	1.78	241.00	112.00
15.00	4.10	8.10	12.20	16.20	20.30	24.30	28.40	32.50	2.02	1.84	250.00	113.00
16.00	4.20	8.40	12.60	16.70	20.90	25.10	29.30	33.50	2.09	1.89	258.00	115.00
17.00	4.30	8.60	12.90	17.30	21.60	25.90	30.20	34.50	2.15	1.95	267.00	117.00
18.00	4.40	8.90	13.30	17.80	22.20	26.60	31.10	35.50	2.22	2.01	276.00	119.00
19.00	4.60	9.10	13.70	18.30	22.80	27.40	32.00	36.50	2.29	2.07	284.00	120.00
20.00	4.70	9.40	14.10	18.80	23.50	28.20	32.90	37.60	2.36	2.12	292.00	122.00
21.00	4.80	9.60	14.50	19.30	24.10	28.90	33.70	38.60	2.43	2.18	300.00	123.00
22.00	4.90	9.90	14.80	19.80	24.70	29.70	34.60	39.60	2.49	2.24	308.00	125.00
23.00	5.10	10.10	15.20	20.30	25.40	30.40	35.50	40.60	2.56	2.56	315.00	127.00
24.00	5.20	10.40	15.60	20.80	26.00	31.20	36.40	41.60	2.63	2.35	323.00	128.00
25.00	5.30	10.60	16.00	21.30	26.60	31.90	37.20	42.60	2.70	2.41	330.00	130.00

INTERCOOLER COOLANT TEMP = 40 DEG F

v	1000	2000	3000	4000	5000	6000	7000	8000	PR	DR	T2	IC OUT
0.00	2.20	4.40	6.60	8.80	11.00	13.10	15.30	17.50	1.00	0.99	80.00	48.00
1.00	2.30	4.70	7.00	9.30	11.70	14.00	16.40	18.70	1.07	1.06	94.00	50.00
2.00	2.50	5.00	7.40	9.90	12.40	14.90	17.40	19.90	1.14	1.12	108.00	53.00
3.00	2.60	5.30	7.90	10.50	13.10	15.80	18.40	21.00	1.20	1.19	122.00	56.00
4.00	2.80	5.50	8.30	11.10	13.80	16.60	19.40	22.20	1.27	1.25	134.00	58.00
5.00	2.90	5.80	8.70	11.60	14.60	17.50	20.40	23.30	1.34	1.32	147.00	61.00
6.00	3.10	6.10	9.20	12.20	15.30	18.30	21.40	24.40	1.41	1.38	158.00	63.00
7.00	3.20	6.40	9.60	12.80	16.00	19.20	22.40	25.60	1.48	1.44	170.00	65.00
8.00	3.30	6.70	10.00	13.30	16.70	20.00	23.30	26.70	1.54	1.51	181.00	68.00
9.00	3.50	6.90	10.40	13.90	17.40	20.80	24.30	27.80	1.61	1.57	191.00	70.00
10.00	3.60	7.20	10.80	14.50	18.10	21.70	25.30	28.90	1.68	1.63	202.00	72.00
11.00	3.80	7.50	11.30	15.00	18.80	22.50	26.30	30.00	1.75	1.70	212.00	74.00
12.00	3.90	7.80	11.70	15.60	19.40	23.30	27.20	31.10	1.81	1.76	222.00	76.00
13.00	4.00	8.10	12.10	16.10	20.10	24.20	28.20	32.20	1.88	1.82	231.00	78.00
14.00	4.20	8.30	12.50	16.60	20.80	25.00	29.10	33.30	1.95	1.88	241.00	80.00
15.00	4.30	8.60	12.90	17.20	21.50	25.80	30.10	34.40	2.02	1.94	250.00	81.00
16.00	4.40	8.90	13.30	17.70	22.20	26.60	31.00	35.50	2.09	2.00	258.00	83.00
17.00	4.60	9.10	13.70	18.30	22.80	27.40	32.00	36.50	2.15	2.07	267.00	85.00
18.00	4.70	9.40	14.10	18.80	23.50	28.20	32.90	37.60	2.22	2.13	276.00	87.00
19.00	4.80	9.70	14.50	19.30	24.20	29.00	33.80	38.70	2.29	2.19	284.00	88.00
20.00	5.00	9.90	14.90	19.90	24.80	29.80	34.80	39.70	2.36	2.25	292.00	90.00
21.00	5.10	10.20	15.30	20.40	25.50	30.60	35.70	40.80	2.43	2.31	300.00	91.00
22.00	5.20	10.50	15.70	20.90	26.20	31.40	36.60	41.90	2.49	2.37	308.00	93.00
23.00	5.40	10.70	16.10	21.50	26.80	32.20	37.50	42.90	2.56	2.43	315.00	95.00
24.00	5.50	11.00	16.50	22.00	27.50	33.00	38.50	44.00	2.63	2.49	323.00	96.00
25.00	5.60	11.30	16.90	22.50	28.10	33.80	39.40	45.00	2.70	2.54	330.00	98.00

Chart 5-1: When inputting computer program data, you need to make some assumptions about the combination. Our target is 400-horsepower at 8,000 rpm. We assume 80-percent intercooler efficiency in an air-to-air unit with less than 1 psi pressure drop. We're at sea level with an average barometric pressure and temperature and we're making 25 psi boost with a 70-percent efficient compressor. Hugh McGinnis laid out the physics equations for turbochargers in his book on turbochargers. Turbonetics has a program that crunches the numbers and will give us the airflow on an 80-degree day with 29.9 barometric pressure through a four-stroke engine with 100 percent volumetric efficiency and a compressor efficiency of 70 percent blowing through an 80-percent efficient intercooler. The software crunched the numbers shown above. Compare these numbers with those for an 80-percent efficient air-to-water intercooler with 40-degree coolant. The mass flow for each RPM data point is given in lb/min.

How to Read a Compressor Map

Compressor maps are rather easy to understand once you get some of the blanks filled in. First off, let's define what we're looking at.

Within the map coordinates, we have several reference lines. The curved horizontal lines with six-digit numbers attached signify the speed of the compressor wheel in RPM. The islands with percentages attached are called efficiency contours. Efficiency contours (the area inside the enclosed shape) depict the regional efficiency of the compressor set. This efficiency is simply the percentage of turbo shaft power that converts to actual air compression. When sizing a turbo, it's important to align the proposed VE/RPM line with a high-efficiency range on the map.

The X-Y coordinates, the horizontal and vertical values that the lines within the map reference, signify mass flow and pressure ratio. The horizontal X-axis shows the amount of air mass the turbo is flowing relative to shaft speed. The vertical axis shows the pressure ratio. The pressure ratio (PR) is a measure of how much the compressor is compressing the air above the ambient air pressure.

Most maps use lbs/min as the unit of air mass flow. These can be converted using the flowing ratios:

0.1 m3/sec = 211.888 cfm
10 lbs/min = 144.718 cfm

The PR is related to boost pressure. For reference, a PR of one is equal to zero psi boost. In other words, if the ambient air pressure equals the boosted pressure, the ratio between them is one.

For example, standard air pressure (barometric pressure) at sea level is 14.7 psi. To get a PR of two at standard sea level pressure, you'd have 14.7 psi of boost. That pressure is in addition to the ambient (in this case, doubling it), so if the density of the compressed air were the same as the ambient air, the compressor would now be flowing twice the mass than at a PR of one. If the ambient pressure falls, then all values for a given PR fall as well. For example, if the ambient barometric pressure were 13 psi, then a PR of two would be 13 psi of boost. What that means is that even turbocharged engines lose some power and efficiency at lower barometric pressures.

The surge region, located on the left-hand side of the compressor map, is an area of flow instability typically caused by compressor inducer stall (the compressor wheel can't compress any more). The turbo should be sized so that the engine does not operate in the surge range. When turbochargers operate in surge for long periods, bearing failures may occur.

The choke line is on the right-hand side of the compressor map and represents the flow limit. When a turbocharger is run deep into choke, turbo speeds will increase dramatically while compressor efficiency will plunge (very high compressor outlet temps), and turbo durability will be compromised.

The arrows on this compressor map show how to use the coordinate system. At a PR of two in the efficiency contour of 74 percent, the compressor will flow 36 lbs/min of air mass. These mass flow rates are assumed to occur at standard sea level barometric pressure at 545 degrees Rankin, or 86 degrees Fahrenheit. These atmospheric conditions are the standard that Garrett uses to produce its compressor maps.

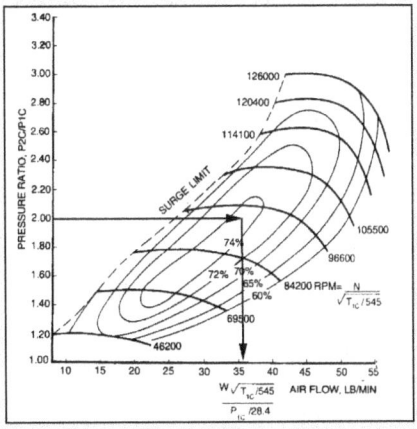

While matching the compressor to a particular set of performance goals is moderately easy, the turbine match is purely based on experience, though there are some general guidelines. Rick knows what works from experience and from working with racers who use the product. In fact, other than choosing a compressor that'll flow the air you need to make your power level, most of it comes down to experience and good judgment.

A good example of how theory and practice for turbo combinations is more art than science is camshaft selection. For a turbo car, in almost every case you don't want a lot of overlap or duration. The guideline used to be turbo motors like lift, but keep the duration to a minimum and keep the lobe separation wide. Well, we've found that in some racing applications, you can throw that right out the window. Some very serious high-horsepower turbo combinations use big cams with long duration and lobe separation angles closer to what you'd see on a naturally aspirated combination. And they work. Basically it comes down to air and fuel flow – how much can you get through the motor and what do you have to do to get more? If it requires longer duration cams, then that's what you do – if it works. If it goes backward on you, I guess you know not to do it.

We gave our hypothetical application, in Chart 5-1, 100 percent volumetric efficiency on gasoline. If you're burning gasoline with 100 percent volumetric efficiency, then one pound of air per minute equals 10 horsepower, and 10 lbs/min equals 100 horsepower. And so it follows that 40 lbs/min is 400 horsepower, which is our target. On a 1.8-liter engine at 8,000 rpm, it'll take 23 psi to reach our goal, which means we'll need a pressure ratio of 2.56:1. We can see on the flow chart that the intercooler temp inlet is 315 degrees F and with an 80 percent efficient air-to-air intercooler, you get 127 degrees F outlet to the motor. Chart 5-1 also shows that you'll see an improvement with the same compressor and an air-to-water intercooler with 40-degree coolant. Notice that with the same 315-degree F

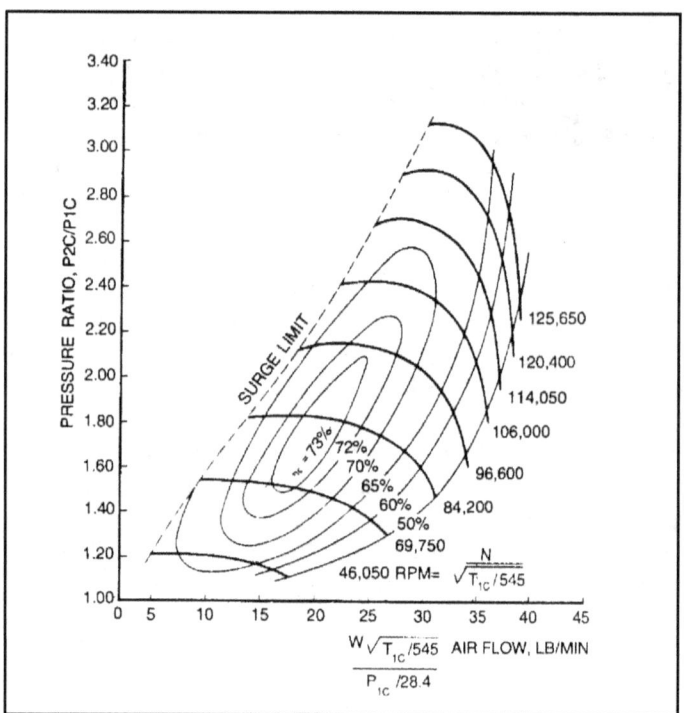

Figure 5-2: The T04B-S-trim compressor map shows it is more efficient at lower mass flow and boost levels compared to the V2 trim. This compressor would be a good choice for a quick spooling street turbo.

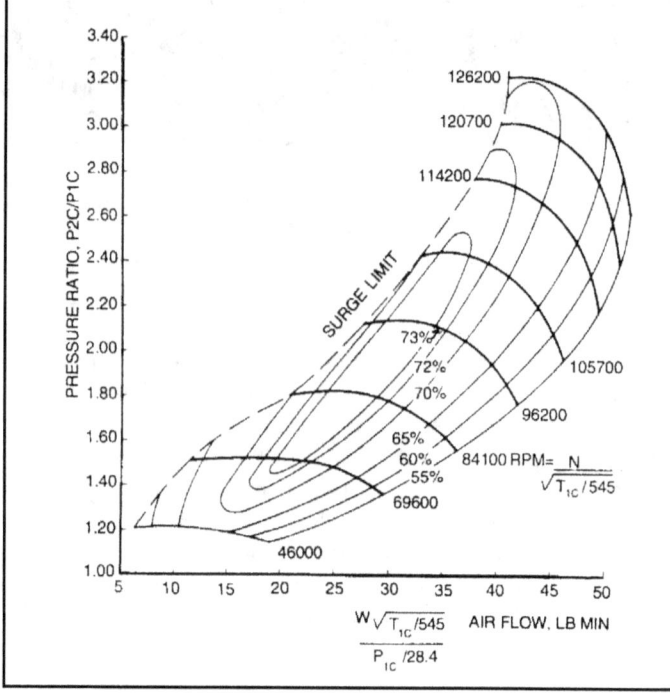

Figure 5-3: The T04B-V2 trim is a good match for power target: At 580 cfm and a 2.5 pressure ratio, we're in the 72-percent island with a shaft speed of 108,000 rpm. We're in between these two speed lines, which looks pretty good for our imaginary combination.

compressor outlet temperature, the air-to-water intercooler brings the temp down to 95 degrees F and increases charge density. An efficient intercooler always makes more horsepower and can even cover up a slight compressor mismatch, but Rick likes to give his combinations a little room, so he'd use the less efficient air-to-air intercooler to base the compressor choice.

Now we compare compressor maps. Rick thinks a V-trim is probably going to do it, but to compare, let's look at an S-trim map first (see Figure 5-2). Some of the maps are in cfm. To convert lbs/min to cfm, divide by .07.

$$(40.6 / .07 = 580 \text{ cfm})$$

At that cfm flow, this compressor is really inefficient. The compressor is over-revving; it has to spin almost 122,000 rpm to achieve the flow and pressure we need. This is not a good match. The shaft RPM is so high it'd probably cavitate and cause durability problems.

So it looks like we need a bigger compressor. Here's a V2 (Figure 5-3) trim at 580 cfm and a 2.5 pressure ratio, which puts us in the 72-percent island with a shaft speed of 108,000 rpm. We're in between these two speed lines, and this looks pretty good for our hypothetical application. (Use maps as an application tool, but they're not exact.) All we do with the map is find out if the turbo is even close to what the engine needs.

Here are a few things to look for. You want to stay to the right of the surge line. The turbo spins right up to the limits; as you're shifting, it's darting over towards the surge line. Each time you clutch, the turbo jerks over towards the surge line, then goes back, so you wind up here in the most efficient island at wide open throttle. If you get past it, the compressor surges. In other words, it's trying to move more air than the engine can use at a given time, so the air will revert backward through the system and come back out the compressor wheel, creating a popping sound. This will also happen on deceleration when you slam the throttle shut.

Surging can get pretty violent and can cause early wear or even damage to turbos with older bearing styles, but modern turbos are pretty tough and can stand more abuse. However, the surging is difficult for the fuel injection computer to compensate for. And if the mass flow isn't even, it can confuse the computer enough to force a lean condition when you can least afford it, and bam! – There goes a piston. So size the compressor correctly and make power with a little less worry.

Before high-quality cylinder sleeves were available, most sport compact engines couldn't take super-high boost levels. Without sleeves you're limited to 15 psi and below, so T04B maps are really good for these engines. The T04B performance envelope is pretty broad. To illustrate the different characteristics of compressors, compare two wheels that flow nearly the same amount of air. For serious drag racing, a peaky, high-pressure mapped compressor will make more power, but you've got to run it at a high boost pressure. They're usually a six-bladed fan instead of seven, and they're more stable at higher boost pressures. The shaft sizes are usually bigger because they're capable of high shaft speeds, and the compressor fans are generally of a much larger diameter.

If you have a smaller motor that you have to operate at a certain boost to get your required power, then you'd want a compressor that's stable at higher boost pressures. If you tried to run a T04B at those boost pressures, you'd have durability problems arising from the higher shaft speeds.

Two things raise shaft speed: higher boost pressure and running all the air out of the compressor. Look at the speed lines on a compressor map, and notice how they roll off to the right. You can have a compressor generate 30 psi or above and you'll have to spin it at 112,800 rpm. At 15 psi with the same mass flow, the shaft speed falls into the same speed line, so you can overspeed a compressor with too much boost, or by trying to flow too much air through it, at any boost pressure. This is why sometimes you'll see shaft speeds spike up at the top end, and even though the boost pressure is maintained, it's running out of air. Plus, it's heating up the air, because it's just beating it, not compressing it.

When the compressor is running out of air, you're approaching the choke line. The maximum centrifugal compressor volume flow rate is normally limited by the cross-section at the compressor inlet. When the flow at the wheel inlet reaches sonic velocity, no further flow rate increase is possible. The choke line can be recognized by the steeply descending speed lines at the right on the compressor map. When this condition occurs, you'll usually see a horsepower drop as well because the faster the compressor spins, the hotter the charge air gets, and the harder the intercooler has to work, making the entire system less efficient. Conversely, less shaft speed generally means denser charge air by bringing the efficiency of the whole system to a higher level.

Here's what happens when you run out of compressor. At first, you can turn up the boost and power comes up accordingly; then you reach a point at which, even though you continue adding boost, the power doesn't do anything. It either stays flat or falls off. That's when you know you're running out of compressor.

While we're talking about the limits of the compressor, it's a good time to get you familiar with a common turbo term: "trim." You'll notice that the term "trim" is applied to both the compressor and the turbine. Turbo makers and customizers use trim as a code to describe how much mass each side of the turbo is able to flow. The calculation is based on the inducer and exducer bore diameter. The larger the bore diameter (cross-section), obviously, the more it can flow. On the compressor side, the trim has a significant influence on where the choke line occurs. On the turbine side, the trim has influence on how much work the turbine can transfer to the compressor.

To make 400 horsepower at 23 psi, which compressor should you use? At that point, the S-trim setup is really close to the surge line, with 113,000 rpm shaft speed. It'll do it, but the shaft speed is getting pretty high. Come over here to the V2 trim, and bam, we're right in the 75-percent efficiency island at around 86,000 rpm shaft speed. This is much better for drag racing. It'll spool up more quickly because it has six blades instead of seven, and the overall diameter of the wheel gives it more tip speed, like a larger gear, so the pressure rises faster.

That's the basic strategy for choosing a turbocharger compressor. You choose between two ways to get to the same place. A compressor wheel of smaller diameter performs better at low pressures and higher volumes. In contrast, a wheel with larger diameter keeps shaft speed down, enabling it to be more efficient at high pressures. If you have a smaller engine requiring higher boost pressures to achieve a given power level, you might opt for the wheel that's more stable at the higher boost pressure, even though the two wheels will flow the same amount of air. You'll want the one that's more stable at your boost levels – it'll be more efficient with the least amount of shaft speed.

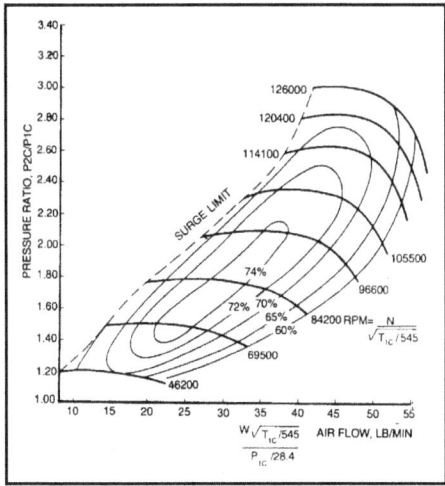

Figure 5-4: On the compressor maps, any position within an efficiency island is that percent efficiency. For example, using the map above, you can see an extremely broad 72-percent efficiency island.

If you study different compressor maps, you can see why smaller engines have to run at high boost pressures to make a lot of power. You want the compressor that is stable at that boost pressure while delivering the required mass flow rate. A big V-8 at 10 psi boost making 400 horsepower may need another turbo. Most people must factor in the cost per horsepower, though, and turbos can get expensive, particularly the super-highly-efficient designs.

When reading compressor maps, remember that any position within the island is that percent efficiency. For example, using Figure 5-4, you can see an extremely broad 72-percent efficiency island. It provides the airflow efficiently at a low shaft speed and builds boost quickly, meaning it has more boost on the low end. The effect is to broaden the area under the curve.

Housing Aspect Ratio = Aspect Ratio = Area / Radius

Before we continue our discussion on matching a turbocharger to an engine, we need to explain what the A/R is in order for the following observations of turbine housing choice to make sense.

The turbine, i.e., the exhaust side, needs to make the compressor side spin fast enough to generate the desired airflow at the desired boost level. A small turbine tends to accelerate to a given shaft speed more quickly than a larger turbine. The tradeoff is that it develops more backpressure for a given mass flow rate through the engine, which is logical since the turbine is a restriction to the exhaust flow. What you want to find is a turbine that spins fast enough at the RPM and load desired in order to generate the necessary boost response and airflow with the least amount of backpressure in the exhaust.

A turbine housing is shaped like a snail shell. Unwind the shell and the taper of the runner resembles a cone. Cut off the tip of the cone and you've got a hole at the end. The cross-sectional area of this hole is the "A" in A/R. The turbine housing A/R (area/radius) ratio is equal to the area of any turbine inlet scroll cross-section divided by the distance from the center of that cross-section to the center of the turbine shaft. A smaller "R" tends to produce higher-shaft RPM to the turbine for a given exhaust flow rate; a larger R gives the turbine shaft greater torque to drive the compressor wheel because the lever arm "R" is longer. The upshot of this is simply that larger turbines, with larger A/R ratios, have the potential to make more power than smaller turbines.

The turbine's A/R (area/radius) ratio basically determines where the turbo starts to accelerate. The hole size is important since it determines the velocity at which the exhaust gases exit the turbine scroll and enter the turbine blades. For a given flow rate, the smaller the hole, the higher the velocity, which is why it spools up more quickly, but with the tradeoff of greater restriction to exhaust-gas flow.

In practical terms, the aspect ratio is a window of operation – the points between which the turbo functions best. We know that a turbo with a lower A/R value accelerates more quickly than one with a higher value, but it theoretically peaks sooner, too. For example, a turbo with a .50:1 A/R will accelerate more quickly than a .95:1 A/R, but it also peaks faster, which means the turbo with the .95:1 A/R will make more top-end power. This is all theoretical, and it doesn't always work in the real world. Some combinations behave unexpectedly better or worse than predicted. The only way to really find out is to put a car on a track. Dyno numbers are closer to reality, but you've got to test it in the real world. Rick has gained a lot of experience over the past nine years working with different combinations on the dyno at Ken Dutweiller's shop and going to the track. He has a good feel for what'll work, but the ultimate judge is the track timer. He says he likes to keep track of the guys who do really well at the racetrack with his product, then work with them to find out how to make their combination perform even better. The books and the turbo maps are important as guidelines to get you in the ballpark, but ultimately, you must go out and experiment.

High-RPM, multi-valve motors affect turbo efficiency. If you look at a two-valve slant six-cylinder engine and the intake and exhaust ports are on the same side of the head, it obviously isn't very efficient. Cross-flow heads are much more efficient, and a four-valve head is even more efficient. The turbine wheel doesn't know that, of course — it just reacts to flow. You've got a whole system to get dialed in, and the turbo is only one part of it. The real question is how efficiently the system can operate.

On the turbine side, you don't really have an application guide. That's where experience comes in. For sport compacts in the 2-liter engine size range, many people are using a standard wheel – a T3 turbine wheel – which you can find in the turbo Saab, 2.3-liter Ford, and the Renault. A small motor might call for an A/R around .36 or .48:1. For a larger motor, you would use a turbo with a .63 or .82:1 A/R with the same wheel. The window of operation is different for each A/R ratio. Turbonetics makes a bigger T3 wheel it calls the Stage 3 for power levels over and above 280 horsepower, the point where the standard turbine wheel starts to get in trouble. The Stage 3 wheel goes much further in terms of flow, so it's not going to be a problem. If you take an engine and you make 250 horsepower with one combo and 400 horsepower with another, you'd use different turbos to do it.

The following chart is what Turbonetics recommends as a beginning guide to match a turbo to your combination:

ENGINE DISPLACEMENT	COMPRESSOR TRIM	TURBINE TRIM TURBINE HOUSING	A/R
60-100 ci	T3-50 Trim	T3 Standard	.36 to .48:1
100-150 ci	T3-Super 60	T3 Standard	.48 to .63:1
150-200 ci	T3-Super 60	T3 Standard	.63 to .82:1
200-250 ci	T4-S3 Trim	T4 "O" Trim	.58 to .69:1
250-300 ci	T4-V1 Trim	T4 "P" Trim	.69 to .81:1
300-350 ci	T4-V1 Trim	T4 "P" Trim	.81 to .96:1
350-400 ci	T4-H3 Trim	T4 "P" Trim	.96 to 1.30:1
400-450 ci	T4-H3 Trim	T4 "P" Trim	1.30:1

One of the systems the A/R influences but is rarely discussed is the exhaust system. If you've ever wondered why street turbo systems tend to run fine with what look like inefficient log-style manifolds and why racers use cool looking high-tech coated and insulated headers with merge collectors, this is the reason: In a turbo system, the turbine is the ultimate restriction. The cross sectional area of the little hole (the divisor in the A/R ratio) is what all the exhaust mass has to flow through, so the usual relationship of exhaust tube diameters and runner length doesn't apply directly.

For a racing engine, the best exhaust setup is equal-length tubes with a merge collector. Again, the header dimensions aren't as critical as with a

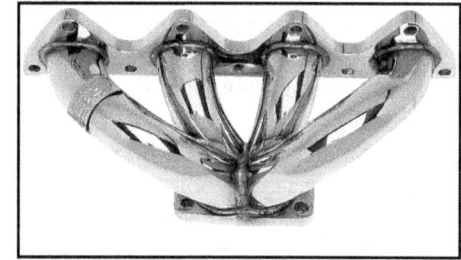

Tubular turbo manifolds, such as this one from DC Motorsports, improve performance and are typically designed for use with either T3, or T3-T4 hybrid turbos. Most high-quality designs are made from mandrel-bent tubing and will have beefy 1/2-inch-thick machined flanges. Depending on the design, they can be used with either internal or external wastegates, but you'll usually have to specify the wastegate you intend so the mounting can be made to order.

Turbocharging Theory

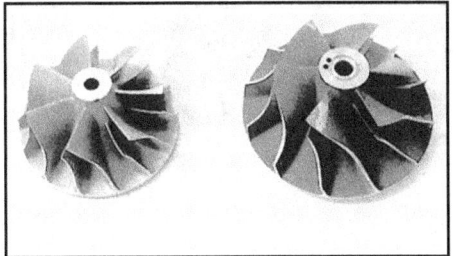

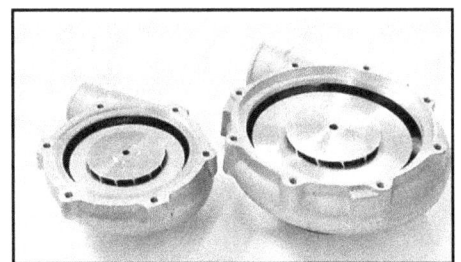

The wheel on the left is good for low boost pressures but high volume. The one on the right produces high boost pressures and high volume. The high-pressure wheel is a six-bladed, six-splitter design; the low-pressure wheel is a seven-bladed, seven-splitter design. The boost performance window is not only determined by the blade design, but is also affected by the diameter of the wheel. A smaller-diameter compressor wheel will perform better at low pressures and higher volumes. In contrast, a wheel with a larger diameter keeps shaft speed down, enabling it to be more efficient at high pressures. That's the basic strategy of turbocharging. These wheels perform equally on the same car, but you get more durability and better boost stability and efficiency using a turbo that is sized to give you the least shaft speed for your boost and flow requirements.

A larger housing has more diffuser area. The diffuser is the flat surface between the edge of the wheel leading into the ram's horn. It slows the air down before it's collected in the housing as pressure. With a diffuser in place, the air doesn't hit the housing wall as hard and generates less turbulence and heat energy — which equals more efficiency.

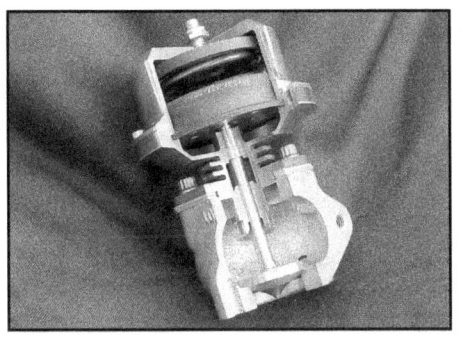

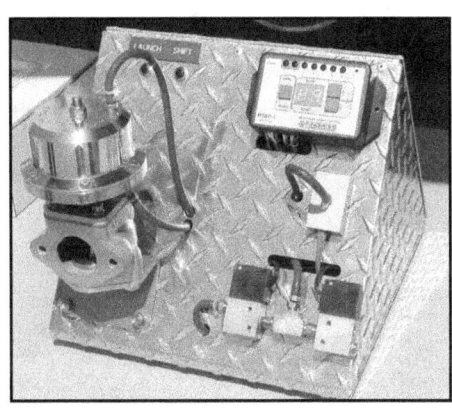

Two different wheels generate two different power levels. The wheel on the left goes to 250 horsepower easily, but 300 is pushing it. The one on the right is a later-generation model. It has more diameter on both the OD and on the exducer, putting its flow characteristics much higher. The exducer is the portion of the wheel where the gas actually comes out. The compressor wheel is opposite — the inducer is the OD.

This is a cutaway display of an Innovative Turbo wastegate. Wastegates control boost and compressor speed by relieving exhaust pressure to bleed into the unpressurized side of the exhaust system on street cars, or directly to the atmosphere on racecars. A vacuum-actuated feedback loop controls the level of boost.

Innovative Turbo designed this electronic boost controller to work with the company's racing wastegates. It's programmable, so you can set boost levels to match traction on launch and several other options. This is the advantage of turbos over a crank-driven supercharger. You can manipulate the mass flow as you're driving or racing — no stopping to swap belts and change ratios for turbo cars.

naturally aspirated or supercharged engine, but there is still an advantage in total mass flow, which leads to higher horsepower output. The advantage of a header system seems to be optimized with turbos with high A/R ratios, which is why they're more important for race engines with huge turbos. But any time you make the whole system more efficient, you'll see a benefit. In this case, the benefit is that it enables you to use a larger turbo, and it'll spool much more quickly with a properly designed exhaust. Most street turbo kits use a log manifold to package the turbo and keep the accessory drives. On a racecar, you don't have to worry about that: you just want more power.

More important for a turbocharged combination is the backpressure after the turbine. Larger-diameter exhaust tubes and low-restriction mufflers, if any at all, yield the best results. As for a muffler choice, stay with a straight-through design. Muffler designs that change airflow direction cause backpressure and take the edge off your turbo.

As for the use of heat insulating coatings and wraps, these help the turbo spool more quickly, and they are a fine-tuning technique when you need to find the last few hundredths of a second in your e.t. For street drivers, insulation is more important in managing heat in the engine bay and exhaust routing through the chassis.

Turbocharging Basic Equations
(Courtesy of Garrett Turbochargers)

Turbine Expansion Ratio

Exhaust manifold pressure (EMP) = 15 psi
Turbine outlet pressure (Outlet P) = 1 psi
Atmosphere (Atmos) = 14.7 psi at sea level

$$ER = \frac{EMP + Atmos}{Outlet\ P + Atmos} = \frac{15 + 14.7}{1 + 14.7} = 1.89$$

This equation is used to help size the turbine to a particular application. The gas expands because it is under pressure in front of the turbine wheel and it is rushing to a lower pressure area behind the turbine wheel. The amount of expansion is one of the measures of available force (work) at the turbine wheel to compress air. You don't need to concern yourself with this – we decided to present it so you can see one of the equations that engineers use to help design the turbo. The turbine maps, and hence the sizing choices, is an area that turbo makers, such as Garrett, don't usually like to give out, since it gives them a competitive advantage.

Turbine Corrected Flow

Engine air flow (Actual Flow) = 50 lb/min
Exhaust manifold pressure (EMP) = 25 psi
Exhaust temperature (Gas Temp) = 1500° F
Barometric Pressure (Baro) = 14.7 psi

$$Corrected\ Flow = \frac{Actual\ Flow \sqrt{([Gas\ Temp + 460]/519)}}{(Baro + EMP)/14.7}$$

$$Corrected\ Flow = \frac{50 \cdot \sqrt{([1500 + 460]/519)}}{(14.7 + 25)/14.7} = 36\ lb/min$$

This is another equation that allows engineers to predict turbocharger performance – if they know the temperature and pressure at the turbine inlet. Again, unless you have access to a dyno with the proper sensors and probes, this stuff is purely academic. But it's sort of cool to know there is an equation that explains and predicts performance in relation to certain mass flows through the engine.

Pressure Ratio

Intake manifold pressure (Boost) = 12 psi
Pressure drop, intercooler (P*Intercooler*) = 2 psi
Pressure drop, air filter (P*Air Filter*) = 0.5 psi
Atmosphere (Atmos) = 14.7 psi at sea level

$$PR = \frac{Boost + \Delta P Intercooler + Atmos}{Atmos - \Delta P Air\ Filter}$$

$$PR = \frac{12 + 2 + 14.7}{14.7 - .5} = 2.02$$

This equation tells you that if there is less pressure at the compressor inlet, i.e., you're at a high altitude, the boost pressure will also be less. Also the reverse is true. More pressure at the inlet means higher boost at the outlet.

Corrected Airflow

Air Temperature (Air Temp) = 60° F
Barometric Pressure (Baro) = 14.7 psi
Engine air consumption (Actual Flow) = 50 lb/min

$$Corrected\ Flow = \frac{Actual\ Flow \sqrt{([Air\ Temp + 460]/545)}}{Baro/13.95}$$

$$Corrected\ Flow = \frac{50 \cdot \sqrt{([60 + 460]/545)}}{14.7/13.95} = 46.3\ lb/min$$

This formula helps you find the corrected mass flow rate of air, taking into account air density (ambient temperature and pressure).

Trim

$$Trim_{Turbine} = \frac{(Exducer\ Diameter)^2}{(Inducer\ Diameter)^2} \times 100$$

$$Trim_{Compressor} = \frac{(Inducer\ Diameter)^2}{(Exducer\ Diameter)^2} \times 100$$

Trim is an area ratio used to describe both turbine and compressor wheels. Trim is calculated using the inducer and exducer diameters. As trim is increased, the wheel can support more air/gas flow.

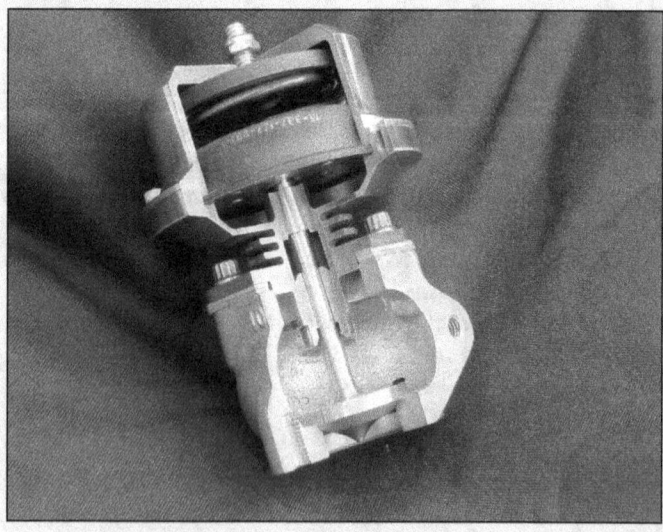

This cutaway of the Innovative Turbo racing wastegate gives you an inside view of the inner workings of a wastegate. This unit is designed for a high-horsepower system flowing lots of mass. Using this on a stock engine would be overkill, but a wastegate that's too small won't be able to control boost pressures, which could hurt your engine.

CHAPTER 6

TURBOS FOR SPORT COMPACTS

HKS

HKS began in October 1973 when two talented young engineers decided to design and build high-performance engines and components that major OEMs could not, or would not, produce.

If you ever wondered why the company is called HKS, here's the story. Hiroyuki Hasegawa, a former engineer for Yamaha Motor Company, and his partner Mr. Kitagawa, secured a capital infusion from Sigma Automotive Co., Ltd. They started the company tuning gasoline-powered engines in a dairy-farming shed at the foot of Mount Fuji in Japan. Mr. Hasegawa worked for about a year on an aftermarket turbocharger for passenger cars. It found a market, and the rest is history.

HKS pioneered the Japanese aftermarket performance industry by delivering a host of exciting new products, including the first commercially available electronic turbo timer and boost controller. Other early products included piggy-back fuel computers and sophisticated fuel management tools. Clearly HKS was driving performance trends for Japanese vehicles.

For over a quarter century, HKS products have been put to the test in drag racing, road racing, rallying, and top speed trials. HKS-equipped vehicles have captured numerous racing championships and hold claim to a myriad of competition records, using many off-the-shelf, race-proven HKS components. As a result, "HKS" has been synonymous with "performance" in the automotive aftermarket industry for the past 29+ years.

HKS USA, Inc. was established in 1982, in order to deliver performance, customer service, and quality products to consumers in North America. HKS recently purchased a new 35,000+ sq. ft. headquarters building for North American sales, marketing, warehouse, R&D, and manufacturing operations. The company also has a 100,000 sq. ft., state-of-the-art manufacturing and R&D facility at the foot of Mount Fuji.

Every HKS turbo, turbo kit, and other turbo-related component is race proven and engineered with the highest standards in performance, function, and reliability.

HKS GT Full Turbo Kits consist of properly sized HKS GT Ball-Bearing Turbocharger unit(s) that offer power and response, as well as all the appropriate related hardware. This Supra TT kit uses GT2835 turbos, stainless-steel manifolds, external wastegates, and flanged downpipes.

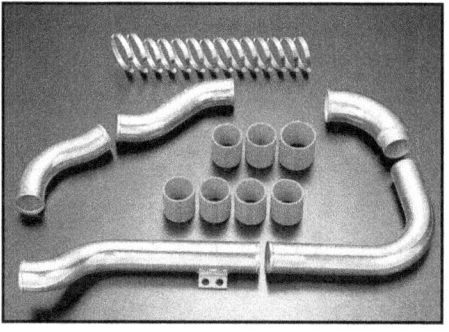

HKS intercooler pipe upgrade kits increase efficiency and performance over the factory intercooler pipe system. The use of metal intercooler piping offers increased durability, consistently higher boost pressure, improved response, and an attractive appearance.

Applications:
- 1993-96 Mazda RX-7 Turbo; T04E, cast manifold, racing wastegate (off-road use only)
- 1993-96 Mazda RX-7 Turbo; T04R, stainless-steel manifold,

Chapter 6

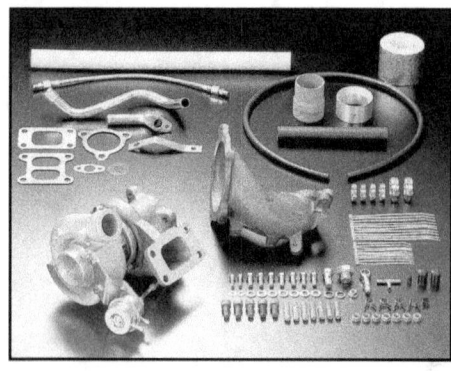

HKS Sport Turbo Upgrades are bolt-on turbo upgrade kits for factory turbocharged vehicles. These kits consist of new, larger turbos designed to bolt directly on to the stock manifold(s). HKS Sport Turbos are designed and sized to promote good mid-range response and provide maximum airflow throughout the RPM band. Each turbo kit is crafted to provide higher-than-stock levels of performance and quality.

HKS GT Ball-Bearing Sport Turbo Upgrades step up to the higher-end HKS GT Ball-Bearing turbos.

racing wastegate (off-road use only) – requires intake manifold modification
- 1993-96 Mazda RX-7 Turbo; T51R-KAI, stainless-steel manifold, GT wastegate (off-road use only) – requires intake manifold modification
- 1993-98 Toyota Supra Turbo; T04R, stainless-steel manifold, GT wastegate (off-road use only)
- 1993-98 Toyota Supra Turbo; T51R-KAI, stainless-steel manifold, GT wastegate (off-road use only)
- 1993-98 Toyota Supra Turbo; T51R-SPL, stainless-steel manifold, GT wastegate (off-road use only)

Applications:
- 1990-96 Dodge Stealth R/T
- 1995-98 Eagle Talon TSI, TSI AWD
- 1989-91 Mazda RX-7 Turbo
- 1990-99 Mitsubishi 3000 GT Turbo
- 1995-99 Mitsubishi Eclipse GST, Spyder GST, Spyder, GSX

Applications:
- 1991-99 Nissan 180SX RPS13
- 1990-95 Nissan 300ZX
- 1991-93 Nissan Silvia PS13
- 1994-98 Nissan Silvia S14
- 1999-02 Nissan Silvia S15
- 2002 and up Subaru Impreza WRX

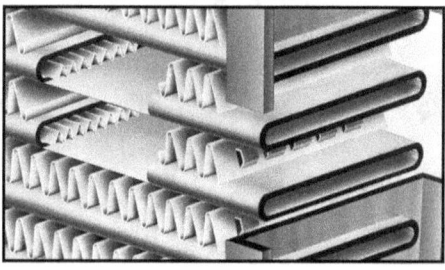

HKS intercooler cores are available in various sizes and thicknesses for various custom applications. From the HKS Core #1 to the new S-Type Core, these are the same high-quality units used in the complete HKS intercooler kits. An array of intercooler end tanks is also available to tailor the intercooler to specific needs.

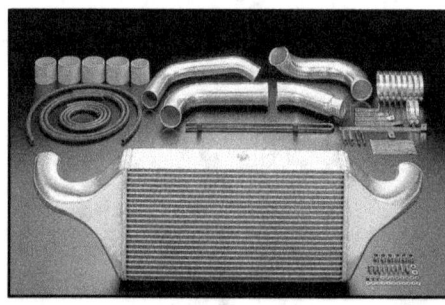

HKS intercooler kits are application-specific upgrade kits for factory intercooled turbocharged vehicles. Intercooler size and placement are calculated for maximum efficiency and performance.

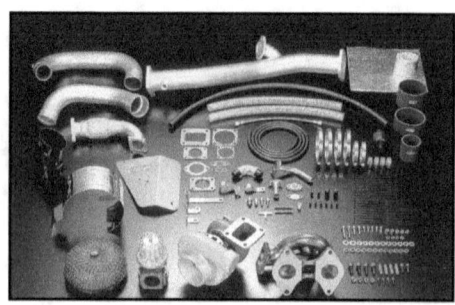

HKS Full Turbo Kits consist of large HKS turbos, manifolds, external wastegates, and flanged downpipes. They offer phenomenal top-end horsepower and good response.

Applications:
- 1990-98 Dodge Stealth R/T
- 1986-88 Mazda RX-7
- 1989-91 Mazda RX-7
- 1993-96 Mazda RX-7, (for HKS single turbo upgrades)
- 1993-96 Mazda RX-7, S Type (fits stock and HKS single turbo), (R134 A/C only)
- 1990-99 Mitsubishi 3000GT
- 1981-83 Nissan 280ZX
- 1984-87 Nissan 300ZX
- 1988-89 Nissan 300ZX
- 1990-96 Nissan 300ZX
- 1990-96 Nissan 300ZX, (front mount w/SMFs, off-road use)
- 1990-9/93 Toyota MR2
- 10/93-1995 Toyota MR2
- 1986.5-92 Toyota Supra
- 1993-98 Toyota Supra, (fits stock and HKS turbo upgrades)
- 1993-98 Toyota Supra, (intercooler fitment kit for stock turbos)
- 1993-98 Toyota Supra, S Type (fits stock and HKS turbo upgrades)

Applications:
- 1990-98 Dodge Stealth R/T, (for HKS intercoolers only)
- 5/89-5/90 Eagle Talon TSI, TSI AWD, (will not work with factory airbox)
- 6/90-2/94 Eagle Talon TSI, TSI AWD, (will not work with factory airbox)
- 1988-92 Ford Probe GT
- 1993-96 Mazda RX-7, (polished aluminum)
- 1990-99 Mitsubishi 3000GT, (for HKS intercoolers only)

HKS offers an array of silicone hose joints in varying diameters and lengths for custom intake and intercooler applications.

The HKS GT II wastegate is the second generation in the high-performance HKS wastegate line. It's available in 50- and 60-mm sizes and its new, more-compact design continues to offer the V-band inlet and outlet flanges for high-capacity exhaust flow and precise boost management. HKS has wastegates that support power levels from 300 hp to over 1,000 hp.

- 5/89-5/90 Mitsubishi Eclipse GS, GSX, (will not work with factory airbox)
- 6/90-2/94 Mitsubishi Eclipse GS, GSX, (will not work with factory airbox)
- 1990-96 Nissan 300ZX, (polished aluminum)
- 5/89-5/90 Plymouth Laser RS, (will not work with factory airbox)
- 6/90-2/94 Plymouth Laser RS, (will not work with factory airbox)
- 1993-98 Toyota Supra, (polished aluminum)

Garrett

Garrett is one of the leading innovators of turbocharger technology. The company's systems save fuel and reduce

If you're taking a factory turbo car and running way more boost and mass flow through the engine, these HKS external-poppet wastegates might be what you're looking for. They're high-performance units for extreme levels of power and boost. External wastegates are used when reliability is needed in high-performance applications because they offer a greater exhaust flow capacity and increased ability to regulate and maintain proper levels of high boost pressure. These units are constructed with a stainless-steel valve, a die-cast mount base and valve seat, a fully sealed shaft, and a heat-resistant diaphragm. It's available in three different types: Standard, Racing, and GT. The standard wastegate uses a 40-mm valve and is rated to applications producing upwards of 500 horsepower. The Racing Wastegate uses a 50-mm valve and supports up to 1,000 horsepower. The GT Wastegate is the largest of the series and has a 60-mm valve to support applications producing well over 1,000 horsepower. Each wastegate can be outfitted with several different spring rates for various boost pressure levels, and you can get universal base flanges, flexible outlet tubes, barb fittings, and gaskets for custom applications.

emissions, with the added bonus of providing an increase in engine performance. Garrett's turbocharging business traces its roots to an aerospace company established in California by entrepreneur Cliff Garrett. Over time, the turbocharging business spun off to establish itself as a serious player in the

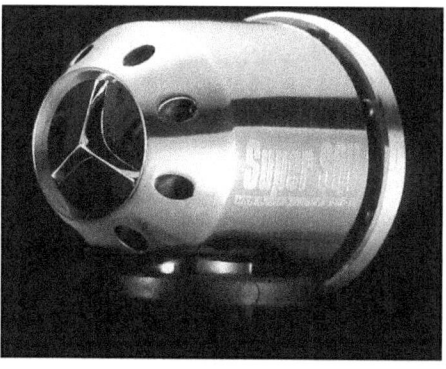

The HKS Super Sequential Blowoff Valve (SSQV) is a dual-stage pull-type relief valve. It's designed not to leak under high-boost conditions or under vacuum at idle. Because of its pull-type valve structure, the SSQV cannot physically leak under any level of boost because boost pressure also keeps the valve closed against its seat. The SSQV is actuated by pressure alterations instead of the level of pressure or vacuum in the line. On typical blow-off valve designs, a large valve is used in order to accommodate high-boost, high-horsepower applications. However, these large valves tend to react slowly and require high activation pressure to open, and therefore are not able to activate and prevent compressor surge at light-load conditions. On the other hand, smaller, faster-reacting valves do not discharge the airflow capacity required for high-horsepower applications and tend to creep open and leak as the boost pressure overpowers the spring. The HKS SSQV gets around this limitation by using both a small primary valve for ultra-quick activation and a larger secondary valve for additional discharge capacity.

engine-boosting industry. Alongside companies like AiResearch, AlliedSignal, and Honeywell, Garrett has sustained its reputation as one of the best companies in the segment. From its long list of industry firsts to its leading-edge ball-bearing turbos, Garrett develops and manufactures cutting-edge boost. Most of the world's top engine and car manufacturers employ Garrett turbochargers to boost their engines, and with 27,000 turbos produced every day, you know they must be building them right. Finally, through the Garrett

Chapter 6

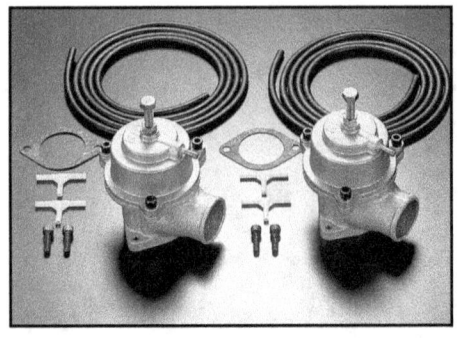

The HKS Racing Blow-off Valve Type II is a pull-type blow-off valve for highly tuned applications. Similar to the construction and function of the HKS SSQV, the Racing Blow-off Valve Type II uses a large, single-stage, aluminum pull-type valve to handle the extreme pressure and airflow discharge volume associated with high-boost, high-horsepower applications. It's supplemented with a light vacuum-aided spring that improves response at light load conditions, and it is engineered to accommodate up to 3.0 bar (43.44 psi) of boost on vehicles up in the 800+ horsepower range. A sleek 29-mm discharge port contributes to a smooth discharge and allows the discharged air to be routed back into the intake stream.

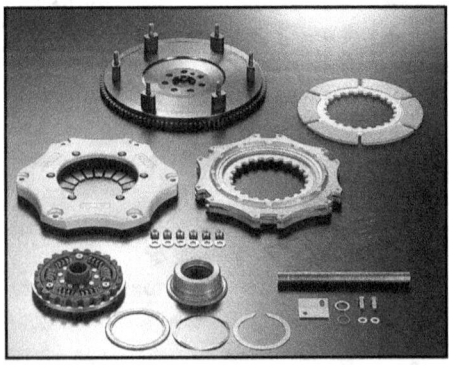

HKS GD Clutch Max Twin-Plate performance clutch kits are vehicle-specific pull-type racing clutches designed for street-car use. Special spring dampening between plates allow for progressive engagement, which enhances driveability. HKS also offers lightweight flywheels to enhance low-RPM throttle response to help RPM matching when downshifting and counter low torque at low RPM levels. The durable chrome-moly material allows a thinner flywheel without sacrificing integrity.

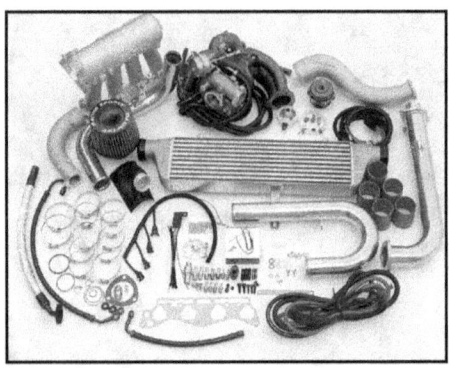

The Garrett 1996-2000 Honda Civic kit is for the D16Y8 SOHC engine. A GT28R ball-bearing turbocharger and the intake manifold, intercooler, TiAl blow-off valve, Ni-Resist exhaust manifold, and turbo-link piggyback ECU are all included — plus, it's emissions certified in all 50 states. The Garrett ball-bearing turbo gives great response, efficiency, and durability, and the absence of a thrust bearing helps eliminate failures at high boost levels.

network of Master and GT Performance Distributors, Garrett's turbocharging product line is readily available for you to install on your vehicle.

Greddy

Greddy is the North American business unit of Trust. The company distributes and supports a wide variety of performance products for the tuner market, with an emphasis on turbocharging and electronic engine management. For the turbo market, Greddy has factory upgrade kits, as well as retro-fit turbo kits.

The logic of upgrading the factory turbo comes from the fact that vehicles with factory turbochargers usually have much more potential for power. Big gains can be found by upgrading the exhaust, intake, blow-off valve, and intercooler, and adding more fuel and boost. But you can take it one step hotter by replacing the stock turbocharger with a properly sized turbo upgrade kit. Greddy kits are designed for some of the most popular vehicles, and they offer various sizes of turbo kits from mild upgrades to full-on race-ready kits with the company's SUS manifolds and external wastegates.

In the same light, installing a bolt-on turbo kit will improve the performance of your naturally aspirated machine much more cost effectively than a hotter naturally aspirated combo. With a bolt-on turbocharger kit, you can obtain instant horsepower gains with less time and money, while still having the potential for upgrading. Greddy says its kits are designed specifically for driveability

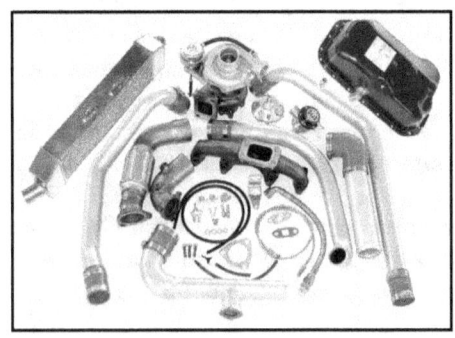

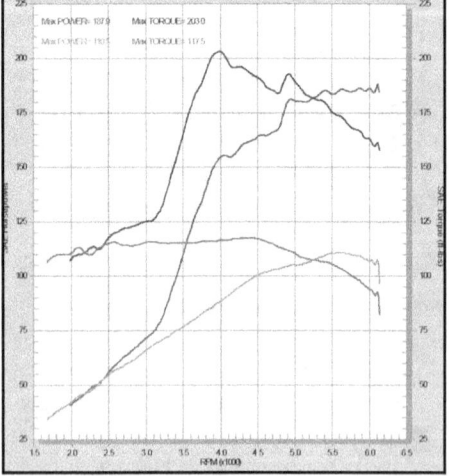

This Garrett turbo kit is a drop-in upgrade for the 1993-98 2.0-liter 8-valve VW Golf, Jetta, GTI, and Cabrio. This kit contains a Garrett T3 Turbocharger and all of the necessary components to install the kit in your own garage. The kit is a direct 3- to 4-hour bolt-on, not including EPROM time. You do need to send in your EPROM certificate at least four working days before installing the kit — you will not be able to complete the installation in one day without it. Check out the great gains on the dyno graph.

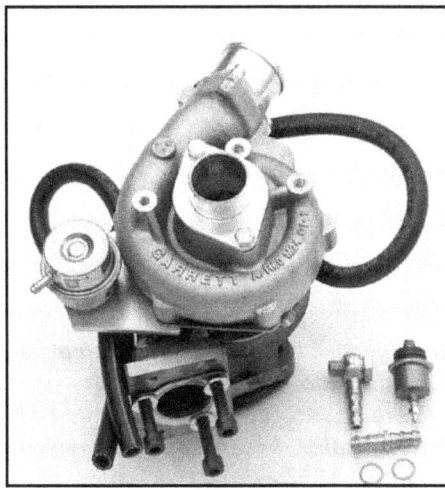 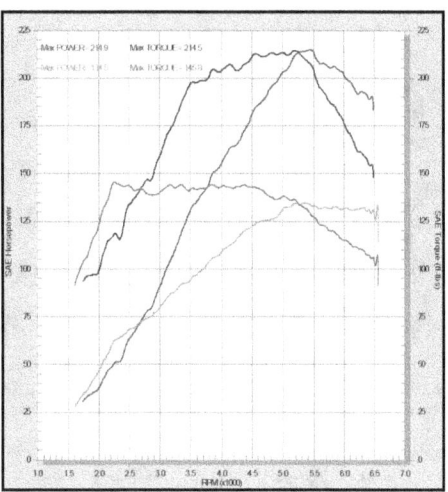 

All GReddy Turbo and Turbo Upgrade Kits exclusively use GReddy-Spec Mitsubishi Turbochargers. The kits are designed and tested to match the application. This means you get good response, smooth driveability, performance that can still be upgraded, and lasting reliability.

This Garrett turbo kit is a drop-in upgrade for the longitudinally mounted 1997-02 1.8T VW Passat and Audi A4. This upgrade is designed to keep most components on the stock 1.8T engine, such as the exhaust manifold, inlet pipe, pressure pipes, and oil return line. This upgrade doesn't alter or remove any emissions-related components. The kit contains a Garrett GT28R ball-bearing turbocharger and all of the necessary components to install the kit. Also: Don't forget to plan for extra downtime while your car's ECU is reprogrammed.

 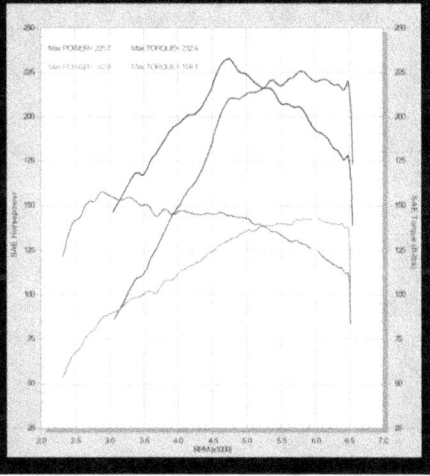 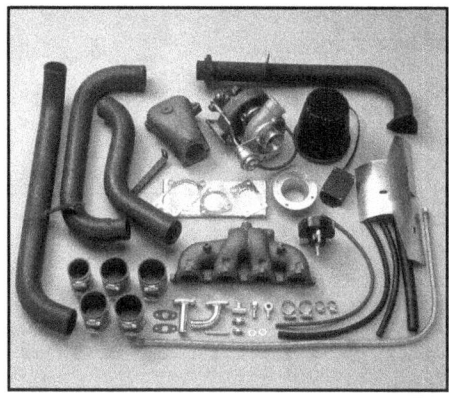

This GReddy Honda kit is for the 1992-95 Civic EX VTEC. It includes a cast exhaust manifold, ECU, air intake, piping, hoses, oil lines, and miscellaneous hardware. The Civic Si 1999-00 kit includes the cast manifold, ECU, 320-cc injectors, air intake, piping, hoses, oil lines, and miscellaneous hardware. The 1997-99 Prelude non-SH kit includes a cast manifold, ECU, 370-cc injectors, air intake, piping, hoses, oil lines, and miscellaneous hardware.

This Garrett turbo kit is a drop-in upgrade for the transversely mounted 2000-03 1.8T VW Golf, Jetta, GTI, and Beetle. Aside from the different applications, this kit is basically the same as the A4/Passat kit.

and reliability, as well as performance. And since they are based completely on stock engines, these kits come with all the necessary basics, including fuel enrichment. Also, many of the kits are covered under CARB E.O. numbers, which makes them 50-state street legal. You also have the option to improve the kit with upgrades such as intercoolers, blow-off valves, fuel management and boost controllers, to boost the power output even further.

Applications:

Acura:
- 1993-95 Integra GSR
- 1996-99 Integra GSR
- 1996-99 Integra LS/RS

Toyota:
- 1990-96 MR-2 Turbo
- 1993-97 Supra Twin Turbo
- 1987-92 Supra Turbo

Nissan:
- 2003-up 350Z
- 1990-96 300ZX Twin Turbo
- 1995-98 240SX

Applications:

Mazda:
- 1989-93 Miata 1.6-liter
- 1987-88 RX-7 Turbo
- 1989-92 RX-7 Turbo
- 1993-96 RX-7 Twin Turbo

Chapter 6

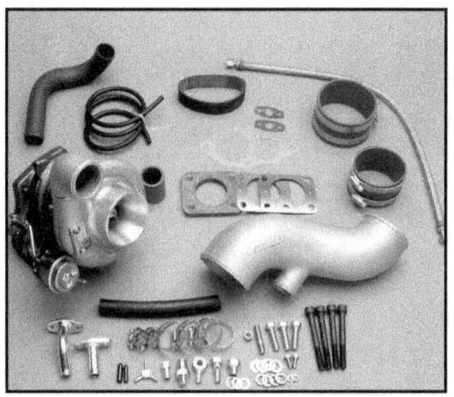
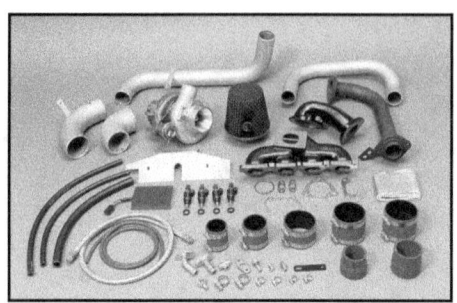

GReddy turbo kits are very complete. They include a cast or stainless-steel manifold, ECU, upgraded injectors, air intake, piping, hoses, oil lines, and miscellaneous hardware.

The GReddy turbo kit for the 1990-98 Mitsubishi 3000GT VR-4 includes upgraded twin turbos, hoses, oil lines, and miscellaneous hardware. The Eclipse GST/GSX 1995-98 kit includes a turbo, cast adapter, cast intake adapter, piping, hoses, oil lines, and miscellaneous hardware. The 2002-up Subaru Impreza WRX kit includes the turbo, hoses, oil lines, and miscellaneous hardware.

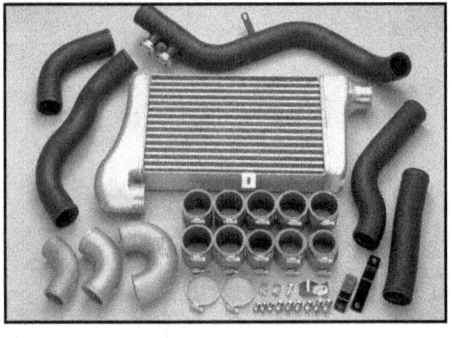
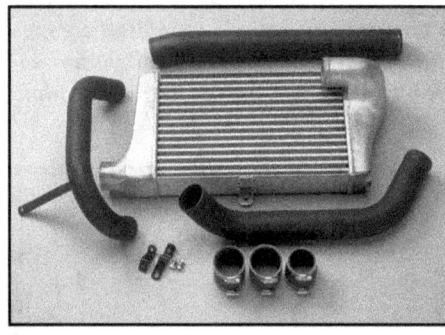

GReddy also has turbo kits for Mazda that includes cast or stainless manifold, FMU, piping, hoses, oil lines, and miscellaneous hardware.

For Eclipse drivers wanting to tune for extra power, GReddy's intercooler is a key component upgrade. GReddy says this intercooler (EO#D-397-2) allows less of a pressure drop than the 1995-97 factory unit it replaces, so it's capable of stuffing more mass in the chambers for more power at the crank. The front-mounted design helps exchange heat since it is exposed to the maximum flow of fresh air. GReddy also has kits for most popular sport compacts.

BorgWarner

BorgWarner Turbo Systems North America's line of aftermarket high-performance engine-boosting components is known as AirWerks.

BorgWarner says it has seen such an increase in consumer demand for high-quality aftermarket turbo upgrades and high-performance retrofits that the company created a product line to serve that market. The AirWerks line features an assortment of BW's K and S series turbochargers that are designed to meet a wide array of high-performance engine requirements. Plus, AirWerks is working with some of the top turbo tuners in the market – for example: Area 51 and Innovative Turbo Systems – so the kits will benefit from the input. AirWerks is also designing installation kits with the intention of making them as easy to install and tune as possible. AirWerks products aren't as widely available as other brands, but they are available from Area 51 and Innovative Turbo Systems.

For example, the AirWerks T3/T4 Hybrid Turbo is available through Innovative Turbo Systems. This T04E 46 Trim Hybrid Turbo is great for medium-displacement six-cylinder engines, and it delivers over 375 hp worth of air using a T3-style turbine mounting flange.

GReddy Blow-Off Valves are easily adjustable to prevent both premature boost leakage and compressor surge. They have durable cast and billet aluminum frames, and the valve-to-diaphragm ratio provides performance that cheap piston types cannot offer. The spring stiffness adjustment screw and two available sizes give you options to get the right blow-off valve for your vehicle. GReddy's Blow-Off Valves are also available in easy-to-install kits for most Japanese turbocharged vehicles.

Sized to produce good spool up and boost for a 2-liter engine, this BorgWarner turbo is made for OE applications.

One of the most important components in a well-designed turbocharged engine is a properly sized wastegate. Too small of a wastegate can cause boost creep, while too large of a wastegate will increase boost lag and decrease performance. GReddy external wastegates are made from high-quality materials to assure both stability and durability in boost control. Each unit is adjustable as well as rebuildable, and they're available in four sizes and various spring rates.

This view of a relatively small BorgWarner turbo shows the integrated wastegate that flows into one exhaust pipe.

AirWerks is the aftermarket business division of BorgWarner Turbo Systems that supplies the aftermarket companies that use BorgWarner Turbo Systems products. BorgWarner also makes Schwitzer turbos and 3K turbos.

This 3K turbo from BorgWarner Turbo Systems is designed to fit a bi-turbo Boxer engine (Porsche). It's made with an internal wastegate.

Turbonetics

In 2004, Turbonetics expanded its staff and product line by acquiring F-Max and the talents of Jhame Peters. Turbonetics also hired Dick Vincent, former head of all automotive turbocharger design for Honeywell, as director of engineering and business development. Turbonetics is one of the best in the business in performance turbocharging, with the greatest breadth and depth of aftermarket turbo applications, from full kits to custom-built turbos and supporting components.

T3/T4 Hybrids

All T3/T4 hybrids are custom matched for specific applications, with airflow ratings from 250 to 450 horse-

The performance Turbonetics T3 series turbocharger is ideal for small-displacement engines with around 150 to 325 horsepower. These are available in any combination of compressor trim (including the exclusive Turbonetics Super 60) and turbine section in standard, Stage II, or Stage III turbine wheel trim.

power. Turbonetics presents a complete lineup of T3/T4 hybrid turbochargers, consisting of a T3 turbine section, (standard, Stage II, or Stage III trim) and a T4 compressor section (T04B trim or T04E trim). The hybrids offer the low inertia and fast boost response of the lightweight T3 turbine wheel and the high airflow characteristics of the T4 compressor family, making them a good choice for high-performance applications.

For the ultimate street/strip performance import enthusiast, the Turbonetics Ceramic Ball-Bearing T3/T4 Hybrid series offers even faster spool-up coupled with outstanding durability.

T4 Series

The Turbonetics TO4B and the TO4E series are the most versatile turbochargers available to the performance aftermarket. The TO4B/TO4E family can support power levels from 250 to 650 horsepower for single turbo applications, and over 1,000 horsepower for twin turbo applications on engines from 100 to 500 cubic inches. All TO4B/TO4E turbos are available with carbon or dynamic seal and wet or dry bearing housings. Standard configuration includes the on-center turbine housings, but a full line of tangential-style housings is also available. TO4B/TO4E turbos are also available with Turbonetics' exclusive Tuff-Turbo and ceramic ball-bearing options.

60 Series

Representing the careful marriage of a unique high-flow, high-efficiency compressor section teamed up with a T4 turbine section, the 60-1 has proven itself in every competitive motorsports application from drag racing to Bonneville. Available with either the standard (4-inch inlet, 2.5-inch discharge) compressor housing or the 60-1 HI-FI (2-3/4-inch inlet, 2-inch discharge) compressor housing, the 60-1 will outflow any standard T04B with ease! The 60-1 HI-FI will deliver approximately 90 to 95 percent of the flow capacity of the standard 60-1.

The 62-1 represents Turbonetics' efforts to produce a premium turbocharger for the engine builder looking for that extra edge of power. Based on hand-selected compressor components and computer-controlled machining centers, the 62-1 delivers an honest 10-percent increase in airflow over the standard 60-1. A turbo like this isn't for everyone, but if you can handle its potential, the expense will be well worth it.

T Series

Turbonetics offers custom-matched, custom-built turbochargers for serious competitors. The T Series incorporates the latest aerodynamics and durability advances for the maximum performance engine builder. The T Series is available with a wide range of flow capacities – TS04, T61, T64, T66, T70, T72, and T76 – capable of supporting 550 to 1,200 horsepower with a single turbo.

All T Series turbos include the Tuff-Turbo option and dynamic seal. You can have your choice of an O or P trim turbine, dry or water-jacketed bearing housings, and on-center or tangential-style turbine housings. Q trim models and ceramic ball bearings are also available.

Y2K Series

The Y2K was specifically created to answer the need for a turbo to be used in pairs capable of supporting 2,000+ horsepower applications. These turbos feature a newly designed compressor wheel matched to a high-flow turbine wheel to dramatically reduce backpressure. The Y2K also features a durable heavy-duty commercial bearing system in a lightweight frame, but it is also available with ceramic ball bearings.

Racegate

The Racegate is a high-flow wastegate that'll control engines that develop 900+ hp. It uses a 1.625-inch (42-mm) stainless-steel valve and the

Turbonetics NewGen swing-valve wastegate (operates like a tradition throttle) is interesting technology. The company says its NewGen swing-valve design is unique in that it offers a clear exhaust path to regulate backpressure in the exhaust, which makes it more effective in maintaining and controlling boost pressure. The NewGen wastegate features V-band type connection, a billet cap, a cast stainless base, and a 2-inch Inconel swing valve. It's rated up to 1,000+ horsepower, so boost creep shouldn't be a problem with this baby. Turbonetics also claims that during testing, the NewGen wastegate out flowed the nearest competitor by 50 percent.

The Edelbrock street-legal Performer X turbo kits come with everything you need to go from stock to fast as heck. Look at the attention to detail Edelbrock put into these kits – ceramic-coated pipes come standard! (Photo Courtesy of Edelbrock)

proven Deltagate actuator to eliminate boost creep on all but the most outrageous combinations. Plus, you can still use it with the Variable Boost Control Regulator.

Deltagate

This is the wastegate most sport compact buyers will be using for engines that develop 300 to 400 hp. The Deltagate is designed for durability, using a 1.250-inch stainless-steel valve, a nomex/silicone diaphragm, and a unique "stand-off" actuator section. When used with a Variable Boost Control Regulator (PN 10402), the Deltagate is fully adjustable over a very wide boost range.

Turbonetics now offers black silicone hose in addition to its immensely popular Blue and Red lineup. Turbonetics hoses are made from high silicone content (400-degree heat resistance) and feature 2-ply reinforcement (250 psi pressure rated).

The new Raptor midsize blow-off valve from Turbonetics offers physical size and airflow characteristics that fill the performance gap between the Street and Strip and Godzilla valves. Kit includes mounting hardware, flange and fittings.

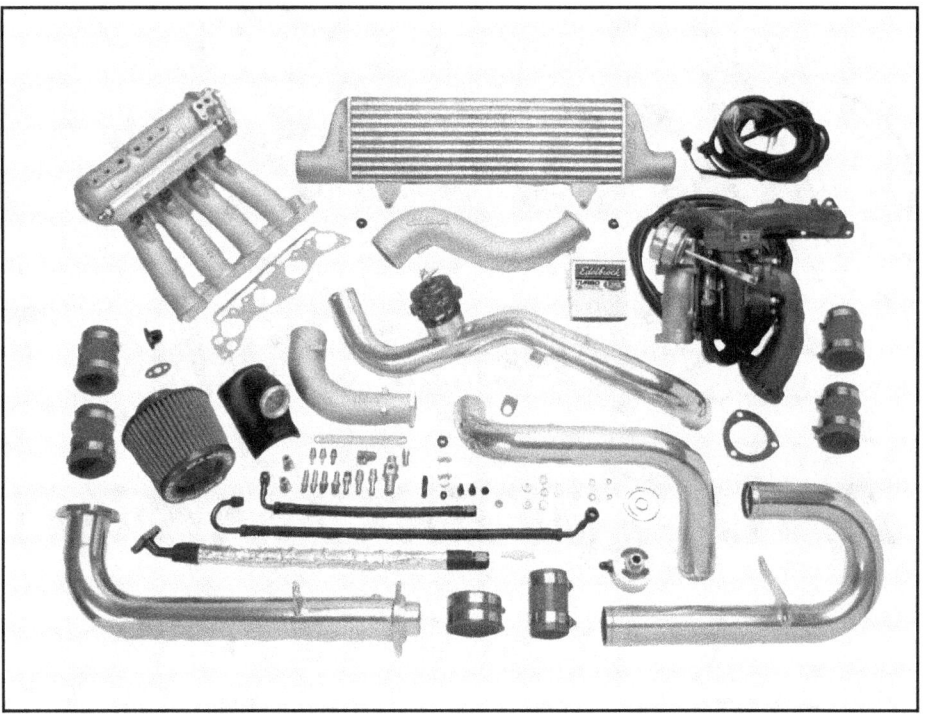

Here's a detail shot of what comes in the box with Edelbrock's turbo kits. Have you ever come across a turbo kit that comes with a Garrett turbo, Spearco intercooler, Tial blow-off valve, and CARB/EO number? (Photo Courtesy of Edelbrock)

Edelbrock

Edelbrock is a high-performance aftermarket manufacturer that's been around since the early days of hotrodding, and it has the experience and high-quality products to prove it. Recently, Edelbrock has been breaking new ground with its sport compact parts. Besides intake manifolds, fuel rails, throttle bodies, and nitrous kits, Edelbrock has also put together a few turbo kits – Performer X kits for street cars, and Open Track kits for hard-core racers. Something very cool about the Performer X kits is that Edelbrock is going through the expensive and time-consuming process of making them 50-state legal. Double-check with Edelbrock to find out which kits have received CARB and EO approval. Edelbrock's Performer X street kits include a Garrett T28 turbo, Performer X intake manifold, cast exhaust manifold, Tial blow-off valve, Spearco intercooler, plus all the necessary tubing, lines, and hardware. Even at only six or seven psi, these kits can add 60 percent more power.

Applications:
- #1500: 1996-00 Honda Civic EX (D16Y8, SOHC)
- #1501: 1999-00 Honda Civic Si (B16A2, DOHC)
- #1502: 1992-95 Honda Civic EX/Si (D16Z6, SOHC)

Edelbrock also offers a line of Open Track turbo kits designed for competition use only (i.e., not emissions legal). These Open Track kits do not come with any of the fuel calibration electronics that come with the Performer X kits, so you'll have to tune it on your own. But if you're at the 240 to 250 crankshaft horsepower level obtainable with these kits, you'll probably know how to take care of that.

Applications:
- #1503: 1992-95 Honda Civic (D16Z6, SOHC)
- #1504: 1996-00 Honda Civic (D16Y8, SOHC)

Chapter 7

Supertuning Turbo and Supercharged Engines

In this section we'll go over how to supertune a super/turbocharged engine. We'll restrict the tuning to items we can alter without cracking open the engine. As we get into cam choices and head and port work, at some point they'll affect both performance and reliability, so we'll save that stuff for the next chapter.

In the broadest sense, you can only increase the power output from an internal-combustion, four-stroke engine by: increasing the force of the power stroke, reducing friction within the engine, and reducing rotational inertial losses and parasitic losses from driving external accessories. That is really all there is to it, in spite of all the hype from performance product advertising. Of course, theory doesn't always line up with reality.

For super/turbocharged engines, the basic strategy is the same: stuff more air and fuel into the engine and light it off at the optimum time in the compression stroke in order to maximize the

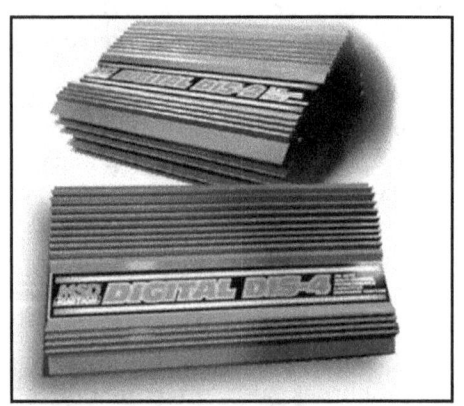

MSD Distributorless Ignition System (DIS) ignitions feature the race-proven capacitive discharge, multiple-spark design of the MSD 6 Series ignitions. Each spark of the MSD Digital DIS Ignitions is packed with up to 115 millijoules of spark energy, resulting in more efficient combustion to produce more power. This is especially important on boosted engines, where the spark can be blown out at high boost levels. MSD engineers included MSD's proven multiple spark discharge feature to improve low-speed throttle response, smooth out the idle, and stop low-speed spark plug fouling. This race-tested design produces a series of full-power sparks that last for 20 degrees of crankshaft rotation to ensure complete combustion of the fuel mixture.

This view of the GM Vortec I-5 engine is with the piston at TDC on the power stroke. You can see the exhaust cam is rotating to open the exhaust valve. As you can see, the intake and exhaust are very smooth and efficient. The factories do not leave much on the performance table these days. The easiest way to increase power is to add boost.

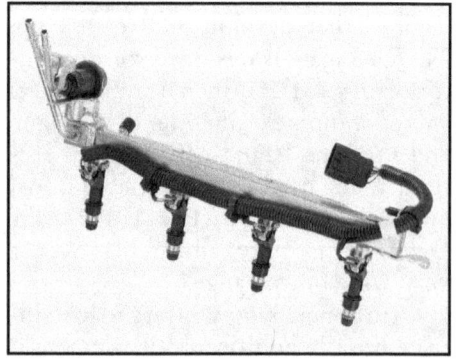

Making more power means flowing more air, but it also means delivering more fuel. Stock injectors have a limited reserve of fuel flow to compensate for atmospheric pressure variations. When you pump in more air than the stock injectors can match, then you have to find ways to deliver more fuel. Larger injectors or higher fuel pressure across the injectors are some of the tactics available.

average pressure in the power stroke. The tactics, of course, are different for each method of pressurizing the intake.

For crank-driven superchargers, a popular method is to install a pulley that'll spin the compressor lobes faster, which in turn increases the boost pressure. The trick, of course, is to get a set of pulleys that don't spin it too fast, which will merely heat the air and expand it, reducing density.

You can also step up to a more efficient supercharger unit. The latest Eaton units are efficient for Roots types, but the Lysholm superchargers on the market are even more efficient. Moving to a more efficient compressor allows you to increase the density of the charge and therefore add more fuel to create more heat and pressure in the cylinder. Hence, the average pressure goes up, and you get more power to the crank.

For turbocharged cars, you can get boost controllers that will override the factory settings and let the turbo build more boost. If the system is intercooled properly, you'll get more mass airflow into the engine. Better yet is to step up to a high-efficiency turbo unit that supplies more boost and mass flow with less heat. Check HKS, GReddy, Turbonetics, Innovative Turbos, and other sources in the buyer's guide for the very latest upgrades. Keep in mind that if you add mass flow, you'd better make sure you have the fuel delivery to support it; otherwise, you'll trash your engine, quickly.

Intercoolers: Do they Really Make Power?

Intercoolers are a hot topic (excuse the pun), and in addition to turbos, crank-driven superchargers can benefit from intercooling. Magnacharger's Radix System is an example of an aftermarket kit that uses an intercooler. The Radix System uses an air-to-water heat exchanger placed between the compressor and the intake ports. On a centrifugal supercharger, you can use an air-to-water intercool or an air-to-air unit. Centrifugals have this design flexibility, where a Roots or Lysholm type doesn't.

Most enthusiasts have a misconception regarding intercoolers of both crank-driven superchargers and turbochargers. The common wisdom is that intercoolers make power by increasing the density of the intake charge. While it is true that the density is increased, it is also true that you get a pressure drop on the other side of the intercooler. Some of the pressure drop is caused by friction from the air having to bounce around through the small tubes of the heat exchanger, but most of it actually results from the charge being cooled. When the charge is cooled, the density is increased, so the same mass takes up less space and therefore exerts less pressure. Remember the Gas Law?

Anyway, the key here is to think in terms of increased mass flow. An intercooler can raise the density of a given amount of air, but density is only how much of something you have in a given space. In other words, the intercooler takes 1 unit of air that is taking 2 units of space before the heat exchanger and turns it into 1 unit of air that takes up 1.5 units of space. You still have only 1 unit of air, but it is now only occupying 1.5 units of space; therefore its density has increased, but its mass hasn't.

Even though the charge air density has increased, the amount of air has not. If we had one pound of air taking 2 cubic feet of space before the intercooler, then after the intercooler we now have one pound of air taking up 1.5 cubic feet of space. The conclusion here is that the intercooler by itself doesn't increase the mass flow entering the engine. So the answer to the question that heads this section is no, intercoolers by themselves don't make power.

What intercoolesrs do is allow you to tune for more power. With a cooler intake charge, the tuner can choose the temperature of the charge air in the cylinder before it is compressed. This is critical in designing your system, because each fuel has a temperature at which it will ignite. Gasoline ignites on its own at a little over 500 degrees F, but this varies slightly with the octane rating. What you strive for, then, is to cool the charge to a specific temperature, so that when it is compressed and heats up during the compression stroke, it will

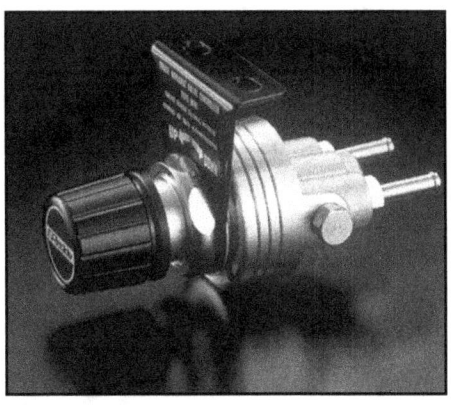

Stock turbocharged vehicles have preset boost pressures. These are lower than the boost pressure the turbocharger is capable of. This means that you cannot obtain any further boost pressure than the level already set. Installing variable boost controls allows you to use the full capacity of the turbocharger. Several manufacturers make these units. The one shown is from GReddy.

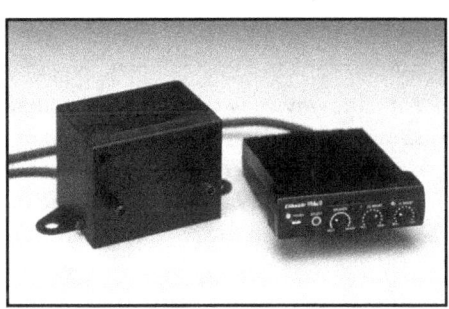

The GReddy PRofec B-spec is one of the simplest, easiest-to-use electronic boost controllers on the market. The B-spec uses a twin-solenoid valve control motor and features two presets labeled Lo and Hi as well as a balance knob to alter the wastegate boost response. This unit also can be used with both factory integral actuator type or external poppet-style wastegates. It's good for twin and sequential turbo setups and is compatible with GReddy's Remote Switching System.

be at a specific temperature when the ignition sparks. As you can probably see, the more the air is compressed (remember the Gas Law), the hotter it will get. This is why compression ratio is so important with a boosted engine – but more on that later.

If you didn't cool the intake charge, more than likely the gasoline would

Chapter 7
Four-Stroke Basics

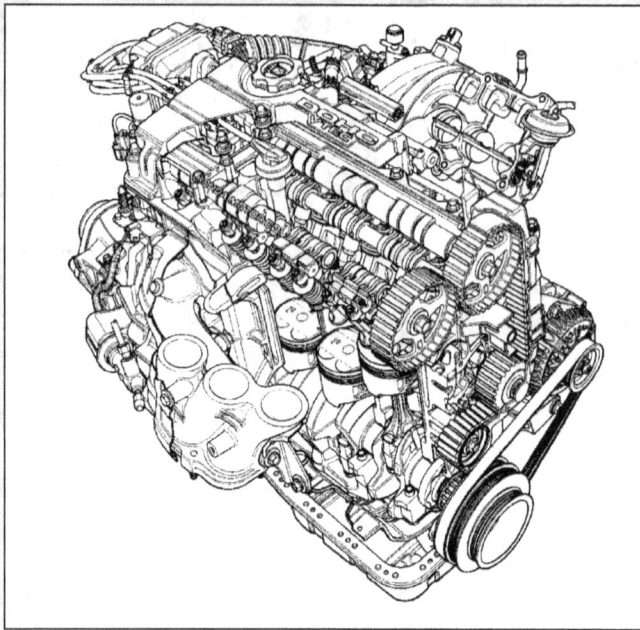

This cutaway view of a 1996 GS-R engine with VTEC head shows the relationship and location of the major components of the modern Honda/Acura high-performance production engine. Note that there is no turbocharger or supercharger on the engine — yet.

The bottom end of your engine consists of the block, crankshaft, connecting rods, pistons, and lubricating system. In general terms, the function of the bottom end is to turn the heat energy released in the combustion chambers into the mechanical energy that drives your wheels. Ideally, you want it to do this as efficiently as possible while being as reliable and long-lived as possible.

The engine block is the structure that provides mounting positions for the crankshaft, the cylinder bores, the head, and the rest of the subassemblies that produce power and allow the engine to keep running. Essentially, that's done by the three-dimensional shape of the metal from which it's made. The engine block must have the correct shape to allow all the different parts to move in a harmonized and specific way. It must also be strong enough to manage the forces generated within the combustion chamber in order to convert heat energy into mechanical energy.

The top end of the engine consists of the components designed to mix fuel with air, contain the heat from the chemical reaction of the air/fuel mix, and then expel the spent gases as quickly as possible. The top end generally consists of the intake track from the air cleaner to the intake valve; the combustion chamber formed by the head; and the exhaust track from the exhaust valve to the end of the exhaust pipe. These components form the airflow path. The rate at which these components flow air determines for the most part how much horsepower your engine can make.

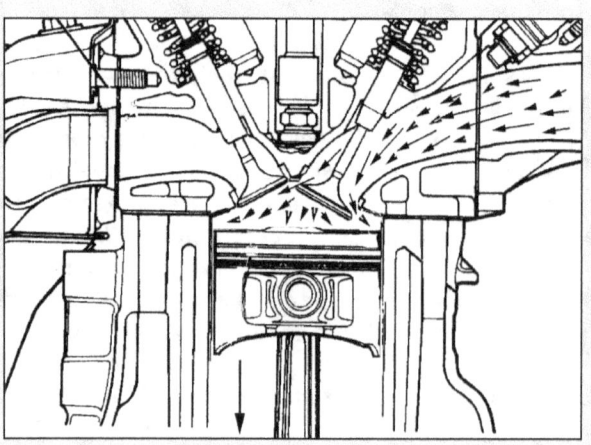

INTAKE STROKE
1. The intake stroke uses the atmospheric pressure or the pressure of a boosted intake track to push the air/fuel mixture into the cylinder through the open intake valve as the piston is pulled down the cylinder bore by the crankshaft. The points at which the intake valve opens and closes influence how much intake charge the cylinder captures. The timing of the intake and exhaust valve opening and closing events in relation to the piston's travel are controlled by the camshaft design.

auto ignite at higher boost levels, which is a fancy way of saying the engine is detonating. Detonation is a condition you want to avoid at all costs.

Intercoolers use either ambient air or a liquid coolant to draw heat from a super/turbocharger's charge air. Which is best? That depends on what you're using it for. An air-to-water intercooler is more efficient. For example, assuming equivalent efficiency levels, an air-to-air cooler's surface area would have to be up to 14 times larger than an air-to-water unit's surface area. That's because the heat transfer coefficient between a liquid coolant (such as water) and aluminum is 14 times greater than the heat transfer coefficient between aluminum

Four-Stroke Basics (continued)

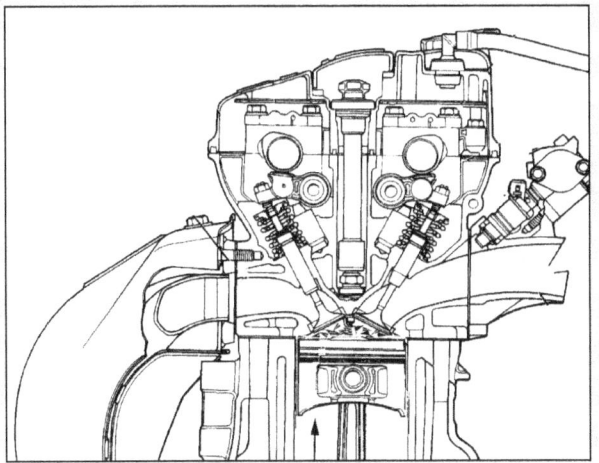

COMPRESSION STROKE
2. The compression stroke compresses the air/fuel mixture captured in the cylinder between the now-closed intake and exhaust valves and the piston. As the crankshaft pushes the piston upward in the cylinder bore toward the head, it reduces the cubic volume between the head and the piston. The amount of compression is indicated by the compression ratio. The compression ratio is determined by dividing the volume of the cylinder with the piston at its lowest point (bottom dead center, BDC) by the volume with the piston at its highest point (top dead center, TDC). If the cylinder's volume is 100 cc with the piston at BDC and only 10 cc when the piston is at TDC, then the compression ratio is 10:1. Note that this is the static compression ratio.

POWER STROKE
3. The power stroke occurs when the compressed air/fuel mixture is ignited by the spark plug and the chemical reaction produces heat. The heat expands the gas trapped in the combustion chamber and the pressure forces the piston down the cylinder bore of the engine. On the power stroke, most of the work is done in the first 90 degrees of crank rotation. As the piston gets near bottom dead center, it's not putting as much pressure on the crank to spin it. The gases are still hot and expanding, but for the most part their job is done.

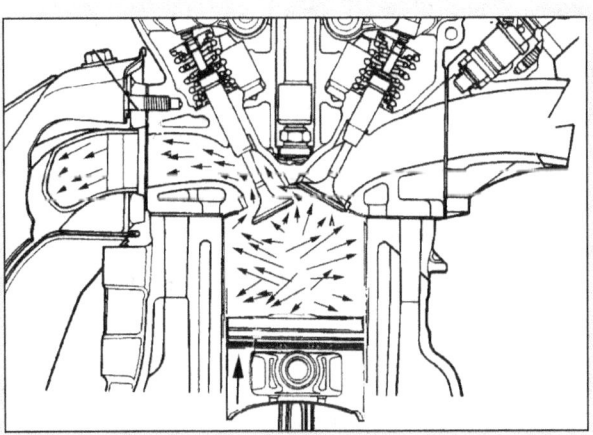

EXHAUST STROKE
4. The exhaust stroke pushes the leftover products of the combustion process harnessed in the power stroke out through exhaust valve into the exhaust system.

and air. However, eventually the liquid coolant heats up (the ice melts, or the supply of cooler water is used up), so air-to-water units are typically used where the cooling effect is needed for only a short time, such as in drag racing or land speed racing, or in marine applications where there is a constant supply of fresh, cool water. Cars that are used for road-racing or are driven on the street should use an air-to-air intercooler, because there is usually always enough fresh, relatively cool air around to transfer heat into.

The basic performance demand of the intercooler is that it must be large enough to achieve the target temperature drop, while minimizing any pressure drop. If you can use an air-to-water unit, you can shoot for 70 percent or greater efficiency and about 1.0-psi boost pressure drop through the unit. For a street car combo, packaging compromises may force up to a 2.5-psi pressure drop and efficiencies as low as 60 percent. If you can reach 70 percent efficiency, that means that if the charge-air temperature from the super/turbocharger going into the intercooler is 300 degrees F, and the ambient temperature of the coolant medium is 100 degrees F, the charge-air temperature exiting the intercooler will be 160 degrees F. This is shown by the equation:

$$E = (T2-T3)/(T2-T1)$$

Where: E = efficiency (percent); T1 = ambient air temperature; T2 = compressor discharge temperature (intercooler inlet temperature); T3 = intercooler outlet temperature (intake manifold temperature).

Notice that this formula doesn't give us the pressure drop, at least not obviously. But it's there. It's there in the temperature drop. The larger the temperature drop, the larger the pressure drop as well. It's the Gas Law.

Why is the pressure drop so important? After all, can't you compensate by turning up the boost an equivalent amount? Sorry, it just doesn't work that way. If you raise boost by more than about 1 psi to compensate for pressure losses, you'll get a slight increase in the temperature of the air going into the intercooler. Unfortunately, it's a downward spiral that reduces the system's efficiency. Therefore, you have to design the system including the intercooler and boost levels to work together.

INTERCOOLER FLOW CHARTS

Just as compressor maps help you select a turbo, Turbonetics/Spearco has efficiency charts for its standard intercooler cores. The charts are calibrated for engines running 10-psi boost at 6,000 rpm. (For 15 psi, increase pressure drop about 10 percent; for 20 psi, increase by 30 percent; for 5 psi, reduce by 25 percent.) For example, this chart for Turbo-

Anatomy of the Power Stroke

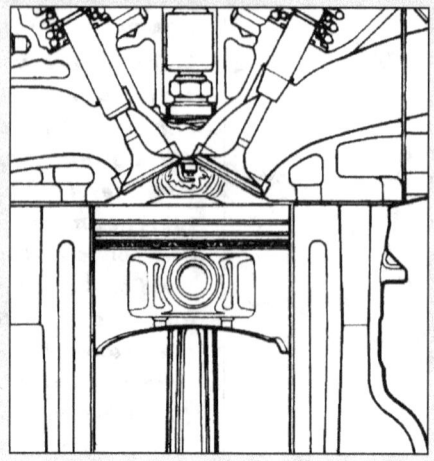

The power stroke can be thought of as beginning a few degrees before TDC. The fuel and air has to be ignited before the crank angle rotates to between 12 to 14 degrees ATDC because it takes time for the fuel to react and raise temperature and pressure. Theoretically, the optimum pressure rise during combustion is typically 20 to 30 psi per degree of crankshaft rotation. The rate of pressure rise is tuned for the most part by choosing compression ratio, cam timing, fuel octane, boost pressure, intake charge temperature, and rod-to-stroke ratio. These factors will influence how much power an engine makes.

The faster the fuel burns, the more power an engine can make. This is because if the combustion pressure can rise more quickly, it has more time to exert pressure on the piston. In the lab, the flame speed of gasoline is between 35 and 50 cm/sec. The actual rate will vary in response to the changing conditions in the combustion chamber. In practice, the flame speed can be much faster in combustion chambers with squish areas or in engines using super/turbochargers that increase turbulence.

The flame speed corresponds to a rise in pressure, but this rise is not constant. Theoretically, the optimum pressure rise during combustion is typically 20 to 30 psi per degree of crankshaft rotation from the point of ignition to about 12 to 14 degrees after top dead center (ATDC). When the crank angle gets past 14 degrees ATDC, the piston begins to travel much faster, expanding the volume of the cylinder. This causes the pressure to drop even though fuel is still reacting and creating heat. Therefore, you want to have peak pressure hit at 12 to 14 degrees ATDC.

Though there is still some power to be gained after about 90 degrees of crank rotation (depending on the fuel and type of induction), most of the work has already been done. A supercharged or turbocharged combination has more fuel to react, so in addition to higher maximum cylinder pressures, the additional fuel can extend burn time and therefore promote a higher average pressure. Alcohol fuels react very slowly compared to gasoline and tend to have more pressure at the bot-

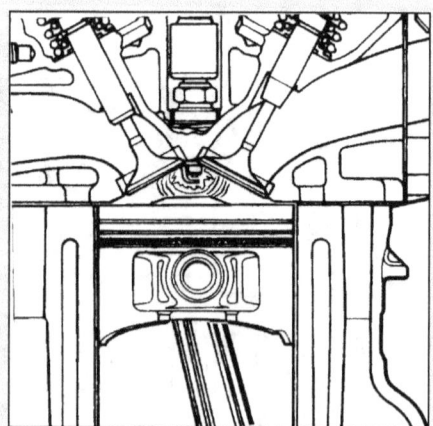

With the maximum cylinder pressure tuned to peak at 12 to 14 degrees ATDC, the rod has rotated to a point that the cylinder pressure acting on the piston will spin the crankshaft instead of putting the force into the rod and main bearings and cylinder head bolts.

Anatomy of the Power Stroke
(continued)

tom of the power stroke than gasoline. Alcohol fuels require different ignition timing and different cam timing.

The limit of pressure rise rate for gasoline is said to be around 35 psi/degree of crankshaft rotation, and once that rate is exceeded, detonation is very likely. The tuning challenge here is to balance the flame-front speeds, the rise in pressure from the heat of combustion, and the changing volume of the cylinder in response to piston travel.

To illustrate, assume a naturally aspirated engine is spinning at 6,000 rpm and ignition timing is at 20 degrees BTDC. Ignition occurs just as the compression pressure is around 200 psi. It starts to build quickly because the piston is nearly at the top of its arc; it'll stall around the top of the cylinder as the crankshaft swings the rod over to begin its downward travel. Because the piston speed is very low at this point, the rate of increase in the cylinder volume is low as well. The flame-front speed will increase more rapidly at this phase in the stroke because pressures and heat are rising at the fastest rate in the combustion cycle. The ignition timing is tuned to produce peak cylinder pressure at 14 degrees ATDC. The actual amount of ignition timing advance has to be tuned to the exact combination; this example is to illustrate the concept only, so don't apply these values directly to your engine. Therefore, we have 34 degrees of crankshaft travel to reach peak cylinder pressure. Doing the math (34 degrees x 30 psi = 1,020 psi added to 200 psi compression pressure) shows we net 1,220 psi.

The tuning scenario above would be very safe and tend to produce good power. However, there's more power available (provided you have the chemical stability of the appropriate octane rating) by advancing the timing a few degrees. For example, 108-octane racing fuel has an acceptable resistance to detonation at a peak cylinder pressure of around 1,500 psi.

Be aware that the amount of timing advance depends on the fuel and your engine's compression ratio. You can push the flame-front speed into the detonation zone by increasing the initial ignition timing advance too much. In that case, you'd see peak cylinder pressure much higher. For example, if you were running unleaded 92-octane pump gas, with the same combination above, you could get into a pressure rise rate of 40 psi/degree. At 14 degrees ATDC, you could theoretically have nearly 1,580-psi peak combustion pressure, which would surely lead to detonation unless it was tuned very rich or the ambient temperature was very cold (or perhaps humid). If the fuel detonates, the pressure would spike way too soon, and your engine (in addition to trying to push itself apart) would be fighting itself, so the power would drop quickly and deeply.

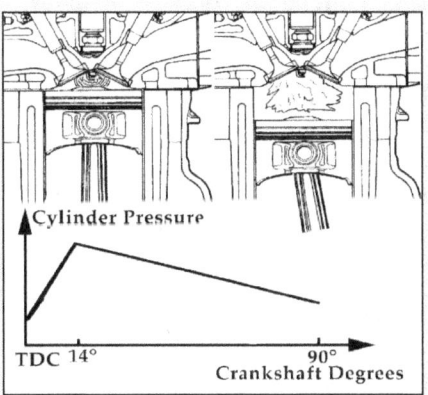

You probably noticed that the peak cylinder pressure is much higher than the mean effective pressure (MEP). Remember that MEP is the average pressure for the entire power stroke. The fact that it is lower than peak pressure is indicative of the pressure curve of the power stroke.

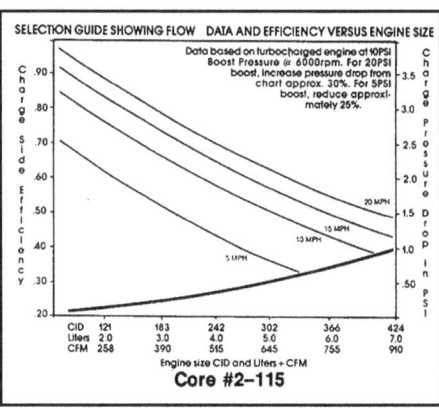

Intercooler Flow Chart.

netics' intercooler shows the unit is suitable for a sport compact engine at 6,000 rpm running 10-psi boost.

Here's how you use an intercooler efficiency chart. First, locate engine displacement along the bottom axis. The cfm values assume 100 percent VE at 6,000 rpm. Draw a vertical line from the engine displacement/cfm value to where it intersects the thick black pressure-drop line. Next, draw a horizontal line from this point to the right-hand axis value to find the pressure-drop. This chart shows the pressure drop across the core only. Depending on the intercooler design and flow rate, the intercooler side-tanks, intercooler inlet and outlet orifice sizes, and ducting may add another 0.3 to 0.5-psi drop.

Now extend the engine/cfm vertical line until it intersects a mph curve (one of the thin black curving lines). Use the 10-mph curve as a baseline unless you can measure the air speed through the intercooler. A horizontal line drawn from this point to the left-hand axis value indicates efficiency – if you can get 70 percent, you're doing good.

THE POWER RECIPE: MORE MASS FLOW

Okay, back to the compressor. So if the intercooler doesn't necessarily give you more power, what does? It comes back to the compressor's design. You want a compressor that will move increased amounts of air mass into your engine's cylinders and do it with the least amount of heat generated in the process. (Because then you've got to intercool it so it doesn't cause detonation. More on this later.) The tactic works like this: Get a bigger compressor that compresses a larger mass of charge air to the same boost level. Then you can intercool it as before. But if you step up to the larger compressor, chances are the intercooler won't be able to handle the increased mass flow, so you have to upgrade to a unit that can and will still lower the charge temp with the least amount of pressure drop. Do this, and the cylinder will be filled with more mass than it would with a smaller compressor and intercooler.

A few more combination suggestions before we move on to the fuel and ignition aspects of tuning. All compressors take air at a given pressure and compress it to a higher pressure. For turbos, this is referenced on the compressor maps as the pressure ratio. You can make more pressure after the compressor by devising a ram-air effect for the compressor intake. Use the motion of the vehicle through the air to artificially raise the intake pressure and you'll see more boost after the compressor whether it's a turbo or a supercharger. That's why you see so many drag cars with an opening for the turbo or centrifugal blower right in the front bumper or hood.

Also, anything you can do to straighten and smooth the airflow through the engine on both the intake and exhaust side will provide additional power. That includes intake tubing from the turbocharger to the intercooler to the intake manifold. In addition, porting the heads and manifold to increase flow works well, though a boosted engine isn't as sensitive to a less-than-optimum port job as a naturally aspirated engine.

ADJUSTING CAM TIMING

For most applications, when you add a super/turbocharger system, you won't have to adjust the cam timing. The pressurized intake works great with stock street cam profiles and timing. However, you can tune how the power comes on by adjusting the cam. Every combination is going to be different, but here are a few tuning tactics to see if you can find power with the cam or cams.

A good super/turbocharged cam has minimal overlap, which means that the lobe centers should be spread as far apart as possible – in the neighborhood of 108 to 115 degrees for most sport compact engines. If you have a SOHC (single overhead cam) engine, that spec is part of the cam grind, so you can't adjust it like you can with a DOHC (dual overhead cam) engine. However, you can advance and retard overall cam timing and that can have some benefit, which we'll talk about shortly. With a DOHC engine (and a set of adjustable cam gears), we use the phrase "lobe phasing" (the phasing between the two cams) instead of lobe center spread. Essentially with a DOHC a good place to start tuning lobe phasing is to align the intake and exhaust lobe centerlines at, for example between 108 and 115 degrees ATDC (after top dead center) for the intake and between 108 and 115 degrees BTDC (before top dead center) for the exhaust, using a degree wheel.

When you widen the lobe centers, or the lobe phasing, you reduce valve overlap at TDC. Overlap is the period during the cam timing cycle when the intake valve has already opened and the exhaust valve is not yet closed. In a naturally aspirated engine, such a situation is preferable because it takes a certain amount of time to get the air moving. But in a boosted engine, the air is under pressure and doesn't require as much duration or lift. As soon as the intake valve opens, the air/fuel mix bursts into the cylinder, filling it rapidly. If the exhaust valve remains open (overlap), part of the air/fuel mix will be pumped out the exhaust valve by the pressure. This is obviously a waste of fuel and power.

In addition to widening the lobe phasing, you can also advance each cam's timing (whether you have one or two). Widening the lobe center spread is usually done by retarding the exhaust cam's timing. What engine tuners have found from hot rods to 4-valves is that you get some power from advancing the cam (or cams) for a super/turbocharged engine slightly (2 to 4 degrees). The net effect is to get both the intake and the exhaust valves open early to get the pressurized air/fuel mix in quickly, get the pressurized exhaust gas out as soon as possible, and to close each valve as soon as possible so that none of the cylinder pressure can leak back out. If the intake stayed open too long, the beginning compression stroke of the piston would want to push the intake charge back out the intake valve. This is similar to reversion in a naturally aspirated engine, except that it would have the effect of backpressure on the blower, which would ultimately reduce its mechanical, volumetric, and adiabatic efficiency. If the exhaust valve stays open too long, as we said, part of the new incoming air/fuel charge will blow out the exhaust port.

SUPERCHARGED EXHAUST

Here's where turbo and supercharged engines vary the most. With a turbocharged combination, the turbo is the highest restriction in the system, so it requires a different mix of components than a supercharged engine.

Supercharged engines do not like backpressure. It's very simple. If you are pumping a greater quantity of air into the engine, you have a greater quantity that has to get out the exhaust side – and you don't want the plumbing backing up. If you plan to run your blown engine in any sort of competition where open exhaust is allowed, you definitely want an "openable" exhaust system. Supercharged engines pick up significant power when uncorked.

A header would be a good choice, especially on a higher-boost engine. In the case of a supercharged race engine, typical header tuning theory does not apply. In other words, the length, diameter, and collector style of the headers is of little consequence. The rule of thumb for blown motors is to use big tubing in the primaries if possible, and keep them as short as possible. Since the exhaust-gas temperature is higher in a blown engine, it will expand more. You may have noticed that supercharged drag cars never run headers that have collectors. They just use short, large diameter "zoomies" to get the spent gas out with the least amount of backpressure.

Even on the street, the object is to keep the exhaust system as unrestrictive as possible. Ideally you would start with a free-flowing header. For the rest of the exhaust system on your blown streeter, use as large-diameter tubing as practical:

DISPLACEMENT	TUBING DIAMETER
1.6 liters:	2- to 2-1/2 inch
1.7-1.8 liters:	2-1/4 to 2-3/4 inch
2.0-2.2 liters:	2-1/2 to 3 inch
2.3-2.5 liters:	2-3/4 to 3-1/4 inch

When choosing an exhaust system, keep the number of bends and the overall length to a minimum, and use a low-restriction muffler. If possible, use a muffler that matches the exhaust tubing diameter all the way through. Remember that an exhaust system is just like any other fluid-flow system – a restriction at any one point affects flow through the whole system.

There's really nothing else to say about getting the exhaust out of a blown engine. Just remember that the capacity of the exhaust system – and the amount of exhaust the engine will have to expel – will be proportional to the amount of air the blower is pumping in. But the exhaust gas is much hotter, and therefore takes up considerably more space (its density is down, its volume is increased). For further information on backpressure, muffler flow capacity, and exhaust system modification, we would highly recommend CarTech's *How to Build Honda Horsepower*, by Richard Holdener, or *High-Performance Honda Builder's Handbook, Volume 1*, by Joe Pettitt.

TURBOCHARGED EXHAUST

On turbocharged engines, the exhaust is important as well, though for slightly different reasons. The turbine will always be the main restriction in the exhaust, so depending on how you size it, you'll change the potential power of your setup. But given that restriction, anytime you can reduce backpressure, you can increase the power output. Racing systems use headers with collectors to reduce internal friction in the exhaust tract, which would increase backpressure above and beyond that generated by the turbo. Also, it is critical to reduce backpressure after the turbine, which will kill the boost. Backpressure behind the turbo will back up the flow of the whole system and slow the turbine down, thus reducing your ability to make boost.

Because of the heat retained in the exhaust, standard mild steel can't be used on turbo headers. The minimum you should use is type 304 stainless-steel tubing with 0.065-inch wall thickness. Again, because the turbine opening is the main restriction, turbo header diameters are relatively small. You shouldn't have to go larger than about 1-1/2-inch ID for the primary tubes. And with the thick walls and a performance ceramic coating, the headers will retain beneficial heat in the exhaust. Equal-length header primary tubes aren't nearly as important on a turbo engine as they are to a naturally aspirated engine. If having equal-length tubes interferes with efficient wastegate mounting, choose the best mount for the wastegate.

FUEL DELIVERY

Superchargers can be set up in two basic kinds of induction systems: draw-through and blow-through. In a draw-through configuration, the blower mounts between the mass airflow sensor and the intake ports, and it pulls air through the mass airflow sensor. With multi-point electronic fuel injection (EFI) almost all super/turbocharger systems are of the blow-through type, plumbing the outlet of the compressor directly to the inlet of the EFI system. In such cases, the tuning of the fuel system is accomplished by increasing fuel pressure, adding larger injector nozzles, adding supplementary injectors, adding larger fuel rails, possibly adding a larger throttle body or mass airflow sensor housing, or reprogramming the existing computer (with a chip) or adding a supplementary fuel management unit (FMU) computer or vacuum-/boost-operated mechanical fuel regulator, as well as the use of computer interfaces.

Some turbo header designs feature downpipes. The downsides of using a tubular exhaust are the increased maintenance and the need for extra space in the engine bay. If you have it, you can find power here. If not, a log manifold will produce good street power levels and offer enhanced reliability compared to tubular manifolds.

First, here's some advice for owners of older sport compacts with (gasp!) carburetors. I know most readers will think carbs are so old school they don't apply to your interest. But before you blow this section off, hear me out. Speaking very generally, the beauty of a carburetor is that it is a responsive device. Which is why in racing applications, a carbureted engine can still be very competitive. (If you're on a budget and you want to build a bad racing motor, don't reject a carbureted combination off hand. Those side-draft Webers and Dellortos still work great on boosted race pieces if you know what you're doing.) The basic function of a carb is to read, or sense, the volume of air passing through it, and to deliver a proportional amount of fuel. The more air going through the carb – for whatever reason – the more fuel the carb delivers. That's how a venturi works. The problem is (1) the typical stock carburetor is filled with pumps, passages, nozzles, and wells that may not operate directly by the venturi effect and are dialed in for naturally aspirated engines, and (2) some carbs, or some parts of some carbs, do not feed a great enough quantity of fuel to feed a healthy boosted engine. Remember that the horsepower output of any engine is directly proportional to the quantity of fuel that it burns. If your boosted engine is set up to make 350 horsepower, its fuel system – including the carburetors, fuel pump, fuel line, filters, and so on – must be capable of delivering at least twice as many pounds per hour of fuel as a 175-hp engine.

As we just mentioned, the rest of the fuel-supply system on a super/turbocharged vehicle is very important. There is little point in reworking the carburetor(s) to supply more fuel, or to add injectors and reprogrammers, if the fuel pump, fuel lines, or filters cannot deliver that quantity of fuel to the engine. Under no circumstances do you want a supercharged engine to lean out from fuel starvation, especially under full throttle at high RPM. Such a situation can result in ventilated pistons in a big hurry.

Each of the components in the fuel-delivery system is equally important, since a restriction at any point between the gas tank and the carburetor float bowl or the injectors will affect the entire system. In other words, a 1/4-inch fuel line from the tank isn't going to cut it on a 600-hp engine. However, even if you replace the entire line with 1/2-inch tubing, but leave the same pickup, screen, and outlet fitting in the tank, you've probably gained nothing.

The same goes for fuel-injected engines, though in addition to line diameter you have to be concerned with the pump's ratings. You want to be sure to have a pump that flows the volume your engine requires at the pressure you'll be operating the injectors. Use the worksheet for fuel injector flows to determine the fuel needs at specific power levels.

I know we've spent a lot of time talking about airflow and hard parts, but if there is one area of your combination that gives your car the speed and power you're looking for, it's the fuel system. Fuel is the source of engine power. The next few paragraphs address how much fuel your engine will demand at various power levels, as well as how to design a fuel system to reliably and consistently supply the fuel.

Turbocharged and supercharged engines require a little richer air/fuel mix compared to a naturally aspirated combination, but let's start with the naturally aspirated fuel needs, because at low or no boost your turbo/supercharged engine will operate in these ranges.

The air-to-fuel ratio (A/F ratio) that is accepted as safe and will produce the most acceleration from a naturally aspirated gasoline engine is 12.8:1. At this air/fuel ratio, if your component combination is good and the engine is tuned properly, you get a brake-specific fuel consumption (BSFC) of approximately .50 lbs/horsepower/hour. Advanced engine tuners can run an A/F ratio of 13:1 and .45 BSFC to get the most steady-state power from an engine. Keep in mind that you're getting closer to the lean side of the fuel curve, and if you're not completely dialed in, you can get into detonation and hurt your engine. By the way, these ratios are for full-throttle, high-load situations. When you're cruising under low-load conditions, you can run right at 14.7:1 (the theoretical ratio that allows complete reaction of fuel and available oxygen) and lower depending on the engine load.

Most tuners experienced with turbo/supercharged combinations recommend an air/fuel ratio in the 12:1 range, which should give you a BSFC of .6 lb/hour. This is on the rich side, but it will give you a very low probability of detonation and yet makes good power. The power-to-air/fuel ratio curve is pretty flat on the rich side but falls off more steeply on the lean side. That tells you that you don't lose much power running a little rich. Given that, it makes sense to run a turbo/supercharged combo with hotter intake temps and higher compressed temperatures a little rich, which cools the charge a bit to resist detonation. It's a little like mixing the gas with octane booster.

With a super/turbocharged engine, Harold Bettes of SuperFlow Corp. says you should plan your total flow rates at .7 BSFC. You need to have some mass flow reserve, so if you calculate the demand with a tenth higher BSFC, you'll have a reliable fuel delivery system. If you use methanol you'll have to double the flow capacity because that fuel's energy density is about half that compared to gasoline.

Use this chart to help determine the flow rate you'll need to support your horsepower goal. Be sure to measure the flow at the pressure you need at the injector.

How to Design a Fuel System

There are two types of fuel pumps produced for gasoline engines: low pressure (4 to 10 psi) and high pressure (30 to 90 psi).

Low-pressure pumps are intended for carbureted engines. Common examples are the 110- and 140-gallon-per-hour (gph) units marketed by a number of manufacturers. These pumps are rated under free-flow exit conditions (no outlet restriction). When the outlet of the pump is restricted (under real-world conditions), the flow capacity is usually significantly less than the rated performance. Low-pressure pumps are the most economical to produce. In most carbureted applications, a low-pressure pump will provide adequate performance and enjoy a cost advantage. Flow

Edelbrock's new 80-gallon-per-hour fuel pump can support about 835 horsepower at 45 psi. Inline electric pumps like this one, along with an adjustable fuel-pressure regulator and high-performance fuel lines and fittings, may be necessary on a high-boost setup. The last thing you want to do is run lean and damage your engine. (Photo Courtesy of Edelbrock)

Fuel Consumption Per Horsepower @ BSFC = .7

Horsepower	Gas lbs./hr	Gas Gals./hr	Gas Gals./min.	Mins. to flow 1 gal.	Secs. to flow 1-gal
500	350	56.45	0.94	1.06	63.77
480	336	54.19	0.90	1.11	66.43
460	322	51.94	0.87	1.16	69.32
440	308	49.68	0.83	1.21	72.47
420	294	47.42	0.79	1.27	75.92
400	280	45.16	0.75	1.33	79.71
380	266	42.90	0.72	1.40	83.91
360	252	40.65	0.68	1.48	88.57
340	238	38.39	0.64	1.56	93.78
320	224	36.13	0.60	1.66	99.64
300	210	33.87	0.56	1.77	106.29
280	196	31.61	0.53	1.90	113.88
260	182	29.35	0.49	2.04	122.64
240	168	27.10	0.45	2.21	132.86
220	154	24.84	0.41	2.42	144.94
200	140	22.58	0.38	2.66	159.43
180	126	20.32	0.34	2.95	177.14
160	112	18.06	0.30	3.32	199.29
140	98	15.81	0.26	3.80	227.76
120	84	13.55	0.23	4.43	265.71
100	70	11.29	0.19	5.31	318.86

capabilities of high-pressure pumps are specified at typical real-world pressure levels. This results in pumps performing much closer to the manufacturers' claim than most low-pressure units.

High-pressure pumps will work well in carbureted applications when matched with the correct bypassing fuel-pressure regulator. Never attempt to use a high-pressure pump with a dead-heading fuel pressure regulator. High-pressure pumps are constructed with closer tolerances and more-costly production techniques. High-pressure pumps will tolerate more severe operating conditions and last longer than low-pressure units.

How to Choose the Right Fuel Pump

When purchasing a fuel pump, there are two factors to consider: performance and cost. By correctly matching a fuel pump to your requirements, you can fill your needs without spending money needlessly. Using the tips below, you should be able to choose the correct pump for your vehicle.

1) Determine the horsepower the pump will have to support (be realistic – no inflated values).

2) Estimate the number of gallons of fuel per hour required to support the horsepower from step 1. Note: these figures are for gasoline; double them if you're using alcohol. Multiply horsepower by .08 to .095. The result is the number of gallons of fuel per hour (gph) required.

$$300 \text{ hp} \times .08 = 24$$
or
$$300 \text{ hp} \times .095 = 28.5$$

3) Determine the fuel pressure the pump will operate at. For carbureted engines, this should be 6 to 10 psi. For fuel-injected applications, you'll have to determine the required pressure. Determine the fuel pressure requirement by using the fuel injection flow rate.

4) Examine the flow-versus-pressure curve included with the pump you are considering. Your flow requirements should be on or below the pump's plotted performance.

Note: In some instances, it is impractical to use a single fuel pump. It's possible to run two pumps in parallel, resulting in an approximate doubling of flow rate if done correctly. In high-pressure applications, two pumps may be run in series. This occurs when trying to increase the fuel flow rate in a late-model, fuel-injected vehicle. The resulting flow of this arrangement (pumps in a series) is not equal to the sum of the two pumps' flow rates (it will be less).

If you're really hardcore, here's a more detailed method for designing your fuel system. First, all reputable pump manufacturers rate their fuel pumps at gallons per hour at some pressure. What you should do first is estimate the horsepower of the engine you are trying to feed. Divide the estimated horsepower by 2 to get a fuel-flow rate required to support that maximum horsepower at a BSFC of .50 (boosted engines could operate at more like .70). Once you have your theoretical fuel requirement in lbs/hr., convert it to gallons per hour by dividing pounds of fuel by 6.2 to 6.8 lbs/gallon, depending on the density of the fuel. Now we take this number (let's use 100 gal/hr) and divide it by 60 to get our required flow in one minute (which in this case would work out to be 1.66 gal/minute). If we take the reciprocal of this (1 divided by 1.66), we would get the fraction of a minute required to flow 1 gallon. This would be .6 minutes or 36 seconds.

Now we get practical. Plumb a pressure gauge into a fuel line just before the carburetor or injectors followed by a small petcock or needle valve. Once you have safely attached the fuel line to a sealed vented measuring container of at least two gallons, turn on the pump and adjust the petcock valve until the pressure reads whatever pressure the pump is rated at. At this point, stop the pump, drain the container, and then get ready to measure the time required to fill one gallon in the container with flow at rated pressure! This method will ensure accurate results and cut through all the claims and counter claims.

"Make sure that you monitor voltage to the pump and make sure that the hot wire feeding the pump and ground wire will carry the amperage necessary to achieve full rated flow. Once you qualify your entire fuel delivery system using this method, you will be amazed at how many 'gremlins' disappear." – From *Uncommon Sense in Engine Development* presented at the 1997 SuperFlow Advance Engine Technology Conference.

Now Let's do the Math

Let's calculate the fuel delivery requirements of 400 hp.

400 x .7 = 280 lb/hr

An adjustable fuel-pressure regulator, like this one from Edelbrock, might help you tune your setup just right. This particular model features a vacuum port for boost reference, and a gauge port, which you'll need if you want to hook up a gauge to monitor your fuel pressure. (Photo Courtesy of Edelbrock)

Convert to gallons per hour by dividing the lb/hr value by the density of the fuel. We'll say our fuel weighs 6.2 lbs/gallon.

280 / 6.2 = 45.16 gallons/hour

Divide that by 60 to get the required flow per minute.

45.16 / 60 = .7526

This tells us we need our fuel pump to flow slightly over 3/4 of a gallon in one minute. To make it easier to measure using a gallon container, take the reciprocal to get the fraction of a minute it takes to flow this amount:

1 / .7526 = 1.33 minutes

Convert to seconds by multiplying 60 seconds by 1.33:

60 x 1.33 = 79.8 seconds

Now set up your test instruments on the fuel system as indicated above and run it for 79.8 seconds and you should have at least a gallon of fuel in the container. If you do, you know you've got the fuel to feed the power.

How to Choose the Right Pressure Regulator

There are two types of fuel pressure regulators available: dead-heading and bypassing regulators. When working with a low-pressure pump, either type can be used successfully. When using a high-pressure pump, you must also use a bypassing regulator. Using a dead-heading regulator with a high-pressure pump will result in premature pump failure and/or ruptured fuel lines. Regardless of which type of regulator you choose, it is important that the regulator be matched to the flow capabilities of your fuel pump. Listed below are the characteristics of the two types of regulators available.

Dead-Heading

A dead-heading regulator works by regulating fuel pressure in the line down to a set value using a diaphragm/spring arrangement. Only the fuel that passes through the regulator will pass into the engine. If fuel requirement goes to zero, such as when the engine stops, fuel flow through the regulator ceases. If the fuel pump remains on, the fuel pressure in the line upstream of the regulator will climb to the value at which the pump stalls or the lines burst. This is why they should not be used in high-pressure, fuel-injected engines. Dead-heading regulators are relatively inexpensive, and they provide acceptable performance in most carbureted applications.

Bypass-Style Regulators

A bypassing regulator controls fuel pressure by returning excess fuel to the fuel tank or the fuel line upstream of the fuel pump. This offers several advantages over the dead-heading unit. Stress on the fuel pump is reduced by lowering the fuel pressure at which the pump operates (the fuel pump will not see pressures above that of the regulator setting). Fuel pressure is also more constant with a bypassing regulator, which is why they are preferred for fuel-injected applications.

Stock (non-turbo model) Fuel-Injection Regulators Compensate for Boost (a Little)

In addition to using a bypass-style regulator, sport compact fuel-injection systems calibrate themselves by using a known fuel pressure differential across the injectors. To maintain that pressure, a manifold vacuum-referenced fuel pressure regulator adjusts fuel pressure at the injectors in proportion to the pressure in the manifold. Therefore, at part throttle when pressure is low, it reduces fuel pressure; at wide-open throttle, when manifold pressure is high (ambient air pressure plus boost pressure), the regulator raises the pressure accordingly. Even on cars not originally equipped with a super/turbocharger, at low to moderate boost levels (5 to 8 psi), the regulator should increase fuel delivery in proportion to the boost level. This is usually enough to keep the fuel ratios right for the additional power levels, though an intercooler or additional injector wouldn't be a bad idea if you want to increase boost above this level.

Rising-Rate Regulators

For cars not factory equipped with a super/turbocharger, it's hard to say how much each factory fuel pressure regulator will adjust. Some aftermarket firms offer what is called a rising-rate fuel-pressure regulator, which compensates for pressure in the intake at rates higher than the one-to-one ratio stock regulators do. For example, a 1-psi increase in manifold pressure gets you a 2-psi increase in fuel pressure at the injector. This is designed to address higher boost levels and can be a useful technique, but it comes with a few caveats.

Since fuel delivery increases as the square of the fuel pressure, you'll need four times the pressure to double the flow. If you're trying to double the flow, you need to step up to larger injectors and recalibrate your engine-management computer. This is because fuel injectors, hoses, and fuel pumps are designed to operate within a pressure window, and in general, quadrupling the pressure is going to be outside that window. Raising the rate this high will also severely reduce the life of a stock pump, and the injectors will most likely not operate properly, usually a little toward the lean side, which is not good for your engine's health. Also, you don't want that much fuel pressure anyway, because the results of a fuel leak and fire will be that much more devastating. Therefore, if you need to bump the fuel ratio up a little, a rising rate is okay, but if you're raising the pressure more than 50 percent or so, you'd be better off taking another course.

You could simply have your injectors checked to see how they flow at the pressure you need, but the right way to do it is to use a fuel-pressure regulator designed for super/turbocharged operation and appropriately sized injectors with the proper recalibration of the engine management computer. If you take this approach, remember that usually your OE regulator is good for about 500 horsepower. You can flow a bunch of fuel through a 5/16 hole at 40 psi or higher, so generally you don't need to install larger fuel lines or massive regulators unless you're building a 500+ horsepower monster. Regardless of what you decide about the regulator, don't forget to upgrade the fuel pump.

How to Calculate the Proper Size Injector for Your Combination

Up until now we've talked mainly about the flow and pressure capability of your fuel pump, but as you've probably guessed, the injectors are just as important. An injector consists of a solenoid that moves an internal plunger when the magnetic windings are energized. The plunger opens a given-sized orifice, allowing pressurized fuel to flow through the created opening. The size of this orifice determines the amount of fuel that can flow out when the plunger is opened. The critical element is the injector's ability to maintain linear fuel flow from very narrow pulse widths to very wide pulse widths, so that the dynamic range of fuel delivery remains accurate for any given RPM and load requirement. The injector's metering orifice is designed to spray the fuel in a cone-shaped pattern of 15 to 30 degrees F for optimum fuel atomization.

Fuel flow is controlled by varying the pulse width or duty cycle of the injectors. Pulse width is the time in milliseconds that the injector is open, while duty cycle is the injector's overall percentage of open time. A 70-percent duty cycle means that the injector is open 70 percent of the injector's maximum cycling time.

Ultimately, to find the optimum injector size for a given application, you have to test it. You can map it out on a dyno, sizing the injector based on observed maximum brake horsepower (BHP) and brake specific fuel consumption (BSFC) at peak power. You can also use a wide-band oxygen sensor that tells you the air/fuel ratio at the load points you're tuning for. The following formulas will get you close to the correct size injector for wide-open throttle performance. Driveability and idle require a little more finesse, and we'll talk about that later.

$$\frac{(BHP \times BSFC)}{No.\ of\ Injectors \times 0.8} = \text{Injector or Size (Flow Rate)}$$

The scaler 0.8 adjusts the calculated injector size to produce the fuel necessary for peak power at 80-percent duty cycle. An accurate BHP figure is critical for proper injector sizing, but not all dynamometers have fuel flow instrumentation, so BSFC is often estimated at approximately 0.5 lbs/bhp-hr. for naturally aspirated engines, and 0.6 lbs/bhp-hr for turbocharged engines.

For example, look at an engine with a known BSFC of 0.49 making 300 horsepower. Applying the formula we derive:

$$\frac{300 \times 0.49}{4 \times 0.8} = 45.9\ lbs/hr\ \text{(req. injector flow rate)}$$

If you need to convert cc's/min to lbs/hr, just divide by 10.5. To convert lbs/hr to cc's/min, just multiply by 10.5:

45.9 lbs/hr × 10.5 = 482 cc's/min

You can also calculate the maximum horsepower a given injector size can feed by plugging a known injector size into the formula using either the measured or estimated BSFC.

$$\frac{\text{Flow Rate} \times \text{No. of Injectors} \times 0.8}{\text{BSFC}} = \text{HP}$$

or

$$\frac{50 \text{ lbs/hr} \times 4 \times 0.8}{0.49} = 326.5 \text{ HP}$$

Running an engine on a dynamometer to determine its performance statistics isn't practical for most of us, so BHP is often estimated by using quarter-mile performance and one of the performance slide rules or "dream wheels."

Tips for Tweaking and Tuning Your High-Pressure Fuel System

Building and tuning a performance sport compact is a process that involves chasing down and correcting "weak links" in the performance chain. On the mechanical side, a car is a collection of systems that work together to produce power and motion. If any of these systems fail to deliver a required function, the performance of the whole machine suffers.

As displacement, RPM, and boost pressure increase, so does the engine's need for fuel. If the fuel system on your car fails to deliver an adequate fuel supply to the injectors, the air-to-fuel ratio will be affected, usually toward the lean side. However, it is possible to have too much pressure, leading to an over-rich condition. Lean air/fuel ratios tend to cause cylinder temperatures to rise and can, in extreme conditions, lead to detonation and destroy your engine, while a rich condition lowers cylinder temperatures and, if it's extremely fat, reduces power output.

There are three basic concepts regarding fuel delivery. One is the rated volume of the pump, the second is the inside diameter of the fuel line, and the third is the pressure, measured in pounds per square inch (psi). Pressure and volume are related in that a higher pressure, for a given diameter of fuel line, will yield more volume, at least up to a point. And obviously a larger diameter line will have a higher volume capacity.

How to Read Plugs

When you're at the racetrack, skill in reading spark plugs will help you produce power and keep you from damaging your engine. We can't give you all the info you need right here, but this will get you started right.

The first thing you need to know about reading plugs is how to run the engine right before you pull the plugs to read them. No tricks here: Make a full-throttle, fully loaded pass at the strip or on a chassis dyno or Dynojet. At the end of the pull, kill the ignition, immediately push in the clutch, and put the trans in neutral. You don't want the engine to cycle without the ignition on, and you don't want to idle down. The idea is to leave the plugs colored as they were at full-throttle, high load.

Check the plugs with an inspection light. This tool has a magnifying glass integrated with a light that lets you see deep into the pocket of the plug at the base of the porcelain. You're looking for the "footprints" of the combustion process, which will allow you to verify the fuel mixture.

For example, black sooty porcelain bases on the plugs mean you're way too rich on your fuel mixture. When you start seeing gray and whitish deposits, you know you're too lean. Sometimes you'll get a glazed, brownish color, which indicates a lean mix or too hot a plug heat range. If you get really lean, and your engine is equipped with forged aluminum pistons, you'll start to see specks of aluminum deposited on the electrode and the porcelain. This is a danger signal; you need to add more fuel to your mixture. If you're running close to the best mixture, the porcelain should be clean and white. From there, fine-tune using your mph at the end of the quarter-mile to dial in the best mix.

Always be on the alert for detonation damage. In addition to the specks of aluminum mentioned above, if you notice that one or more of your plugs have a melted or chipped electrode tip, it's a sure sign of intense detonation. Find out the cause immediately before making any more passes. Check the fuel ratio, timing, plug heat range, and cooling system — anything that could cause the engine to detonate.

Delivering an adequate supply of fuel requires that the system overcomes the forces of gravity (since it must be pumped up to the intake against earth's gravity) as well as against the pressure of the boost (since the boost pressure in the manifold will be trying to keep the fuel in the injector), the acceleration of the car, and the friction within the fuel line. As a general rule, a low-pressure system with a fuel line with a horizontal length of 13 feet between the tank and injectors will lose 4 psi per g of acceleration. High-pressure fuel-injection systems lose less pressure, but they still drop off, so be aware and have lots of reserve capacity. Losing pressure means you are also losing volume, and that means you might be losing performance.

The solution to this performance problem is to design a system that has an adequate reserve of pressure to overcome the effects of gravity (and the g's during launch) and to install a fuel line that is of adequate diameter and is as free of needless bends as possible. Bends in the fuel lines and connections are a source of turbulence and friction and reduce flow.

If you want a state-of-the-art fuel system, the following ideas will help you achieve it. Of course, you'll still have to do the testing and tuning, preferably at the racetrack.

1. Delivering a consistent supply of fuel begins with choosing a proper fuel tank or modifying one to work right. A proper fuel system has a tank with baffles to keep the fuel from sloshing away

A stock fuel filter might get the job done in a stock fuel system, but when you up your flow and pressure requirements, all your components need to be up to the task. High-flow fuel filters, like this one from Aeromotive, get the job done without adding a restriction and keep contaminants out of your engine. (Photo Courtesy of Tony Huntimer)

from the outlet during acceleration. It should also have fuel outlet bungs that are positioned such that the force of acceleration feeds fuel into the fuel line before the pump. So if you're making serious power with hard leaves off the line, you'll need to find a racing-style fuel tank to fit your street car. FuelSafe and other manufacturers make tanks to fit production-based racers. These might work for you.

2. Electric fuel pumps do not pull fuel well; they're better at pushing it. So the less restriction you have before the pump, the more efficient and stable your fuel supply will be.

3. You can reduce the turbulence in the fuel line exiting the fuel tank by massaging the insides of the fitting to improve flow (similar to porting heads). Drill out the inner diameter (ID) of the fitting, then hand blend the angles of the male and female fittings. You have to be careful not to enlarge the ID too much or you'll compromise the integrity of the seal.

The inner diameter of the fuel line should be as big as the inner diameter of the fuel pump fittings. If two lines need to be split or joined in a "Y" or "T" arrangement, the cross-sectional area of the two lines should be equivalent to the cross-sectional area of the single line. Fuel lines should be kept as short and free of tight bends as practical.

4. You want to filter debris from the fuel before the pump. That way the debris can't become lodged somewhere and cause a restriction or perhaps hurt the pump. It's also best to position the filter so it is easy to inspect and clean. Use a filter with lots of capacity reserve so it doesn't offer much restriction to the system before the pump.

5. Pros use high-torque pumps to generate reliable high pressure. A weak pump will tend to stop at lower pressure, and when it does it will draw more current from the battery and wear out quickly. Pump pressures are related to the amount of voltage available. If you need more pressure, you could run a 16-volt battery, though it might be heavier. Another tactic is just to use a 10-gauge wire from the kill switch directly to the pump to deliver the max amount of voltage offered by the battery. As you raise the power level higher and higher, you'll eventually reach a point at which the wiring can act as a restriction and reduce fuel pressure and flow. You can also use a device such as the Kenne-Bell boost-a-pump to raise the voltage to increase pumping pressure and flow rate.

Ignition

Timing the ignition to get maximum power is part art, part science, because you're chasing a constantly changing combustion chamber condition. Light-load, part-throttle; high-load, part throttle; and high-load, full-throttle conditions each have their own timing requirements.

That's why almost all stand-alone engine management systems have a starting map with basic timing and air/fuel ratios provided. If you had to program the whole thing from the start, you'd be retiring before you made your first blast. Better still is to use the factory computer programming and alter it to your needs. You can simply have the factory computer program flashed (reprogrammed), or try one of the popular interface units such as the

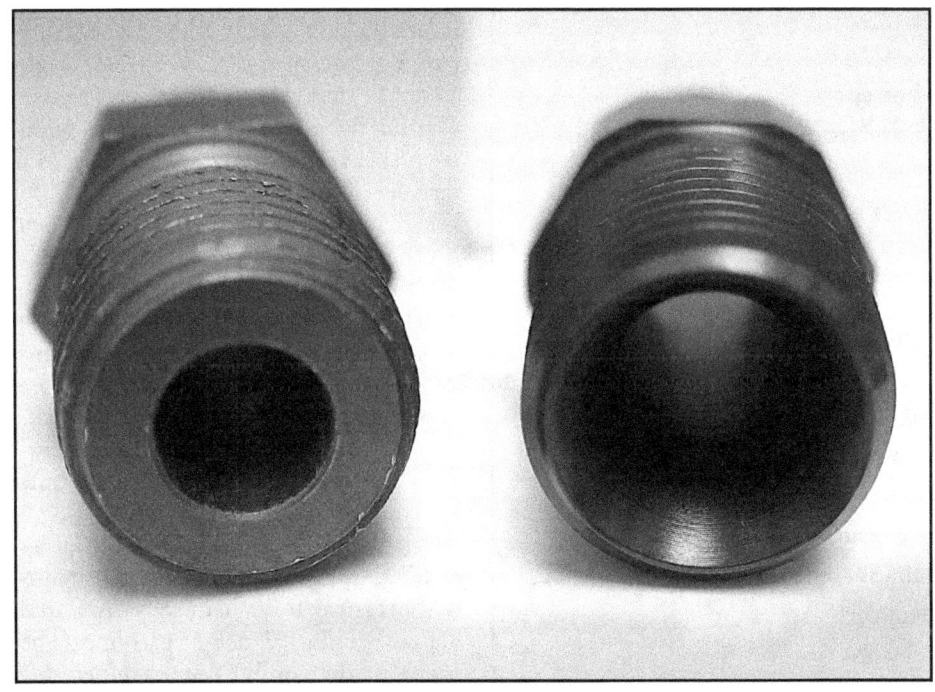

Not all fittings are created equal. The XRP fitting on the right has a much larger cross-sectional area for better flow. When you're building a high-performance fuel system, keeping restrictions to a minimum is key. That way your pump won't have to work as hard, and your engine will be less likely to be starved for fuel. (Photo Courtesy of Tony Huntimer)

Jim Bell's Supercharged / Turbocharged Rules of Thumb

This chart comes from Jim Bell of Kenne Bell. It lists most of the important relationships between fuel, boost pressure, and compression ratios. This data is intended as a guide only. It's the result of thousands of dyno runs and street testing that Kenne Bell has performed on Ford, Mazda, Dodge, GM, Buick, and Syclone/Typhoon turbocharged vehicles.

- 1 psi boost = .5 point CR (effective CR)
- 1 point CR = 2 psi boost (cylinder pressure)
- 1 point CR = 2% horsepower
- 1 psi boost requires 1-1.5 octane (minimum)
- 1 psi boost = 6.8% horsepower max (1 ÷ 14.7 = 6.8%)
- 1 point CR = 3 - 5 octane points
- 1 point change in the A/F ratio = 2 octane points
- 1° advance = 1/2 - 3/4 octane point
- 10° engine coolant (160° -180° range) = 1 octane
- 20° ambient = 1 octane point
- 1 can NOS Octane Boost = 1.5 - 3.6 octane points
- 1,000-feet altitude = -1 octane point
- 1,000-feet altitude = .5 psi (2" Hg)
- 6° F temp change = 1% air density
- 30% humidity = 1 octane point
- 10° air charge temperature = 1% horsepower
- 20° charge temp reduction through intercooling = .5 psi additional boost with same octane
- 3/4 psi drop = 5% pressure (5% x 14.7 = .75 psi)
- engine cfm = $\frac{ci \times RPM \times VE^*}{2 \times 1728}$

*70% VE for the average engine, 90% for racing engines

- 10% horsepower increase = 7% A/F ratio
- (based on 70% VE) or 10% AF ratio with 100% VE
- 10 psi fuel pressure = 8% A/F ratio: 5 psi = 4% AF ratio
- horsepower = CFM (int @ 28") x .257 x no. cylinders
- 10 horsepower = .1 sec/1 mph in the 1/4 mile
- 100 lbs = .1 sec/1 mph in the 1/4 mile
- RAM PSI = $\frac{Ad \times V^2}{4287}$

where: Ad = atmospheric density .076 lbs/cu ft at sea level
V = speed in mph

HKS AFC. In the latter case, the unit alters the existing instructions to the engine from the computer to accommodate higher boost, cam changes, etc. When flashing the factory computer, the programmer gets in with editing software and changes the existing program in specific areas to accommodate the performance mods. As the tools come online, editing the factory computer is fast becoming the preferred method of tuning both air/fuel ratios and ignition timing.

The advantage of using the factory timing programming is that for 85 to 90 percent of your street driving, you won't be making boost and the stock tuning will be absolutely perfect. All you have to do is edit the timing required for the boosted condition. Unless you're editing for a known combination, you'll have to do some trial-and-error tuning. Understanding what's going on in the combustion chamber will help you make the right choice.

If the air/fuel ratio is right around 12.5:1 all the way through the RPM range, you can concentrate on getting the timing right. Ideally, you want to ignite the mix so that you get maximum cylinder pressure at a crankshaft angle 12 to 14 degrees after top dead center. Getting the ignition timing to this point is just as important as getting the air/fuel ratio right.

Many guys with their engines tuned on the ragged edge are lifting the heads off their motors because they get too much cylinder pressure at the wrong time. When you're talking about cylinder pressure, you must consider the rate at which the fuel burns, i.e., how quickly the cylinder reaches maximum pressure after ignition, and what that time lag equates to in crankshaft degrees.

It takes between 20 and 30 degrees at 6,000 rpm to reach maximum cylinder pressure for a naturally aspirated engine running 91-octane gasoline. (The shape of the combustion chamber also influences how quickly cylinder pressure rises, and we'll talk about that in a second.) So, with a naturally aspirated combo with a pressure rise time of 25 degrees at 6,000 rpm, you'd want to light off the cylinder at around 12 degrees before TDC. If it takes a few more degrees, you can advance the timing accordingly.

But keep in mind when I'm explaining this that when you turbo, supercharge, or inject nitrous, it takes less time for each cylinder to reach maximum pressure. The time difference is because pressurizing the intake and/or adding nitrous increases the burn rate of the fuel mix, i.e., these processes add oxygen and turbulence and increase the dynamic compression ratio. What you need to do now is delay or retard your ignition timing to keep the spark happening at the optimum time.

To give you a baseline timing mark, Rob Smith, a savvy engine tuner and owner of Turbo Clutch, likes to run 20 degrees total timing on a maximum-boosted motor. He's found that spec by running a computer program that simulates this timing and shows that if he has 23 to 24 psi boost, with 18 degrees timing advance, he'll see the cylinder pressure at around 1,800 psi and 300 horsepower. Bump the timing up to 26 degrees and the cylinder pressure jumps up 400 psi – that's a bunch. Though the pressure climbs from 1,800 to 2,200 psi, you only net about 8 to 10 horsepower. The additional psi puts a strain on the engine by beating on the bottom of the main bearings and the top of the rod bearings, and by trying to push the cylinder head off the block. Rob says he usually elects to sacrifice the extra eight horsepower in favor of reliability. We recommend you follow suit.

Tuning the timing is best done on a dyno or a racetrack. You'll want to be watching or recording the scanned data coming from the engine's sensors to do this right. As long as the air/fuel ratio is right, you can focus on the timing. At full throttle under 15-psi boost with high-octane fuel and 8:1 static compression, set the timing near 18 degrees BTDC to begin your tune. If you lose power, or the knock sensor acts up, retard the timing or reduce boost. With a 9:1 engine, drop back to 14 degrees. And from there you can retard timing about 1 degree for every 2 psi of boost. You may also want to increase the octane, depending on what you're trying to accomplish. If you're racing, up the octane and run the best racing fuel you can find. If it's just for fun on the street, back off and save your engine. And while you're doing this, watch closely for any indication that the engine is detonating. If it does, figure out what's wrong before continuing.

That's the basic scoop on timing; and here are a few suggestions on the hard parts to make it happen.

Go with a good set of plugs. We've had good luck with the iridium plugs, but really any premium plug designed to live in the heat you're planning to produce will be good. With boost, you need to pay attention to the heat range. A colder plug transfers heat more rapidly into the head than a plug with a warmer heat range. If you're generating lots of heat and stay at wide-open throttle at max boost all the time, you'll need a pretty cold racing plug. If you're not running that hard, or your combo is running overly rich, you'll want a hotter plug to keep the gap clean and firing consistently.

Upgrading to an aftermarket ignition system is especially important when you're running boost. MSD, Holley, Crane, and others make ignition systems that pump up the voltage. In some cases, the aftermarket systems add multiple sparks to get the fire going in highly boosted combustion chambers. MSD Distributorless Ignition Systems (DIS) work very well on

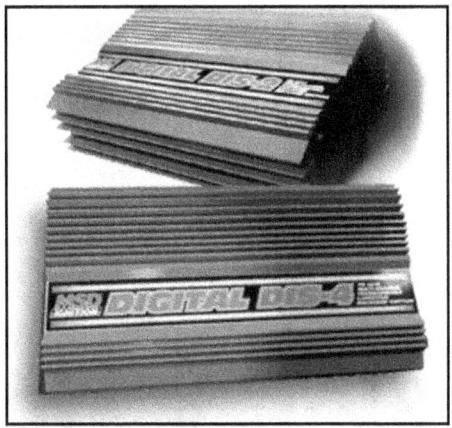

MSD Distributorless Ignition Systems (DIS) ignitions feature the race-proven capacitive discharge, multiple-spark design of the MSD 6 Series ignitions. Each spark of the MSD Digital DIS Ignition is packed with up to 115 millijoules of spark energy, resulting in more efficient combustion to produce more power. This is especially important on boosted engines, where the spark can be blown out at high boost levels. MSD engineers included MSD's proven multiple spark discharge feature to improve low-speed throttle response, smooth out the idle, and stop low-speed spark plug fouling. This race-tested design produces a series of full-power sparks that last for 20 degrees of crankshaft rotation to ensure complete combustion of the fuel mixture.

Precise timing control is essential to producing maximum power. With the addition of nitrous, turbos, or supercharger systems, timing becomes even more critical. To get the most out of your engine, the ignition must be able to compensate for these extreme changes in cylinder pressure throughout the engine's entire RPM range. During low-speed operation, the MSD DIS ignitions use the factory ignition to control basic timing functions. Once maximum timing is achieved, the DIS-2 and DIS-4 can be programmed to retard the timing at a specific rate and RPM point to prevent engine damage due to detonation caused by excessive timing. They also feature an adjustable built-in rev control to protect the engine from over-rev damage caused by missed shifts or broken driveline components. The two-step function allows you to activate a low RPM limit while staging and waiting for the light to turn green. The RPM limit is easy to adjust in 250-rpm increments with switches built into the side of the housing.

Chapter 7

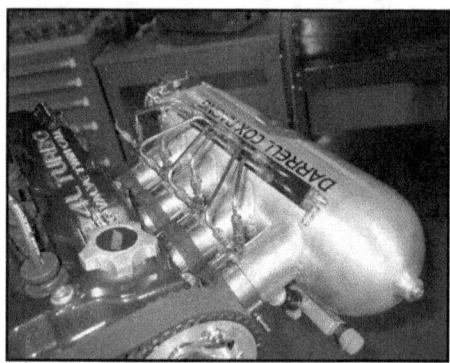

The safest way to add nitrous oxide injection to a supercharged or turbocharged application is to use a direct injection system. This allows you more precise control over nitrous and fuel delivery. If you do this, be sure to inform the nitrous oxide manufacturer that you intend to install the system on a boosted engine, and have them jet the nitrous oxide and fuel-enrichment nozzles accordingly.

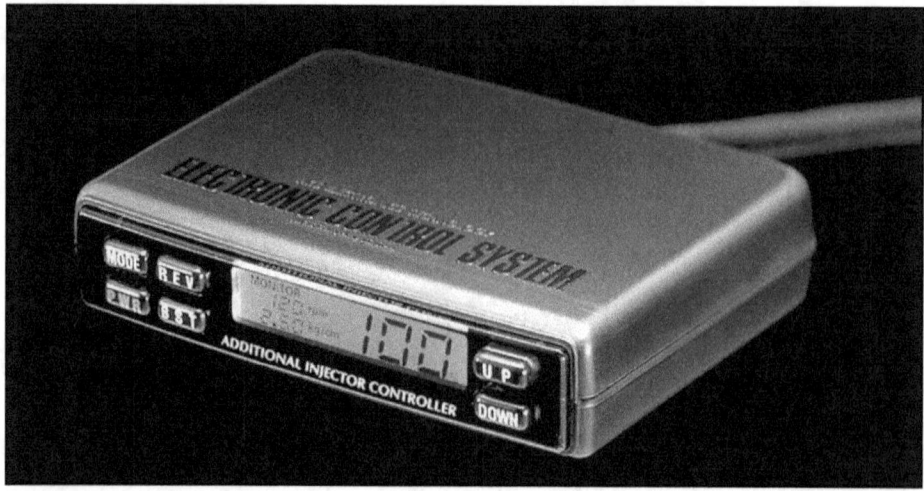

The HKS AIC III is a stand-alone digital fuel enrichment device that is designed to supply, upon demand, the supplemental fuel needed by forced induction vehicles. The AIC is an ideal option for vehicles that require additional fuel but have factory fuel systems that offer limited expandability. The device integrates supplemental fuel via additional injectors mounted in the intake stream or on the intake manifold. The AIC is useable on factory turbocharged applications or aftermarket turbocharged applications.

The HKS Super AFR is an airflow meter correctional device with a built-in CPU. These devices interface between the sensor and the engine management computer and compensate for the additional mass flow of a turbo/supercharged intake. Since the correction will be made to this specific intake volume, the correction ratio of fuel will be precise and proportionally correct. The Super AFR is compatible with virtually any fuel-injected vehicle, and the internal CPU allows it to be versatile and used on many of the newer-type airflow meters.

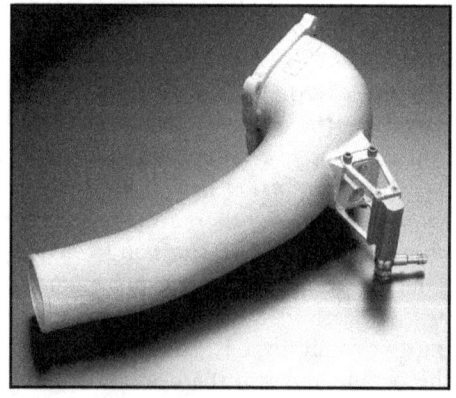

HKS AIC Injector Pipe kits are aluminum, vehicle-specific, high-performance fuel delivery units that are designed to properly supply the additional fuel enrichment needed for high-boost, performance applications. HKS AIC Pipe kits offer proper mounting and integration of additional injectors controlled by the AIC III.

modern ignition systems with one coil per plug.

Don't forget to tie the ignition component together with the highest quality ignition cables you can afford. Ignition cables by themselves don't make power. What they do is offer reliability under very harsh conditions. A high-output ignition system, combined with the heat and vibration of a boosted engine, will require a cable that'll hang on the plug and coil and won't wilt in the heat.

Boost Electronics

The fuel and ignition systems are the relatively easy part of the recipe. The hard part is making sure the A/F ratio is perfect and timing is just right. This is the trick to tuning. It sounds easy, but just wait until you try it. An engine is almost a living thing – what it needs changes throughout the RPM range and according to load conditions. Fortunately for modern tuners, we have very good electronics at our disposal that allow us to monitor and tune the system in real time. Perhaps more realistically for most of us, there are sources that will custom tune the factory computer, or provide an interface to allow the engine management system to take advantage of the hard-parts changes we make.

One example of a piggy-back tuning system is the HKS Super AFR. The Super AFR is a piggy-back system because it manipulates the airflow meter signal going to the factory computer using its own built-in CPU. The advantage of having a built-in CPU is that instead of making pre-programmed

The HKS FCD is an electronic device developed to properly raise the factory-set fuel cut RPM on factory turbocharged vehicles. This device is useful if you don't or can't reprogram the stock ECU to compensate for the higher RPM power-curve you get as you add intakes and exhausts, larger turbos, a boost controller, etc. In some cars the factory fuel cut is often triggered by the higher boost levels obtainable with a boost controller as a failsafe procedure. The FCD installation is designed as a simple integration on to the VPC/F-CON or factory ECU harness. You have to know how to use this product, because you can easily force unsafe boost levels resulting in severe damage to the vehicle's engine or other mechanical parts. We strongly suggest a fuel supplement system or consulting a trained technician before the purchase and use of the FCD.

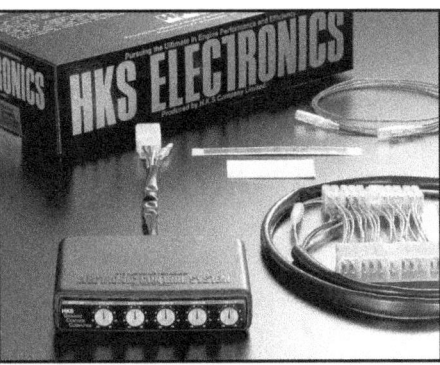

The HKS GCC adds additional flexibility to the fuel-tuning capabilities of the VPC, PFC F-CON, and F-CON S by allowing the user to further adjust the air/fuel ratio at five specific RPM points with an adjustment range of 16-percent rich to 12-percent lean in 2-percent increments.

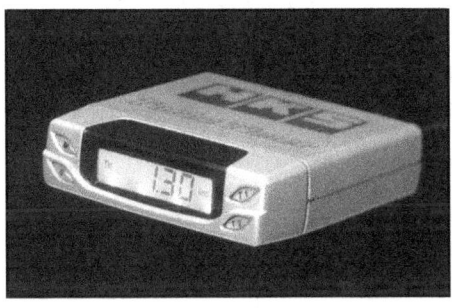

HKS' Turbo Timer Type-1 is a full-featured turbo timer that combines all the features of the Turbo Timer Type-0 with added monitoring and metering functions such as RPM, time to speed/distance, peak hold, warning features, and a stopwatch for lap times.

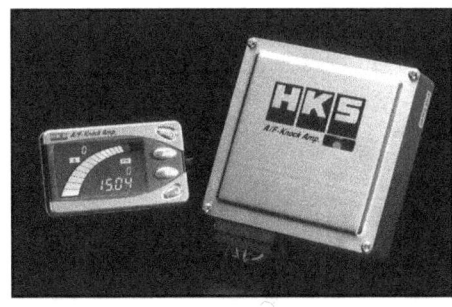

The HKS A/F Knock Amp has a built-in digital display and face-mounted controls, making it ideal for high-performance engine tuning. This wide-band air/fuel monitoring device offers visual and audible warnings for precision tuning.

HKS's all-new EVC features integrated CPUs in each component (Display Unit, Control Module, and Stepping Motor) for more precise control, quicker response, and improved boost-pressure stability. The system is available in kPa and psi measurement and features an LCD panel that can be positioned separately from the control module for driver convenience.

(generic) corrections to the airflow meter and map sensor signals, the signals are inputted into the CPU so it can calculate the most accurate amount of airflow. Since the correction will be made for each specific situation in real time, the correction ratio of fuel will be more precise and proportionally correct. With the Super AFR, you can make fuel adjustments (by percentage over baseline) in real time, and monitor these changes on the LED screen. Of course, you'll want to do this on a chassis dyno, or have a friend drive while you're tuning. Remember to be especially careful on public roads. HKS says the Super AFR is compatible with virtually any fuel-injected vehicle using a 12-volt electrical system with between 2 and 12 cylinders and a hot-wire, Karmen Vortex airflow meter or pressure sensor to measure mass airflow. Other similar examples of piggy-back systems include the Apexi S-AFC and GReddy E-Manage. Apexi also sells a VTEC AFC if you also need to control a VTEC system.

Another category of product interfaces with the factory computer to alter its stock engine management settings. More recent factory computers are being edited using programmers like the DiabloSport that offer a variety of pre-set programs to remove the fuel cut at RPM (rev-limiter) and vehicle speed limiter, and adjust the timing, fuel delivery, etc. Another example, the HKS FCD, can raise the factory fuel cut level on factory turbocharged vehicles as well as compensate for the additional mass flow and speeds attained through tuning and modifications.

A good example of this type of hybrid device is the HKS AIC III. It's a "stand-alone" digital fuel enrichment device that's designed to supply,

Chapter 7

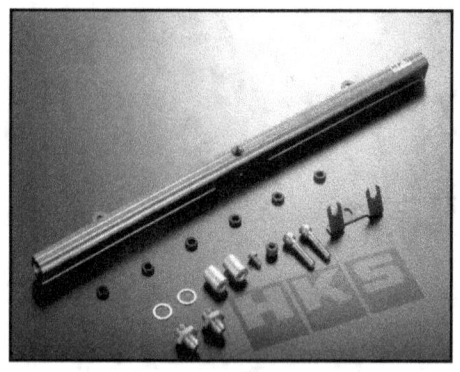

HKS Fuel Rail Upgrade Kits are high-performance fuel delivery units designed to properly supply the additional fuel enrichment needed for high-boost performance applications. HKS Fuel Rail Upgrade Kits replace the factory units with precision, high-flowing anodized aluminum units that also allow for seamless integration of larger injectors. This kit shown is for the 1993-1998 Toyota Supra Turbo, for 680-cc/1000-cc injectors.

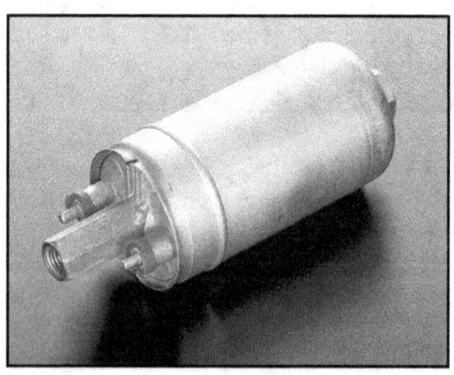

As performance levels increase via greater airflow efficiency or higher boost levels, fuel delivery is crucial in developing maximum horsepower and in maintaining proper air/fuel ratios. The HKS In-Tank Fuel Pump Upgrade replaces the factory pump to increase flow for high-boost applications where the factory injector pulse duration is substantially increased or where additional or larger injectors are used. This particular pump is rated at 71 gph at 45 psi.

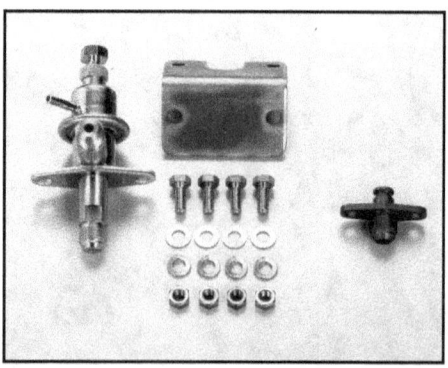

HKS Fuel Pressure Regulators can be integrated to properly increase or maintain correct fuel pressure levels. The fuel pressure regulator can be used to raise fuel pressure levels in order to increase the amount of fuel being injected by the stock fuel injectors. It can be used to adjust the fuel pressure to tune your setup to work with larger injectors.

One of the fundamental limitations to increasing boost is stock injector capacity. The work-around solution is installing higher-capacity injectors. RC Engineering is well known for supplying injectors as well as advising on style, capacity, and other fuel delivery requirements.

upon demand, the supplemental fuel needed by forced induction vehicles as power levels are increased. It's a hybrid system in my mind because it doesn't use the stock ECU, but it doesn't replace it, either. The AIC III is an ideal option for vehicles that require additional fuel but have factory fuel systems that offer limited expandability. The system works on factory or aftermarket turbocharged applications, from 3 to 8 cylinders, by controlling up to eight additional injectors for precise fuel enrichment. The AIC III adds supplemental fuel via additional injectors mounted in the intake tube or on the intake manifold. It seems to be pretty clever, too, offering comprehensive adjustments with two independent fuel curves: boost pressure and RPM. The boost-dependant fuel curve can be calibrated at incremental points, while the RPM-dependant fuel curve has a calibration range from 1,000 to 12,000 rpm in 100-rpm increments. Each fuel curve is independent of the other, yet the two curves overlap, combining their enrichment values at that given condition. With this device, assuming you have the fuel pressure at the injector and the volume capacity to back it up, you should be able to tune a fuel curve that'd be very powerful and reasonably safe. Plus it has real-time monitoring of the RPM, boost, and injector duty cycle for quick reference and adjustments.

This limitation of this device and others like it is that you have to know what you're doing. You have to know what air/fuel ratio you want at each point. Most tuners will tell you you're looking to have 12.5:1 air/fuel ratio to make the best power. If you run a high boost level (say, over 10 psi) you'll need to fatten that up a bit, say to around 12 or 11.8:1. It all depends on if you're getting into detonation or not and if you're making the power you desire.

If you really step up and get a huge compressor that'll jam lots of air at a high pressure through your engine, you'll need more fuel than your stock system can provide, even if you cheat on fuel pressure. At that point you have to make a call on a stand-alone engine management system (not even remotely emissions legal in most states) or an additional injector controller.

There are essentially two levels of stand-alone engine management systems. One is more user friendly, with some automatic programming to allow you to get up and running relatively easily. The second, such as the Motec engine management system, is for pros and serious amateurs. These units have features and engine control ability more appropriate for the purpose-built racecars and experienced tuners.

AEM's Engine Management System (EMS) is a user-programmable system that can plug directly into a vehicle's factory ECU harness and requires no additional wiring or hardware. For some non-factory supercharged combinations, some adapting hardware may

Underdrive pulleys like these AEM True-Power Pullies include a smaller-diameter crankshaft pulley and an accessory drive pulley set. They're an okay modification for naturally aspirated engines but not for a supercharged or turbocharged engine. These pulley sets reduce the drive speed of the accessories in order to reduce the drag they impart on the crankshaft. But with a pressurized engine, you need the water pump and alternator spinning at the proper speed to cool the engine and supply power. Plus, belt-driven superchargers are set up to run off the OEM crank pulley anyway.

Fuel pressure risers use a vacuum signal to control pressure at the injector. The less vacuum it sees (wider opening of throttle) the more pressure it delivers across the injectors. Higher pressure, up to a point, allows the injectors to deliver more fuel to burn with the denser air charge from the pressurized intake.

For a factory supercharged engine, the options for making more power without opening up the engine are basic. You have the choice of driving the supercharger faster and increasing intercooling effectiveness to get the most gains. For incremental gains, try a free-flowing intake and exhaust system. Remember, you may need a power programmer to deliver more fuel to the denser intake charge.

be required. It uses Windows®-based software (2000, NT, 98, 95, ME) to make copying, viewing, and manipulating data simple. The AEM EMS's infinitely adjustable software allows tuners to program virtually any combination of engine control, power adders, and auxiliary devices, and accurately deliver proper amounts of fuel and correct ignition timing for virtually any boost level or operating condition.

AEM designed each EMS part number to fit a specific car. It doesn't use an adapter loom or external jumper harness. It also plugs into the factory sensors. That is a big plus for a production car. About the only negative is using the stock narrow-band oxygen sensor, but it even has provisions to use a wide-band sensor.

The coolest thing about this system is that it's smart. With a wide band oxygen sensor installed, you can set the desired A/F ratios at 350 rpm, manifold pressure, and load points. Then fire up the motor and do some acceleration and the unit will tune the fuel curve itself.

It's also packed with a bunch of cool features, such as programmable traction control, a data logger, the ability to control up to 10 fuel injectors sequentially, rev limiter, two-step launch control, electronic boost control, nitrous controller, knock controller, and several other outputs, as well as idle control and seven switch inputs.

As off-the-hook as the AEM unit is, the MoTeC system is just as staggering. Of course, so is the price. The MoTeC can control the injector in just about any way you can think of: sequential, semi-sequential, and batch fire. It can even time when the injector fires, taking into account the "lag time" between when the injector is energized and when it actually fires. It can also control ignition timing trim for each cylinder. These are only some of the unit's capabilities, but you get the point. For a more complete treatment of fuel injection technology, see my first book with CarTech®, *High-Performance Honda Builder's Handbook, Volume 1* or Ben Strader's new book *Building and Tuning High-Performance Electronic Fuel Injection*.

At any rate, if you're going to be doing any tuning yourself, you'll need a good wide-band air/fuel ratio meter with which to gauge the effectiveness of any fuel system changes. Factory oxygen sensors can give readings only over a very narrow range, and they are virtually useless anywhere else. Wide-band oxygen sensors provide you with a specific definition of the air/fuel ratio at which the engine is currently running. Wide-band sensors are able to depict air/fuel ratios as rich as 10.5:1 and as lean as 18:1. You can use this real-time data to see the results of the adjustments you make to your vehicle's tune. If you use it right, a wide-band oxygen sensor can help you tune for the most power without blowing up your engine.

Most enthusiasts are all up to speed on the latest turbo innovation: more boost, more efficiency, and all that. What they don't tend to pay attention to and what gets them into trouble is the fuel system. The power comes from the fuel, not the boost, not the intercooler...*from the fuel*. It has to be delivered in precise amounts, or you'll toast your motor. You just can't throw a big injector in your stock fuel system and ECU and think you'll be fine.

Case in Point: ESX WRX

To illustrate the process of taking the WRX to a higher state of tune, we'll follow along the modification stages suggested by Tony Rigoli Performance (TRP). TRP is an Australian tuner shop that at the time of this writing has the world's fastest WRX – a 2002 WRX that ran 9.60 @ 144.78 mph with an automatic trans. The car is tuned and the parts marketed by the US dealer Easy Street Motorsports (ESX).

ESX suggests starting with its Stage 1 kit, which includes an Injen 3-inch turbo-back exhaust and an ESX 3.5-inch down-pipe with cat (cat-less option available). These components reduce pressure after the turbo (especially with the cat-less option) to increase the pressure differential across the turbine. This makes the turbo spool up quicker, providing more power throughout the operating range. The Stage 1 kit also includes a dual-stage adjustable blow-off valve that helps get the boost back after each shift in a car equipped with a manual transmission. Finally, an Injen cold-air intake system probably helps a little on the top end with this combination, but it will help more with further mods and increased airflow demands.

The ESX Stage 2 kit consists of an ESX top-mount intercooler and hoses. This is a preparatory step, and as we've talked about, you shouldn't expect to see big power gains with just an intercooler. Any power gains would tend to be in the high-RPM range since the intake tract could then be smoother and more efficient. However, if the intercooler is more efficient and the cylinder sees cooler charge air, that will promote reliability and lessen the chance of detonation, especially if you like to drive hard, which we assume you do.

The ESX Stage 3 is also a preparatory step, even though it consists of a turbo upgrade to an IHI VF-22 (VF-34, Innovative GT60, 66, and 72 available at additional cost) and a larger-diameter ESX up-pipe to handle the additional flow once you're able to boost up and take advantage of the upgraded turbo. The IHI VF-22 flows more mass than the stock unit; the company claims 344 hp with this turbo (plus the ECU tuning in the next step), a significant power increase over the stock WRX's flywheel SAE rating of 227 ponies. Therefore, this is at least half of the real power story of this combination.

The second half of the power story is contained in the ESX Stage 4, which consists of tuning the factory ECU to work with the additional mass flow provided by all the hard parts installed up to this point. ESX uses ECUtek Tuning software and DeltaECU programming interface. To reprogram the ECU, the DeltaECU programming interface is simply plugged into the diagnostic socket of the car. This is the new wave of tuning OBDII engine management systems – it's a quicker, cleaner, and more reliable method of tuning than using the old-style interfaces, signal processors, and conditioners.

There are many advantages to reprogramming the factory ECU. For example, reprogramming the original ECU is by far the cleanest, safest, and quickest way of correctly compensating for engine, induction, and exhaust modifications. The fuel and ignition maps in the factory ECU may be adjusted to cater to virtually any modifications, yet you retain civilized features such as the cold start program and a stable idle. Perhaps more importantly, the performance mapping begins from the already extremely good factory Subaru map. You can forget using questionable boost clamps, bleed valves, boost controllers, and piggy-back modules. By modifying the factory ECU, you can retain all the safety features like sensor checks, fuel cut, boost cut, rev limit, speed limit, and "limp home" mode, though you can alter them to suit the car and its modifications. For example, if the ECU detects a problem (engine over-temperature or failed sensor), it is still in full control of boost pressure and is able to take evasive action to preserve the engine. This is in stark contrast to external controllers and piggy-back modules that either take over control of engine functions or fool the ECU about the state of its sensors.

The company claims that its ESX Stage 4 package will give you up to 344 horses, which, given the weight of the WRX, should be capable of a 12.5-second, 110-mph 1/4-mile time slip. The cost? The MSRP for the hard parts (installed) and dyno tuning is $6,595.

This is about the limit without getting into the engine and reinforcing it – installing heavy-duty cylinder liners, head studs, porting the heads – all the trick hot rod/super tuning stuff you see in the magazines. It's really about at the limits for a civilized street machine. However, civilization is sometimes overrated, so if you really have to go for it all, this is what you have to do.

To take things to the next level, you'll have to build a stronger engine, and while you're doing that, you can increase the stroke of the engine to give it more horsepower. Tony Rigoli knows that torque is important, so he's designed three stroker engine packages for the EJ20 WRX engine. Each increases the capacity, while adding progressively more strength and head porting, to make power at higher RPM. The first two stages are more street oriented, while the third stage is aimed at racers, able to handle 35+ psi and nitrous. The second stage is able to handle up to 30 psi, but if nitrous is used, then a lower boost pressure is recommended. TRP doesn't say how much boost you can use with the first stage, but it should be at least 20 psi.

Here is the parts list for the Stage 1 2.13-liter engine:
- Billet connecting rods
- Forged pistons
- Stroker crank
- Metal head gaskets
- Head studs

As you'll see in the next chapter, Stage 1 is

Case in Point: ESX WRX (continued)

a basic high-performance engine build. It's very analogous to what Subaru did to upgrade the WRX engine for the WRX STi (besides adding to the stroke). The metal gaskets and head studs will also help contain the boosted power stroke events.

Here is the parts list for the Stage 2 2.13-liter engine:
- Billet connecting rods
- Forged pistons
- Stroker crank
- Copper head gaskets
- O-ringed heads
- Head studs
- Ported heads

Stage 2 adds O-ringed heads, which can secure a lot of pressure. This is the reason for the 30-psi boost rating. The heads also get port work to increase the mass flow though the engine. The company uses this engine package as the basis for its ESX 500 package, which includes everything you need to make your car a 500-horsepower street machine. ESX figures that's good for 10.80 @ 128 mph in the 1/4 mile.

The 500-hp combination consists of the following:
- Complete dyno-tested engine via Tony Rigoli Performance (TRP)
- TRP engine internals and stroking
- ESX/TRP front-mount intercooler with aluminum piping
- TRP fuel system
- Micro-tech engine management system
- Innovative turbocharger
- ESX/TRP up-pipe
- ESX/TRP turbo-back exhaust system
- ESX carbon fiber grille badge and three ESX 500 decals
- ESX/TRP ugraded-synchro transmission
- ESX/TRP performance clutch

Notice that the 500-hp level necessitates an aftermarket stand-alone engine management system, a high-tech turbocharger from Innovative Turbo, and extensive fuel-system upgrades. This kit also reached the limit of the stock trans, so ESX/TRP has components designed to withstand the power level. Entry price? – professionally installed and dyno tuned for $24,999 (w/core exchange). Yikes!

Stage 3:
- Street cams
- Billet connecting rods
- Forged pistons
- Stroker crank
- Copper head gaskets
- O-ringed heads
- Head studs
- Ported heads
- Stainless-steel valves
- Heavy-duty valvesprings
- Titanium retainers
- STi Buckets
- Street cams

Now we're in the heavy-duty hot-rod category of engine building. Stage 3 adds the O-ringed heads to improve the seal for the combustion pressures it'll see with over 35-psi boost and nitrous. The same goes for the stainless-steel valves – they're really strong and won't buckle under pressure, plus they have a shape that helps air flow through the port. The titanium retainers are an attempt to offset the weight penalty of the stainless valves, while the heavy-duty valvesprings are required to control the valves with the more aggressive cam in the kit and keep them from blowing off the seat under pressure. This combination of the cams, head porting, and the ability to contain the extreme boost and nitrous pressure makes this a potent combination.

Stage 3 is the base for the ESX 740 package (740 estimated flywheel hp), which was used to take the ESX Subaru WRX to the mid-9 second 1/4 mile @ 145+ mph – the world's fastest WRX.

The ESX 740 package consists of:
- Complete dyno-tested engine via Tony Rigoli Performance (TRP)
- TRP engine internals and stroking
- ESX/TRP front-mount intercooler with aluminum piping
- TRP fuel system
- Micro-tech engine management system
- Innovative turbocharger
- ESX/TRP up-pipe
- ESX/TRP turbo-back exhaust system
- Nitrous oxide injection system (50-hp shot)
- ESX carbon fiber grille badge & three ESX 740 decals
- ESX/TRP full dog-box transmission or racing 4-speed automatic (+ $3,500)
- ESX/TRP performance clutch

This takes the 500-hp package above, boosts it further, and adds a direct port nitrous shot to overcome the exaggerated turbo lag of the big turbo required at this staggering power level. Cost to play at this level? – professionally installed and dyno tuned for $31,999 (w/core exchange), not including the transmission upgrade.

You can find more info by contacting:

TRP Direct
15 Clapham Road
Regents Park, NSW 2143
Australia
Contact: Domenic or Sam Rigoli
Phone: 61-2-9644 3100
Fax: 61-2-9644-3122
Email: info@rigoliracing.com.au
www.rigoliracing.com

Easy Street Motorsports
11834 & 11836 Vose Street
North Hollywood, CA 91605
Contact: Ali Afshar
Phone: (818) 764-9800
Fax: (818) 764-9805
Email: info@easystreetmotorsports.com
www.easystreetmotorsports.com

Chapter 8

Engine Building Tactics that Survive Under Pressure

There are two ways to approach the construction of a boosted engine. In this section, I'm going to use supercharging and turbocharging as equivalent in terms of engine building. The differences in terms of the build are very slight because to the engine a pressurized intake is a pressurized intake. It just has to be built strong enough to handle the power level. If you are going to be adding a modest-boost 'charger (one which will produce a maximum of five to eight psi) to a stock engine, you probably won't need to make any significant changes to the engine before getting started. Most of the Roots, centrifugal, and turbo kits are designed for this type of installation. Rather than pulling the engine out, tearing it apart, and changing pistons, rings, bearings, cam, valvetrain, heads, manifolds, ignition, and so on, you can buy a kit, bolt it on to the engine in an afternoon, and drive away with a strong, usable 40-percent horsepower increase. If an intercooler is included in the kit, even greater power gains can be achieved.

In contrast with traditional, naturally aspirated performance modifications, a super/turbocharger making in the neighborhood of six pounds of boost will greatly increase both horsepower and torque in the midrange (2,000 to 4,500 rpm), where you can really feel it in a street-driven vehicle. Of course, like

As long as your stock engine is in good condition and has a compression ratio of 9:1 or less, the addition of a supercharger in the 5- to 8-psi boost range can really wake it up without further modifications. Electronic fuel injection makes supercharging stock engines even easier — just hook a blow-through supercharger to the throttle body and go.

naturally aspirated performance parts, the boost will continue to produce power right on up the RPM scale. Keep in mind: an engine that uses higher-compression pistons and a longer-duration cam to get the same horsepower increase as the supercharged stock engine will have less power in the lower RPM. In addition to making less power down low, the hopped-up naturally aspirated engine will run rougher and probably be less efficient at street and normal highway speeds.

Since most sport-compact car

engines come with compression ratios in the 8.5:1 to 10:1 range, adding boost is a very practical, relatively quick, and simple way to achieve a healthy performance increase. As long as you keep boost below approximately 8 psi, and you don't rev the engine above 6,000 to 7,000 rpm (sometimes higher for certain models), you shouldn't really have to make any internal modifications to the engine. If anything, you might want to install slightly stiffer valvesprings to help keep the intake valves on their seats (add valvesprings to the exhaust side for turbocharged engines), and you might want to switch to a good super/turbo cam or cams. For DOHC engines, a set of adjustable cam gears to dial in the valve timing for maximum power is also good choice.

Obviously, the above statement – that you can bolt a 5- to 8-psi blower system onto a stock engine without making any other modifications – requires some qualification.

First, of course, we're talking about an engine that's in good condition to start with. But most importantly, you need to figure out at what level the new combination will begin to ping or detonate. This point will depend on the design of the combustion chamber in the particular engine, the efficiency of the compressor, your driving habits, the weight of the car, the gearing, and the quality of gasoline you tune to, among other things.

My point is that the life expectancy of the parts in any street-driven boosted engine these days depends primarily on whether you can safeguard those parts from detonation. To be safe, you'll want to run the highest-octane pump gasoline available. You will have to either reprogram the stock computer (this is currently the best choice) or use interface computers to enrich the air/fuel ratio and tune the ignition (retard the ignition timing slightly). Perhaps you will have to add a water injector, or some other add-on to stop detonation, because you certainly do not want to rattle the pistons in a stock engine. But with adequate octane gasoline (91 or better) and proper air/fuel ratios (12-12.5:1 at full throttle, full load), you will

The great thing about superchargers, positive displacement or centrifugal, and turbochargers is that they're fully adjustable. If you want more power, just turn up the boost. This might mean you'll have to make commensurate modifications to your engine, such as cooling, ignition, or perhaps internal upgrades to handle more cylinder pressure.

On the other hand, if you intend to bolt a big blower on your engine and make some real horsepower, then you had better build the engine to handle it. Several companies offer high-performance crate engines with forged pistons, heavy-duty head gaskets, and upgraded valvetrains if you don't want to build your own.

Chapter 8

Although stepping up to billet mains and cross drilling the block would be preferable for any high-performance engine, it's certainly not a necessity for most boosted street applications. However, most new engines are very well designed, as the main bearing girdle of the new GM Vortec inline engine shows. Engine parts selection depends more on the state of the equipment you're starting with, the amount of boost you intend to run, and the amount of horsepower the engine will make, rather than the fact that it is boosted.

The decision on whether or not to use the stock connecting rods on a boosted street engine has to be based on the design of the stock rods. The bottom end of this Ford Focus engine would probably handle a little boost — though one of the rods in this set is bent. The machinist at L&R Automotive Supply in Sante Fe Springs, California, didn't know how it happened, but you bend rods with cylinder pressure. The bolts break with excessive RPM. For this engine, instead of Magnafluxing, shot peening, polishing the beams, and fitting ARP rod bolts, a set of Carrillo or Crower rods or equivalent should be considered.

If you have any doubts about running 5- to 8-psi boost on a stock low-compression engine, my personal advice would be to go ahead and install the system on the car, being sure to add a boost gauge so that you know exactly how many psi you're making. If you experience knocking or pinging under boost, and you're already using the best gasoline available, the air/fuel ratio is right, and the timing isn't too advanced (you'll have to experiment a little to get it right), then you need to back off the boost or get a better tune.

If the boost is kept in the 5- to 8-psi range, I seriously doubt that you'll have any problems. If, for some reason, the engine can't handle this boost, and you blow a head gasket, burn a valve, or even break a piston land or ring, then you'll have to pull the motor out and go through it. If you're the type of person who would rather be safe than sorry, it certainly wouldn't hurt to blueprint any engine that will see performance use. But with mild blower boost (below 8 psi), and low static compression (9:1 or lower), the instances in which production parts will fail are the exception.

If you fully intend to get your foot into the throttle now and then with boost levels greater than 8 psi, you had better think about upgrading some of the components. Again, if you can keep your charged motor out of detonation, you're not going to have to worry a whole lot about parts damage. Likewise, if you're not going to abuse the engine, over-rev it, or race it every week, you don't need parts like a billet crank and mains, O-ringed heads, and so on. There is a middle ground. Many tuners have bolted street blowers and turbo kits onto relatively stock engines without any problems at all. But once you start making boost in the 10- to 15-pound range, or buzz the motor to 8,000 rpm or more, you are certainly in marginal territory with factory components – especially in terms of pistons, rings, and head gaskets.

Here's the bottom line: if you're boosting your motor to make it a high-performance engine, and you plan to drive it in a high-performance fashion, then sooner or later you'll need to build

find that six to eight pounds of boost is very livable and fun with a stock motor. Further, remember that in a street-driven supercharged vehicle, the compressor very seldom actually gets into boost, and then usually only for short bursts. The rest of the time the engine operates under no greater pressures than normal.

Engine Building Tactics that Survive Under Pressure

Leave the super-expensive, billet-steel custom crankshafts to the professional racers. All a boosted street engine needs is a stock crank, which can be improved with chamfered oil holes, polished journals, and Tufftriding. A factory steel crank would be preferable, but cast cranks will work fine in most street applications.

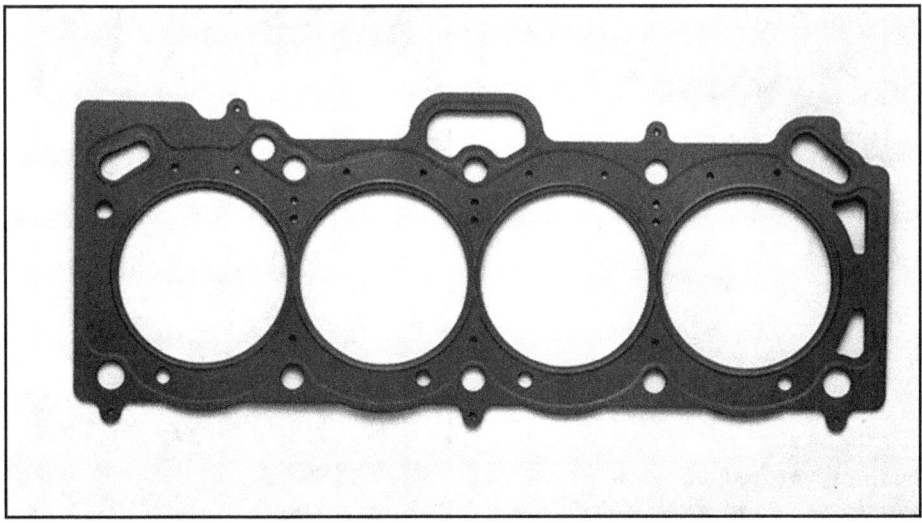

Only on very high-boost street engines will O-ringing the block be necessary. O-ringing means that you cut grooves in the head and block deck and install flat copper rings that surround the cylinder bores. Now several manufacturers offer much better gaskets with integrated "O-rings" in the gasket. The unit shown is from GReddy for a Honda D16Z engine.

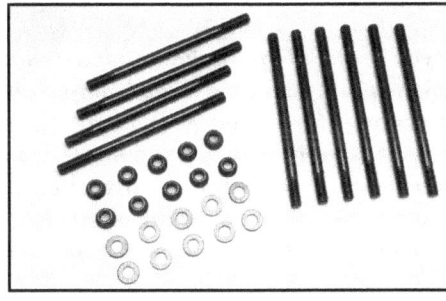

Modern head gaskets and head studs ensure even and positive torque across the head and provide a seal that'll handle more pressure. The head stud kit shown is from AEM.

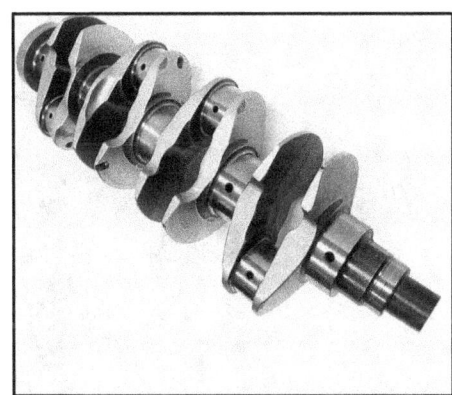

If you're building an engine that's going to see its power doubled by running over 14 pounds of boost, you'd want to step up to a billet crank if you can afford it. Four-cylinder cranks are very stout, with lots of overlap material near the journals. We've seen 500 horsepower with stock cranks. Beyond that, or if you just need to be sure, Crower can set you up with a billet piece.

the engine to high-performance specifications. Any high-performance engine, boosted or not, should be blueprinted – this includes checking and fitting all clearances, matching ports, dialing in cam timing, balancing the rotating and reciprocating assemblies, and so on. It is not within the scope of this book to fully describe engine blueprinting techniques, but the procedures are basically the same as those for any high-performance engine. If you're really interested in blueprinting, you can check out *The Step-by-Step Guide to Engine Blueprinting*, by Rick Voegelin. In the following sections, we will discuss peculiarities in parts selection or assembly procedures unique to a boosted engine.

It isn't practical to run more than 15 pounds of boost on any street engine. In the first place, Roots-type blowers aren't very efficient above this level, and, in the second place, it would be very difficult to find any type of gasoline that would be compatible with such boost on the street. Consequently, few of the problems associated with superchargers or turbochargers in racing applications apply to street engines. You certainly aren't going to be blowing out cylinder walls or breaking crankshafts because of extreme cylinder pressures.

The only real problem to watch out for in a boosted street engine – primarily those set up to make over 10 pounds of boost – is that the compressor will inevitably cause some increase in intake air temperature. This will cause both the cylinder temperature and exhaust temperature to be higher than they would in naturally aspirated engines at similar power levels. However, in boosted street motors this extra heat should be easily handled by a good cooling system, high-quality pistons and rings, good valves, a proper valve job, head studs, and good head gaskets. Remember that even a high-performance boosted street motor still only sees the full stress of maximum boost very rarely – as opposed to a racecar, which is built to operate under constant boost. The rest of the time the engine will be running on a much lower effective compression ratio than a comparable naturally aspirated high-performance engine. Also, keep in mind that when a turbocharged engine is under boost, the denser air charge forced into the cylinder "cushions" the piston/rod/crank

Sport Compact Turbos & Blowers

Chapter 8

Engines boosted above 8 psi or so should get good rods. These Crower H-beams will handle as much boost and RPM as you can throw at them.

Standard cast pistons will work with boost in the 5- to 7-pound range. For any boosted application, however, and certainly for those making over 10 psi, quality forged pistons are recommended. If you're keeping the stock pistons, smooth the sharp edges to reduce hot spots, which can start detonation.

If you're planning to build a boosted engine, don't use pistons that look like the ones on the right. These are forged pop-up pistons for a Dodge Neon that give 12:1 compression — far too much for a boosted engine. Also, don't have the domes milled off of such pistons to lower the compression, since the remaining top surface would be too thin and too weak to sustain even moderate blower pressures. Go with the dished piston design you see on the left. Note the deep dish in the top, and the considerable distance between the top and the first ring groove.

assembly during the overlap cycle. This is the point where you're most likely to break a rod. It's interesting to note that a naturally aspirated, high-compression engine actually sees much higher peak cylinder pressures than a comparable boosted engine, and this can cause greater stress on parts, as well as promote detonation.

BLOCK, CRANK, AND RODS

If you are going to be using a moderate boost system, you probably do not need to tear into the short block. If, on the other hand, you plan to make more than nine pounds of boost and you figure the engine might be seeing some high RPM, then you should plan on a typical performance blueprinting of the entire block and lower engine assembly. Magnaflux the crank and rods, straighten and polish the crank, chamfer the oil holes, shot peen and polish the beams on the rods, resize all the holes and align all surfaces, and so on. A boosted motor shouldn't need anything special above and beyond a regular high-performance engine. However, if you're this deep into the engine, many engine builders feel that you may as well step up to forged connecting and forged pistons designed for a pressurized engine.

If you are using a cast crankshaft, it would be wise to give it a surface-hardening treatment, such as Tufftriding. Since you cannot perform any crankshaft preparation work in your own garage, all you really need to do is give your crank to a good engine shop and ask them to prepare it for the use you expect your engine to see. They should know what to do.

Connecting rods are a difficult issue. Since most sport-compact engines are designed as naturally aspirated units, the rods aren't designed to take a lot of pressure – they're light and made to rev. So if you have the engine torn apart, just step up to a good set of forged rods. As a variety of cranks, pistons, and rods are released for sport-compact applications, they should continue to become increasingly affordable. If you decide to stick with stock rods on a mild street engine, check (Magnaflux, Zyglo, etc.) them for cracks or fatigue as part of the blueprint, and always replace used rod bolts. It is wise and relatively inexpensive to use stronger rod bolts, such as those available from ARP, as a replacement.

For most performance applications, a forged rod, H-, or I-beam is about all you'll ever need. Some special applications use aluminum or titanium, but these are very expensive alternatives and are beyond the scope of this book. In choosing a rod, the lightest, strongest unit is the best. Also, some engine builders prefer H-beam designs over I-beam designs. They reason that the I-beam has more windage drag in the crankcase. Windage is the drag on the crankshaft from the oil fog around it at speed. If you're running a dry sump it doesn't matter, as long as they're strong enough for application. In all cases, follow the manufacturer's instructions regarding rod bolt torque specs and bearing sizing. They'll also supply a recommended RPM limit.

Bottom-end clearances in a boosted engine should not differ from those in any high-performance application. All engine builders that we interviewed for information in this section of the book strongly recommend using a premium rod bearing for a boosted engine. These bearings feature a tri-metal surface with a lead-tin Babbitt overlay on the top, which is softer than that of standard bi-metal bearings, yet still has a higher load-carrying capability.

As a rule, most sport-compact engines have plenty of support engineered into the stock block, but monster race combos will need stud girdles. In fact, Honda engines already have girdles stabilizing the main bearing caps.

Race-only combos that see over 15 psi and that spin above 7,000 rpm could use some block reinforcing. Some racers fill the block's water passages with a reinforcing compound that stabilizes the block and the cylinders at high engine speeds. This reduces the tendency of the rings to leak pressure (the stronger cylinders keep their shape), so you get more power.

One critical block preparation for any boosted engine is to resurface the cylinder deck (and the adjoining surface of the head) to make sure everything is flat so that head gaskets will seal properly. You don't want to take too much off the head, though, because you'll increase the compression ratio. You can always offset that with piston choice, but just be aware of it. On the subject of head-to-block sealing, for high-boost combos, think about using head studs to clamp the head to the block. Head studs have threads on each end. First, you torque them into the head-bolt holes in the block. The head just slides over the studs, and then you torque the heads into place with nuts on the other end of the studs. This method provides more even clamping pressure (not to mention more clamping pressure), as well as providing more stability to the alignment of the head to the cylinder. In addition to studs, O-ringing the block is also good insurance, especially at levels of 30 psi or above.

O-ringing the head gasket involves cutting a circular groove in the head and sometimes the block deck. The groove is sized to receive a thin metal wire that acts as a gasket to seal in cylinder pressure. You can use this technique, in addition to high-quality head gaskets, to provide an almost bullet-proof seal. When done

Any of the major performance piston manufacturers can make custom forged blower pistons to most any specifications you dictate. This Ross piston is designed for an Integra 1.8-liter and has an extra-thick crown to withstand boost and higher temperatures.

right, O-ringed engines will contain so much cylinder pressure that the engine will sometimes hurt the bottom end before blowing the seal.

You may also want to look into installing an oil-cooling system. On any boosted street motor, you want to make sure that lubrication is efficient and adequate. High-performance oil system parts and techniques vary widely from one make of engine to another (once again, follow typical performance engine procedures). However, even moderate-boost street motors can benefit from a remote oil cooler or a larger-capacity oil pan, since the greater volume of circulating oil will help to cool the engine (and the cooler oil will live longer, too). However, this is certainly not a necessity for most street engines.

COMPRESSION RATIO, PISTONS, AND RINGS

This is the primary area in which a boosted street engine differs from a naturally aspirated high-performance engine. Pistons are very important on a boosted engine, because they help determine the compression ratio, and the compression ratio you're running will be directly related to how much boost you can run safely. Let's start with some basics.

First and foremost: you cannot run high-compression pistons with boost. As a very general guide, we'll suggest that the static compression ratio in a boosted engine with iron heads should be below 9:1; with aluminum heads, which is what most sport-compact engines have, compression shouldn't be more than 9.5:1. However, it all depends on the combination you want to run.

How low with the compression should you go? Unfortunately, there just isn't any rule or formula for "balancing" static compression ratio with boost. For boosted street motors, however, nearly all engine builders set the static compression between 8:1 and 8.8:1. Then you can "dial in" the boost to provide the most performance possible up to the point of detonation. For the bigger compressors, you will probably want a compression ratio towards the bottom of this range (8:1), while the smaller units will work well closer to 9:1 or even 9.5:1, since they'll make less boost. Think of it this way: at 9.5:1 you can use 5 to 6 psi; 9:1 up to about 10 psi; and at 8:1 you can go up to 15 psi on premium pump gas, provided the rest of the combo is scienced out. There are many variables involved here, including engine size, combustion chamber size and shape, and so on.

As far as saying which compression ratio is best, we'll go with Ford and Mercedees-Benz. The Ford GT's supercharged engine has a compression ratio of 8.4:1, the M-B SLR McLaren has 8.8:1. JE Pistons makes forged units rated for forced induction and nitrous use in 8:5:1 and 9:1 compression ratios. The advantage of using a lower compression ratio in a forced induction motor is that you can make more power under boost. The disadvantage is that the engine produces slightly less power on the motor alone (no boost).

So how do you find your compression ratio? You can't tell what the compression ratio in the engine is unless you measure it. Factory engines can vary a point or more above or below the rated compression. In fact, factory engines can often vary considerably in CR from cylinder to cylinder – that's just one reason why blueprinting is necessary. Even aftermarket pistons that are rated at a certain compression ratio must be matched with the specific components in your engine. Minor differences in connecting rod lengths, piston pin heights, dome heights, valve-head heights, valve-seat depths, and combustion chamber core shift can all add up to alter the actual compression considerably. Furthermore, "listed" compression ratios for aftermarket pistons are stated for a specific-volume combustion chamber and a certain thickness of head gasket. Combustion chamber sizes vary, even on factory engines. Remember, you may have to mill the heads to flatten the sealing surface, and this reduces the size of the combustion chamber, which in turn raises compression. So, consider that when picking out your pistons.

Figuring the exact static compres-

Calculating Compression Ratio

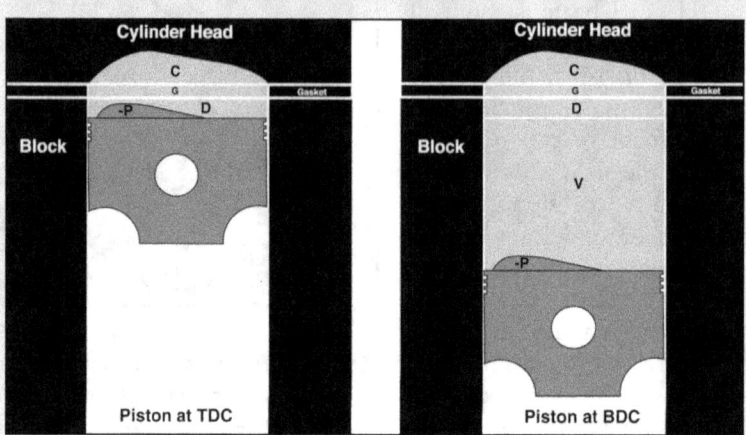

An engine's compression ratio is the ratio between two volumes: The volume of the cylinder and combustion chamber when the piston is at BDC, and the volume of the combustion chamber when the piston is at TDC. But there's more to consider than just cylinder volume and head cc's (cm^3). To get the engine's TRUE compression ratio, you need to know these volumes:

- Combustion Chamber Volume (C)
- Compressed Head Gasket Volume (G)
- Piston/Deck height (D)
- Piston Dish Volume (P) or Dome Volume (-P)
- Cylinder Volume (V)

When the piston is at BDC, the total volume is all of these volumes added together. When the piston is at TDC, the total volume is all of these EXCEPT the Cylinder Volume (V). So, true compression ratio is this:

$$\frac{V + D + G + C + P}{D + G + C + P}$$

Conversion Factors

Combustion chamber volume, dome volume, and dish volume are generally measured in cc's, which stands for cubic centimeters. Cubic centimeters can either be abbreviated as cc or cm^3. The same goes for cubic inches: ci = in^3. If for some reason you need to convert cm^3 to cubic inches, divide the measurement in cm^3 by 16.4.

$$cm^3 / 16.4 = in^3$$

To go from ci to cc's, just divide ci's by 0.06202.

$$cm^3 = in^3 / 0.06102$$

To go from inches to centimeters, multiply by 2.54.

$$in \times 2.54 = cm$$

To go from inches to millimeters, multiply by 25.4

$$in \times 25.4 = mm$$

To go from cubic millimeters to cubic centimeters, divide by 1,000

$$1,000\ mm^3 = 1\ cm^3$$

Cylinder Volume

Finding the cylinder volume is a relatively easy job. You remember the formula for finding the volume of a cylinder from geometry class, right? No worries. As long

Calculating Compression Ratio (continued)

as you know your bore (including overbore) and stroke, you can find it. We've plugged in the values for an imaginary Honda/Acura B18 engine, assuming it needs a 0.5 mm overbore.

Bore x Bore x Stroke x 0.7854 =
Cylinder Volume

81.5 mm x 81.5 mm x 89 mm x 0.7854 =
464,297.26 mm³

To get cubic centimeters (cm³ or cc), just divide by 1,000.

464,297.26 mm³ / 1000 mm³/cm³ =
464.29726 cm³

Combustion Chamber Volume

Combustion chamber volumes for stock heads and aftermarket heads are typically available from the manufacturer. If you can't find the info or if you've modified the combustion chambers, you'll have to measure the volumes (using a plastic deck plate, burettes, and a graduated cylinder) or have your local machine shop do it for you. For our B18 example, we'll assume the cylinder volume is 45 cm³.

Compressed Head Gasket Volume

Compressed head gasket volume is simply the volume of the cylinder hole in the head gasket – think of it as a very shallow cylinder. So, its volume is computed the same way you compute cylinder volume:

B x B x Gasket Thickness x 0.7854 =
Compressed Head Gasket Volume

In this case, the gasket's compressed thickness is 0.9652 mm (.038 inches), so:

81.5 mm x 81.5 mm x .9652 mm x 0.7854 =
4,988.327 mm³
4,988.327 mm³ = 4.988327 cm³

Piston/Deck Height Volume

Piston/Deck height volume is the small volume at the top of the cylinder that is not swept by the piston. Measure piston/deck height with a dial indicator. Bring the piston to top dead center (TDC) and measure the distance from the top of the piston to the deck of the block. If the block deck has been machined, then the deck height will be smaller.

Once again, this volume is a shallow cylinder. Compute its volume by plugging the piston/deck height measurement (D) into the cylinder volume formula:

B x B x D x 0.7854 =
Piston/Deck Height Volume

For our example, let's say this measurement was 0.381 mm, so we plug that value into the formula and compute piston/deck height volume in cubic millimeters. If you want the number in cubic centimeters, just divide it by 1,000.

81.5 mm x 81.5 mm x 0.381 mm x 0.7854 =
1,987.61 mm³

1,987.61 mm³ = 1.98761 cm³

Piston Dome/Dish Volume

The last bit of information we need is the volume of the piston dome or dish (dish includes valve reliefs, too). Because the dishes or domes are irregularly shaped, it's necessary to either measure the volume using burettes and graduated cylinders, or you can usually get the measurement from the piston manufacturer. If the piston is domed, the dome reduces the amount of volume in the combustion chamber, so its volume is subtracted. If the piston is dished, the dish increases the volume of the combustion chamber, so its volume is added. In this example, our B18 has pistons with a dish that measure two cm3 in volume. That two cm³ increases the cylinder volume, so we give it a positive value. If the pistons were domed, the dome would reduce the cylinder volume, so we'd give it a negative value.

So, let's check the true compression ratio for that B18 engine, assuming it has a combustion chamber volume of 45 cm³, a compressed head gasket thickness of 0.9652 mm, and a piston/deck height of 0.381 mm. Here's what we've figured out so far:

V = Cylinder Volume: 464.29726 cm³ (calculated)
C = Combustion Chamber Volume: 45 cm³ (measured)
G = Compressed Head Gasket Volume: 4.988327 cm3 (calculated)
P = Piston Dish Volume: 2 cm³ (measured)
D = Piston/Deck Height Volume: 1.98761 cm³ (calculated)

Now (finally!) we're ready to calculate our true compression ratio, using the formula we developed earlier:

$$\frac{V + D + G + C + P}{D + G + C + P}$$

Plug in the values:

$$\frac{464.29726\ cm^3 + 1.98761\ cm^3 + 4.988327\ cm^3 + 45\ cm^3 + 2\ cm^3}{1.98761\ cm^3 + 4.988327\ cm^3 + 45\ cm^3 + 2\ cm^3}$$

$$\frac{521.273197\ cm^3}{53.975937\ cm^3}$$

When you divide that out, you get 9.6575, or a true compression ratio, for this B18 engine, of 9.6575:1.

sion ratio in an engine involves a lot of measuring and a lot of arithmetic (although it is simple arithmetic), but it is the only way to be sure how much compression your engine really has. If you're starting with a late-model, low-compression engine (in the 9:1 compression range) in good running condition, and you want to add a bolt-on, moderate-boost (5- to 8-psi range) system, there is no need to pull the engine apart either to change the pistons or to check the actual static compression ratio. Add the compressor, dial in the system, and figure that everything is going to work fine. If the engine does experience severe detonation under boost, even though you have taken all of the "external" steps to eliminate it, then consider pulling the heads, measuring the actual compression ratio, and possibly changing to pistons that either make for a lower compression ratio, or are made of higher-quality material, or both.

If an engine has worn pistons, rings, valves, or other components, adding a compressor is only going to aggravate these problems. This is important, so let's say it again: If your engine has any blowby, leaky rings, valves, or guides, sloppy pistons, or marginal head-gasket seal, adding boost is certainly going to worsen the situation. The point is, don't add a blower to a worn-out engine. Furthermore, adding boost to a relatively fresh factory engine, or a standard rebuild, might (in isolated cases) immediately point out the flaws that sometimes creep past assembly-line employees. If so, a rebuild and blueprint is in order.

Forged Pistons

Now, if you're adding a healthy-boost system to the engine, if you intend to be making some exorbitant horsepower and using it, if you think your combination may encounter some detonation or cooling problems, or if you just prefer to be on the safe side, you should consider a set of forged pistons and good rings.

There are two ways to go for forged pistons for boosted applications. One is to order a set of custom-made forgings tailored exactly to your needs by one of several good high-performance piston manufacturers such as Ross, Venolia, BRC, JE, and so on. In the case of less popular engines, this may be your only choice for a low-compression forging. There are a few drawbacks, however. Naturally, such pistons are the most expensive. They must be custom-ordered from the manufacturer, and you must wait for them to be made. If it happens to be racing season (and it always seems to be, somewhere), the length of time it takes to fill your order will usually be proportional to the number of racers who need pistons (and they all do, every week) who have that manufacturer's decal on the side of their car. True forged-aluminum pistons also expand more than cast-aluminum pistons, so they must be installed with wider piston-to-cylinder wall clearances. Piston-to-wall clearances vary depending on the block material, size of bore, and several other factors your machine shop will be up on. Find a good one and work with them. Consequently, forged pistons will audibly rattle in the cylinders when the engine is first started cold, and you must allow the pistons to warm and expand before you go racing, or drive down the road. This can be an annoyance in a street engine; but if you install custom-forged pistons, you must allow ample engine warm-up every time you start the car.

Ultimately, however, such high-performance forged pistons are the best insurance you can get. They are the only type that can be made exactly to your order, and they are an absolute necessity in an all-out high-performance supercharged or turbocharged motor that will see lots of high boost (over 12 pounds) and hard use.

The other choice, and the one that is, in most cases, more practical for a boosted street engine, is to use a replacement-type forged piston. The advantages are that such pistons are readily available across the country, they are less expensive than custom forgings, and they are made in such a way that they expand at a rate similar to cast pistons, and can, therefore, be installed at clearances similar to those for cast pistons (.0025-.003-inch in most street-charged applications).

High-compression pistons should never be milled down to make "turbo" pistons. The practice of trimming the dome of a piston in a mill or a lathe to adjust the compression ratio slightly is common, and acceptable, for naturally aspirated engines. However, this should not be done on pistons for a boosted engine for two reasons. First, milling the dome makes the top of the piston thinner, and turbo pistons need a thicker top to withstand the increased cylinder pressure and heat produced by the blower. In most cases, milling the dome of a high-performance piston enough to lower the compression adequately would severely weaken the piston. Second, milling the top of the piston lower, particularly on low-dome or flat-top designs, will reduce the distance between the piston top and the first compression ring groove. The "shoulder" of the piston top above the first ring land is an area of critical stress in the piston. If the thickness of the piston top above this groove is marginal, the edges of the top are prone to cracking, burning, or even breaking off when cylinder pressures and temperatures are increased. On a blower piston, the first ring groove should be at least approximately .250-inch down from the top.

Rings

As far as piston rings are concerned, the rule of thumb for boosted engines is – use the best. There are three major considerations for the choice of rings in a boosted motor: they must seal the cylinder against higher pressure; they must withstand and dissipate greater heat; and they must have a high tensile strength so that they will not break under heavy load or detonation.

Typical standard production, or "service," rings are made of cast iron. Their major attribute is that they seat quickly and provide fine sealing in standard engines. However, cast iron is brittle rather than ductile, and it has a melting point of 2,000 degrees F. Chrome-plated iron rings are better, having a melting point of 3,212 degrees F,

What Makes a Good Turbo Piston?

The engine component most impacted by boost is the piston/ring assembly. The top of the piston needs to be strong to withstand the high cylinder pressure. It also needs to be smooth to avoid producing hot spots, which can cause detonation. In addition, the piston and rings, among other things, have to seal in cylinder pressure and keep oil out. If you get oil in the combustion chamber, it lowers the octane of the fuel mixture, leading to detonation. Even though this is a concern, you don't need to order special oil rings. On high-horsepower engines, you need to be concerned about sinking the heat out of the crown of the piston. The heat path from the head to the engine block is through the rings.

Unfortunately, this heat and detonation tend to be a common problem for boost addicts. Detonation is a fact of life at super high levels of performance, so you need a piston that'll survive a little bit of it. That is why a strong forged aluminum piston is required. Cast and hypereutectic pistons break more easily under detonation than forged pistons.

When you get into detonation under boost, it easily bends the ring over the ring lands. And since the piston is quite hot, the pressure in the combustion chamber can bend the ring land down and start pinching the ring. One of the more common solutions to this problem is to move the top ring downward, away from the crown of the piston.

However, a solution that seems to be gaining favor is putting more space between the rings. The reasoning is that since the cylinder pressure acts hydrostatically, i.e., the pressure will still be as great no matter how far down the piston you put the ring pack, it isn't necessarily a pressure problem, it is a heat problem. Moving the second ring down puts more land material between the top and second ring and so provides more support for the top ring. This is important because the top ring is under tremendous pressure that tries to bend it down over the land. In severe cases, you can see a shiny ring on the bottom of the top ring that develops from the distortion. You can tell that the ring has been bent over from the pressure and has ridden on the sharp edge of the ring land. When this happens, the ring loses its seal because the ring face is at an angle to the cylinder wall instead of sitting flush.

When the ring is not sitting flush it is still sealing, but it is not transferring the heat from the piston crown to the cylinder case as effectively as before. The reason is that less surface area is now available to transfer heat. This causes the piston to heat to a point that it softens, and combustion pressure forces the ring land to collapse on the second ring. What's weird is that typically when the second ring binds, the top ring remains free with apparently no problem.

If you were to design a stronger piston, one of the things to request is more material behind the rings, since as you move the ring package down, you get into an area of the piston that is thinner. When that happens, the heat then has to flow out of the small cross section of the piston skirt and through the rings. The small areas of the piston will then suffer from a high thermal load, which tends to soften these areas, allowing them to bend. It's like a bottle neck, and as these areas soften, the whole top of the piston will want to come off.

Several engine builders we consulted like to see a little larger ring gap on the second ring than on the top ring. They say they find a better seal with this gap configuration in hot running conditions. Just how hot is hard to say, but you know the engine is too hot when the rings butt together. What happens in this case is the top ring closes more than the second ring, so even if you set both end-gaps at .025 inch, the top ring gap will be smaller than the second ring gap.

It is important for the gaps to be this way, because you want the pressure between the top ring and the second ring to go out the gap of the second ring faster and more easily than it gets past the top ring gap. The reason is that you do not want the pressure to equalize before and after the top ring. If that happens there is no pressure to force it against the cylinder wall and seal the bore. If the pressure is equal here, then all that's sealing the cylinder is the ring tension, which isn't nearly enough. This is advanced stuff, so unless you're sure or have experience with it, we suggest you follow the piston manufacturer's recommendations.

If you're using high boost and not a lot of RPM, you shouldn't use real thin rings, because a thin ring holds the heat in the crown. The heat in the piston crown has to go somewhere, and the only place it goes is out the side of the piston, through the rings, into the cylinder case. Most people think the piston is cooled by oil splashing on the bottom of it. It is true this provides some cooling, but not nearly as much as you'd think, though some manufacturers spray oil on the pistons for this effect. In fact, most piston-top cooling comes from the heat path through the rings into the cylinder case. This is why when you start losing ring seal, you start losing pistons.

So, if you are not spinning your motor past 7,000 or 8,000 rpm, use a wide ring. Even as wide as 5/64-inch would not be detrimental to performance. With forced-induction combos, you don't have to run thin rings in an effort to get the last few horsepower. Instead, go wide and build reliability.

We need to address a few other issues regarding the piston. You should follow the piston maker's guidelines for piston-to-wall clearance. The correct clearance depends on several factors, but mostly the expansion rate of the material from which the piston is made.

As for piston pins, most of the better aftermarket suppliers have case-hardened, high-carbon steel pins with their piston sets. These should be strong enough for all but the most outrageous combinations.

How Detonation Starts and How to Avoid It

Detonation is the sudden and uncontrolled burn of the fuel/air charge in the combustion chamber brought about when the temperature and pressure exceeds the fuel's auto ignition point. The "knocking" or "pinging" sound of detonation comes from pressure waves pounding against the insides of the combustion chamber, cylinder wall, and the piston top. Detonation occurs under specific conditions within the combustion chamber. Here's a theoretical description.

The initial ignition of the air/fuel mixture generates a pressure wave that travels through the unburned fuel and air at the speed of sound, and thus is able to travel far ahead of the flame front and bounce around the combustion chamber. When the pressure waves hit the sides of the combustion chamber and piston tops, they reflect back, just as ripples reflect off the edge of a pool. In areas where the main pressure wave and the reflected pressure waves converge in a constructive interference pattern, the pressure is amplified, and detonation tends to occur first at these points.

The edges of the piston top are prone to such interference patterns. Detonation occurs in these areas because the severe increase in pressure increases the temperature at these points to the ignition temperature of the air/fuel mix.

The chemical reaction that produces the most power is a gradual and controlled release of the heat energy of the air/fuel mix. A measure of this is flame front speed or flame propagation. Flame front speeds for a gasoline/air mixture are on the order of 40 to 50 centimeters per second, which is very slow compared to the speed of sound of the pressure waves, which is approximately 300 meters per second. In most modern engines, flame front speed is higher due to combustion chamber designs that increase the turbulence of the mixture. Basically, the flame is carried across the combustion chamber by the myriad of swirls and flow patterns of the turbulent air/fuel mix. The turbulence also increases the surface area of the flame front, which further increases flame front speed, since more of the mixture is exposed to the larger flame front.

Detonation, then, is the result of myriad little explosions that occur in areas where the heat and temperature allow the chemical reaction between the fuel and air to begin. Once started, they raise the temperature and send out more pressure waves, which cascade into the seemingly instantaneous release of the fuel's energy on the engine's components. The piston top, ring lands, rod and main bearings, valves, and head bolts all take a severe beating from detonation pressure spikes.

Recently, engineers have developed a much more detailed model (in fact several) of detonation. One of the more interesting "discoveries" is a process that

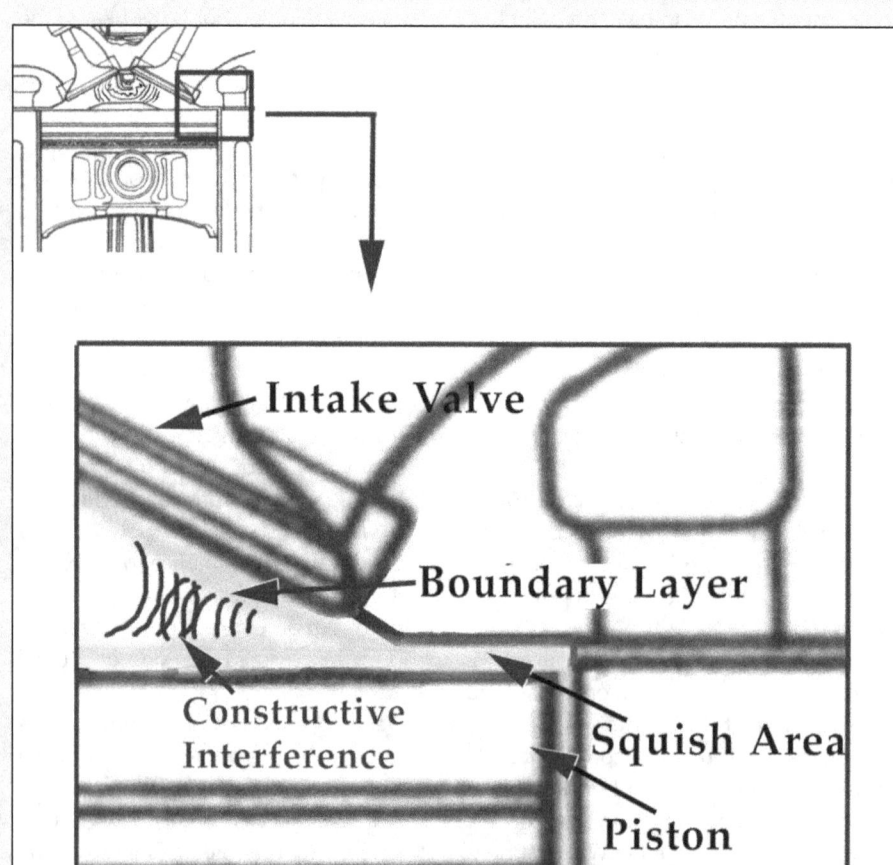

High-intensity pressure waves generated by the ignition pulse can converge and amplify the temperature and pressure of the air/fuel mix to its ignition point. Once a small area detonates, it tends to force other areas to detonate and the whole charge is soon consumed in a potentially engine-killing pressure spike.

How Detonation Starts and How to Avoid It (continued)

occurs during heavy detonation that allows combustion heat to be injected into engine components at destructive levels. Detonation pressure waves have such intensity that at a certain level they will push aside the thin (less than a millimeter) boundary layer of unburned air/fuel mixture that resides near the metal surfaces in the combustion chamber under normal circumstances.

Under normal combustion processes, the boundary layer will not react with the flame front because the cool metal of the combustion chamber and piston surfaces have a temperature below the ignition temperature of the air/fuel mix. This boundary layer serves as an insulating layer, keeping the flame front from directly contacting the engine's metal. When it is brushed aside by severe detonation, the flame front comes in direct contact, which transfers more heat into the engine, often enough heat to destroy the component. This seems to explain why detonation can punch holes in pistons and collapse ring lands. The heat injected into the component is well above its ability to conduct heat into the cooling system. The component begins to change state, softens, and the cylinder pressure does the rest.

The best way to avoid detonation is a properly designed, tuned, and operating engine combination. However, in the performance realm, we're pushing the envelope of our engine combinations, so to achieve max performance, you need to find ways to delay and avoid detonation. Many tuners choose to run overly rich fuel ratios, relying on the excess fuel to absorb and carry away the heat. You can also run a cooler thermostat and use an oil cooler to keep the components that make up the combustion chamber cooler. One of the techniques that is gaining acceptance is using water injection, or a combination of water and methanol. There are several systems on the market that work well.

We've discussed several of the causes, but to recap: you'll get detonation when the effective compression ratio has been taken beyond the pre-ignition point of the fuel. Injecting water works well because it has good heat content, i.e., it absorbs a lot of heat then carries it out of the combustion chamber, and it is extremely effective for controlling onset of detonation, as well as reducing the production of oxides of nitrogen in modern lean-burn engines. You can increase effectiveness and power output by using a mix of 50 percent alcohol.

Premature ignition occurs before the spark plug fires and is usually caused by a hot spot inside the cylinder. Premature ignition is different from detonation, though it often has the same result.

but they are still brittle and they are much more difficult to seat in the cylinders. A popular choice for performance engines today are "moly" rings, which are nodular iron rings sprayed with a molybdenum filling on the face. Molybdenum has a melting point of 4,750 degrees F, and the nodular iron body is ductile rather than brittle, so they seat easily like cast-iron rings. "Double moly" ring sets include moly-filled top and second compression rings, usually with a chrome oil ring. These rings (available from most major manufacturers) would be a good choice for most street super/turbocharged engines.

Super/turbocharged engine builders used to high-boost, high-horsepower combinations, however, prefer stainless-steel rings for such applications. Some like a non-cast chrome or stainless top ring, which they feel keeps the rings from breaking in a healthy boosted motor, followed by a moly second compression ring. They also suggest increasing the end gap on the top ring in a boosted motor slightly (about .005-inch) to allow for greater heat expansion. In any case, with any rings, it is critical to check and fit the end gaps of each compression ring in each cylinder during engine assembly. Most high-performance rings are made slightly longer than necessary so that you can file them to fit. Failing to do so will allow the ends of the rings to butt when they heat and expand, causing them to seize in the cylinder or to break.

To sum up then, with pistons, strength is more important than saving weight. You should maintain at least 1/4-inch dome thickness, and use premium thick-wall piston pins. To fight heat buildup, increase the piston-to-wall clearance slightly, and when ordering custom slugs, spec 'em out with more distance from the piston deck to the top ring land. Also, 60 to 70 percent of the heat carried out from the piston goes through the rings, so use only the best rings, such as Speed-Pro's Hellfire series. Run wider than normal ring gaps, and use standard-tension oil rings to maintain oil control.

CYLINDER HEADS

Modifying the cylinder heads on a super/turbocharged engine can really wake up your engine. The better your heads flow, the more mass you can flow through the engine, and that's how you make power. If you're on a budget, at the very least unshroud the valves by adding bore diameter to the cylinder (don't forget to match the heads), or just remove some material from the head where the combustion chamber walls are closest to the valve heads.

There are some special considerations for cylinder heads on a boosted engine, however. First of all, you want to make sure that the heads seal in the extra pressure pumped in by the compressor. We highly recommend that you have the heads surfaced to make sure they are flat. For the majority of boosted street applications, you will not have to O-ring the heads (or block); this should only be necessary on very high-boost installations, or possibly on engines with poor head sealing to begin with (usually because of too few head bolts surrounding each cylinder). If you feel that O-ringing might be necessary – or you become convinced after a few head gasket failures – you will have to find gaskets to fit your engine that are compatible with O-rings. A steel-faced sandwich head gasket is best (steel on each side with asbestos in the middle); a steel shim gasket will work if you can carefully match the O-ring to the rib on the gasket (this is touchy); solid copper gaskets are best left to racecars since they are prone to water leaks. Of course, the job of cutting the O-ring grooves should be done by an experienced machine shop.

However, few street-blown cars will need to be O-ringed. An excellent compromise these days is new high-performance head gaskets that have a built-in stainless steel "O-ring" seal around each cylinder. These gaskets are expensive, but they are much easier to install than true O-rings, since you don't need to modify the heads or block. Obviously, with these or any other gaskets on a super/turbocharged engine, a careful and sequential torquing and subsequent re-torquing of the heads is advised.

The second consideration for cylinder heads on a supercharged engine is to guard against heat and detonation. While the intake and exhaust ports probably won't require enlarging or polishing, it would be helpful to clean up the combustion chambers to remove any burrs, flash, or sharp edges, which could become hot spots and lead to pre-ignition. On a high-boost motor, you might as well polish the entire chamber, which will not only help reduce detonation, but will also help lower the compression ratio by adding volume to the chamber. Just don't grind so much out of the heads that you weaken the chamber walls – remember that boost can break through combustion chamber walls just as it can break through piston tops.

For valves and valvesprings, there are some important considerations for a super/turbocharged engine that differs from other performance-engine buildups. First, the exhaust sides of boosted engines see much higher temperatures than an average engine. Since the operating temperature of the valve is controlled by its contact with the water-cooled head, and since the valve seat is the area of contact through which heat can be transferred from the valve to the head, it's imperative not to narrow valve seats (particularly on the exhaust valve) very much on a boosted engine. Three-angle and five-angle (two cuts on the valve seat to further improve low lift flow) valve jobs are popular, and effective, for increasing airflow past the valve on naturally aspirated engines. In most cases, however, cutting the valves and seats at three angles greatly reduces the width of the actual valve seat area. If you use three-angle cut seats on the heads of your super/turbocharged engine, be sure to keep valve-seat widths as wide as possible. Remember, the blower will do most of the job of getting air past the valves, but power gains are definitely available with a three- or five-angle valve job. Actually, a standard valve job should be fine for a street-driven boosted engine and would be the best to ensure that the valves did not burn from increased cylinder temperatures.

Regardless of the seats, if you're really boosting the engine, you may want to consider an alloy valve such as those available from Ferrea and other makers. These valves are made of alloys that resist heat better than regular Inconel stainless. Some also have trick sodium-filled hollow-stems that transfer heat better from the seat area to the head.

And finally, any performance engine will usually require stiffer valvesprings to guard against valve float at higher RPM. A super/turbocharged engine will also need greater valvespring pressure on the intake valves to keep these valves on their seats, since the boost pressure will be acting on the backsides of all the intake valves. Turbos also build pressure on the exhaust valves, and they need higher spring rates there too. Admittedly, even 15 or 20 psi isn't enough air pressure to blow an intake or exhaust valve open, even with stock springs, but the addition of blower pressure to the momentum of the valvetrain components at high RPM makes things a lot harder on the intake valvesprings. This is super critical in a wet-flow pressurized intake, such as you might find with an additional injector fuel enrichment system. If an intake valve does not fully close (or "hangs up"), combustion in that cylinder will backfire into the intake manifold and into the blower/turbo, both of which are filled with pressurized, atomized air/fuel mixture – a highly volatile substance. If you have watched Top Fuel racing, you know the explosive results and the reason why the NHRA now requires restraint straps on Top Fuel blowers. Fortunately, virtually all sport-compact street engines are dry-flow fuel-injected engines, so we don't have to worry about that, unless you're using an additional injector or a wet nitrous system installed away from the port.

In general, broken valvetrain parts, like intake valvesprings or valves, can be very destructive, so be sure to invest in good parts from a reputable manufacturer. Most street-boost-level motors won't require special valves, but if you're planning to make some RPM with high boost, we suggest a good set of stronger stainless-steel or other alloy valves. Check with Ferrea on the valve tech, as they're on the leading edge of that technology. Make sure you have good valvestem seals too, as the boost can leak up valvestems. Some applications like running a bit more valvestem-to-guide clearance on the exhaust valves. Check with your machine shop for the latest techniques. Otherwise, head prep for a street-boosted motor is basically the same as for any performance engine, but without all of the time-consuming, touchy, and expensive port and polish work

CAMSHAFTS

Just as it is a definite no-no to run high-performance, high-compression pistons in a super/turbocharged engine, it is equally and emphatically against the rules to use a typical high-performance, long-duration, big-overlap camshaft in a boosted motor. These are by far the two most common mistakes in building boosted street engines, and of the two, over-camming is the more flagrant. We're talking street here, so even though you can get a combination to produce great peak power numbers with relatively high static compression ratios (10:1) and a naturally aspirated racing cam, it'll be very, very peaky.

Typical high-performance camshaft technology has been developed to get unpressurized air into and out of the cylinders. This technology does not apply to engines with pressurized intakes. Actually, camming a blown engine is quite a bit easier than trying to match cam timing and profile to the various components of a naturally aspirated, high-performance engine (especially manifold type, size, and runner length). As we have said before, the super/turbocharger does the work of getting the mixture into the cylinders and much of the job of getting the exhaust out. In short, the boosted motor isn't as touchy about several aspects of engine tuning, including cam timing and profile, as naturally aspirated combinations. In many cases, moderate boost will work fine with the stock cam or cams, as long as you install heavier valvesprings. Stock cams would certainly work better

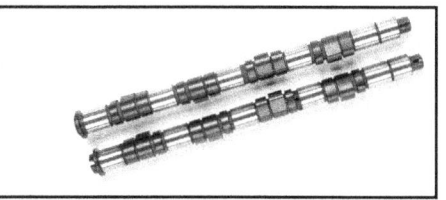

For a healthy boosted street engine, you want a cam that won't strangle the inlet with short duration or blow the boost out the exhaust with long duration and big overlap. There are lots of good cam manufacturers that offer specific grinds for such applications. Crower's New B-Series VTEC Race Core PN 63411T Stage 2 Turbo cam is a special design with short duration, low overlap, and high lift for increased performance. Advertised duration is listed as 280/276 degrees (intake/exhaust); duration at .050-inch-lift is 230/226. Lift is .465/.445-inch with 1.55:1 ratio. The cam requires the PN 84161 spring and retainer kit.

Boosted engines benefit from stiffer valvesprings. The boost in the intake wants to push the intake valves open; the backpressure from the turbo tries to push the exhaust valves open. Higher-pressure springs resist these effects. Keep in mind that street levels of boost aren't enough to force the valves off the seats, but if you're building more than 8- to 10-psi, this mod is for you.

than a typical high-performance cam for regular, street-driving power.

Most cam companies now list specific supercharger and turbocharger grinds in their catalogs, often for varying levels of boost, or else they specify which grinds would be good for certain super/turbocharged applications. Further, many of the supercharger and turbocharger companies offer camshafts and related hardware tailored to work with their systems. In other cases, the manufacturer should be able to recommend a cam profile that would be good for your given application. For a very general rule of thumb, for a super or turbocharged DOHC engine, you want something less than 235 degrees of advertised duration range (stock VTEC high-lift cam is rated at 235 degrees); SOHC engines need to stay open a bit longer, but not over 280° as measured at .050-inch lift, with net valve lift in the neighborhood of .450 inch. These are strictly ballpark figures, but most SOHC moderate-boost combos would be happy with a cam in the 260-degree (advertised) duration range; bigger engines with more boost could use a bit more.

One of the first street-blower manufacturers to do a lot of experimenting with camshaft profiles for blown engines was Jerry Magnuson of Magnacharger. Jerry was Dan Gurney's crew chief and engineer for many years of successful road racing on the international circuit – including winning Le Mans in the Ford GT-40. Magnacharger is the West Coast source for Eaton superchargers that are found in the Roots-type supercharger kits from Jackson Racing and a few others. Through this testing, he developed a cam that he sold to go with his MC-220 blower on small-block Chevys. Its specifications were 224 degrees intake, 226 degrees exhaust duration (at .050 inch lift), .480-inch net lift, on 114-degree lobe centers. This cam was used in a 350 Chevy for a series of dyno tests for *Hot Rod* magazine with the five different street blowers limited to six pounds of boost, and it produced excellent low-end power, an exceptionally flat torque curve, and good power through 6,000 rpm.

The Magnuson cam was manufactured by Schneider Cams of San Diego, California, a respected cam grinder (especially in high-revving circle-track engines) and the company explained the basics behind this, or any, good boost street cam – even for sport-compact engines. The most important thing is that the cam should have minimal overlap, which means that the lobe centers should be spread as far apart as possible – in the neighborhood of 108 to 115 degrees for most sport-compact engines. Use the SOHC lobe center spread as a guide for the lobe phasing for DOHC engines and put the intake and exhaust lobe centerlines at, for example, between 108 and 115 degrees ATDC for the intake and between 108 and 115 degrees BTDC for the exhaust. Overlap is the period during the cam timing cycle when the intake valve has already opened and the exhaust valve is not yet closed. In a naturally aspirated engine, such a situation is tolerable (in fact, preferable) because it takes a certain amount of time to get the air moving. But in a boosted engine, the air is under pressure and doesn't require as much duration or lift. As soon as the intake valve opens, the air/fuel mix bursts into the cylinder, filling it rapidly. If the exhaust valve remains open, part of the air/fuel mix will be pumped out the exhaust pipe by the pressure. This is obviously a waste of fuel and power.

Overlap can be decreased by choosing a cam with less duration of both the intake and the exhaust valve cycles, or by adjusting the lobe phasing on a DOHC engine. However, even though a boosted motor doesn't need as much cam timing as a naturally aspirated motor, you still want to keep as much duration as practical to fill the cylinder as much as possible and to get the exhaust out. Widening (increasing the cam timing between) lobe centers reduces overlap without changing the length of time each valve remains open. However, doing so advances the exhaust valve timing and retards the intake valve timing; or, to look at it another way, it retards the intake valve timing relative to the exhaust valve timing.

Consequently, to get the intake valve timing back to where it should be, Schneider, as well as Russ Collins of RC Engineering, recommends advancing the entire cam for a supercharged engine slightly (2 to 4 degrees). The net effect is to get both the intake and the exhaust valves open early to get the pressurized air/fuel mix in quickly, and to get the consequently pressurized exhaust out as soon as possible. This will also close each valve as soon as possible so that none of the cylinder pressure can leak back out. If the intake stays open too long, the beginning compression stroke of the piston will want to push the "supercharge" back out the intake valve. This is similar to reversion in a naturally aspirated engine, except that it would have the effect of "backpressure" on the blower, which would ultimately reduce its mechanical, volumetric, and adiabatic efficiency. If the exhaust valve stays open too long, as we said, part of the new incoming air/fuel charge will blow out the exhaust port.

Finally, Schneider usually cuts forced-induction cams on a dual-pattern profile, giving the exhaust more duration than the intake (as much as 10 to 12 degrees). Widening the lobe centers and advancing cam timing also helps to make this possible without negative effects. The reason for giving the exhaust more timing on a supercharged engine should be obvious – the blower pumps a whole lot more air and fuel into the engine on the intake stroke, but the exhaust has to get out on its own. Many people (including us, come to think of it) have stated that the supercharger will actually help to "blow" the exhaust out of the cylinder, but this isn't wholly accurate. The blower will increase overall cylinder pressure, since it will pack a greater mass of air and fuel into it. After combustion, this "super charge" of air and fuel expands, filling the cylinder with a greater mass, and greater pressure, of hot exhaust gas than would be present in a naturally aspirated engine's cylinder (that's why you put the supercharger on the engine, remember?). Consequently, when the exhaust valve opens, the significantly increased pressure of the heated gases in the cylinder forces them out the exhaust port at a greater velocity. However, there is more mass of exhaust in the cylinder, so it will still take more time to get it all out. In this instance, the pressurized intake helps evacuate the remaining gases at overlap, but this only occurs for a short time in the cycle.

This recommendation, though developed for racing V-8s, translates almost directly to sport-compact engines. And if you think about it, it's obvious why. A four-stroke gasoline-fueled engine operates the same way. The difference is in the efficiency of the ports, particularly with four-valve heads. But a race-ported two-valve Chevy or a ported two-valve Honda SOHC engine can have very similar overall cylinder-head efficiency. The more mass the heads can flow (or the smaller an engine is), the less duration and lift the cam needs.

Now, just to throw another contradiction at you – if you remember back in the chapter on blower theory – we were talking about mean effective pressure and the thermal efficiency of a supercharged engine versus a naturally aspirated one. Although we ultimately get much more power out of a boosted engine (because its mean effective pressure is higher), its thermal efficiency is, nevertheless, lower than that of the naturally aspirated engine, and it's even less efficient than a turbocharged one. The reason is that all of the extra energy pumped into the engine in the form of fuel simply cannot be converted to heat, then to pressure, and then to work within the cylinder, before the exhaust valve opens. The very fact that the exhaust rushes out of the blown engine under greater pressure, and at a higher temperature, than in other engines, tells us that a greater portion of the potential power is being wasted, unless it's captured by a turbine in a turbocharger system. Of course, all internal combustion engines have terrible thermal efficiency, supercharged or not, so this is not a major point. But to a certain extent, the thermal efficiency, and a fraction of the power, of the crank-driven supercharged motor is determined by the opening time of the exhaust valve. The sooner the exhaust valve opens (the more advanced the exhaust timing), the lower the thermal efficiency, and the more potential work (power) goes out the exhaust pipe. Like we said earlier, the super/turbocharged engine is a mélange of tradeoffs and that is why a turbocharged cam spec, though similar to a supercharged cam, will be slightly different depending on the power profile you're looking to produce.

THE COOLING SYSTEM

One essential component of the total vehicle power package often overlooked by performance engine builders is the cooling system. Any high-performance engine will require increased cooling capacity, since roughly 30 percent of the engine's power is absorbed by the cooling system. Remember that the power (energy) made in the motor is first converted to heat before it is converted to work. The more power your engine makes, the more heat it produces, and the more heat must pass through the radiator.

Super/turbocharged engines not only make more power, but also inherently create more heat because (1) the compressor heats the intake charge a certain amount and (2) a certain portion of the engine's power is used up in driving the blower, unless it's a turbocharger.

Consequently, you are going to need a nice, big radiator for your super/turbocharged engine, and a good water circulation system to feed it. Just how much radiator you need obviously depends on several factors, including how much extra horsepower you are making in the motor, how well the radiator is ducted to fresh air (and how well hot air is ducted out of the engine compartment), and even ambient climactic conditions. We really can't tell you how big a radiator you need. All we can do is forewarn you that a boosted engine is going to run hotter. If your stock cooling system is good, adding five to seven pounds of boost probably won't necessitate any cooling system change (other than perhaps a lower-temperature thermostat). However, if your cooling system is marginal to begin with, the blower is only going to make things worse.

The cooling system situation is compounded in most supercharged vehicles because the blower drive takes up most of the room at the front of the engine occupied by the water pump, fan, fan shroud, and radiator. With turbo systems, the turbine also radiates a bunch of heat into the engine bay. With turbos and centrifugal chargers, you may also have the added heat load of an intercooler mounted in front of the radiator. In no case should you consider eliminating the fan on a blown motor. If you don't have enough room for a good-sized radiator, do not try to get by with a thinner one just to make room for the blower drive. You might have to remount the radiator in the chassis, or have a custom radiator built to handle the situation. But don't skimp here. You plan to enjoy the supercharger on your engine, right? Well, an engine that overheats is no fun at all.

If a supercharger or turbocharger increases the power output of an engine, you will have to increase the fuel input to feed it. Several manufacturers offer injectors of various flow rates that allow you to tune the fuel system to the power levels of your combination.

Chapter 8

Turbocharged Performance Tactics Case Study: Subaru Impreza

Maximum boost pressure: *13.5 psi*
Horsepower: *227 @ 6,000 rpm*
Torque: *217 @ 4,000 rpm*
Fuel/Induction: Sequential multi-port fuel injection (MFI) with *multi-spray injectors* and *tumble generator valves, turbocharger, and intercooler*
Fuel Requirement: *91-octane minimum*

Airflow through this combination: 23-24 lbs/min
MEP: 268.2 psi
Horsepower/Liter: 113.84

Perhaps the best way to demonstrate the proper sequence of modifications to your stock turbocharged vehicle is to analyze the approach taken by Subaru to offer increasing performance packages for the Impreza-based turbocharged WRX and WRX STi.

We'll begin by checking out the specs of the naturally aspirated 2003 Subaru Impreza 2.5 RS Sedan's engine.

Impreza 2.5 RS Sedan
Displacement: 2,457 cc (150 cubic inches)
Valvetrain: Single overhead-cam (SOHC), 4 valves per cylinder
Bore x Stroke 99.5 mm x 79.0 mm (3.92 in x 3.11 in)
Compression ratio: 10.0:1
Horsepower: 165 @ 5,600 rpm
Torque: 166 @ 4,000 rpm
Fuel/Induction: Sequential multi-port fuel injection (MFI)
Fuel Requirement: Regular, 87-octane minimum

Airflow through this combination: 16-17 lbs/min
MEP: 166.9 psi
Horsepower/Liter: 67.16

This naturally aspirated combination uses an over-square bore-to-stroke ratio – the bore is larger than the stroke. This unshrouds the valves, allowing them to flow more air through the port. In addition, they're using the larger 2.5-liter engine size to provide more piston area for the combustion pressure to act upon. Notice that the compression ratio is 10:1 and that it's rated for 87-octane gas. Since the volumetric efficiency is probably around 85 percent, the average dynamic compression ratio is probably closer to 8.5:1, well within the safe range of regular gas. In addition, the aluminum heads transfer heat more effectively than iron heads, which reduces the tendency of the fuel to detonate. In addition, the engine management electronics have detonation sensors to protect the engine. These design features allow the use of cast pistons in production high-output engines.

WRX
(Engine upgrades from the standard Impreza are set off with italics)
Block: Die-cast aluminum with integral cast-iron cylinder liners, five main bearings, *open deck cylinder design*
Displacement: *1,994 cc/122 ci*
Bore x Stroke: *92 mm x 75 mm (3.62 in x 2.95 in)*
Heads/Valvetrain: *Aluminum-alloy cylinder heads with belt-driven dual overhead camshafts (DOHC), 4 valves per cylinder, and solid lifters with valve-lash shims*
Compression ratio: *8.0:1*

The main differences between this engine and the naturally aspirated engine are the intercooler and turbocharger, the reduction in engine displacement and static compression ratio, the dual overhead cams, and tumble generator intake valves. The turbocharger system reaches a max boost of 13.5 psi and allows the 1.994-liter engine to flow nearly 24 lbs/min of air. Notice that the compression ratio is reduced to 8:1 to allow the use of pump fuel at the maximum boost pressure. Since more air and fuel mass is being stuffed into the cylinder, the compressed charge temperature of a 10:1 static compression ratio, even at 85 percent VE, set off in italics, would exceed the detonation limit of 91-octane pump gas. By increasing the combustion chamber size, which reduces the compression ratio, the engine is able to ingest more mass, which equates to a longer, higher-pressure power stroke. This shows up in the higher MEP value. In addition, because the intake is pressurized, the cylinders fill better at higher RPM, allowing this engine to make peak horsepower at a higher RPM.

STi specs
(Engine upgrades from the WRX set off in italics)
Block: *Specially reinforced die-cast aluminum with integral cast-iron cylinder liners, five main bearings, semi-closed deck*

Turbocharged Performance Tactics Case Study: Subaru Impreza (continued)

cylinder design

Displacement: *2,457 cc (150 ci)*

Bore x Stroke: *99.5 mm x 79 mm (3.92 in x 3.11 in)*

Heads/Valvetrain: Aluminum-alloy cylinder heads with dual overhead belt-driven camshafts (DOHC), four valves per cylinder, *Subaru AVCS (Active Valve Control System) variable valve timing, and sodium-filled exhaust valves*

Compression ratio: *8.2:1*

Horsepower: *300 @ 6,000 rpm*

Torque: *300 ft-lbs @ 4,000 rpm*

Fuel/Induction: Aluminum-alloy intake manifold, sequential multi-port fuel injection (MFI) with multi-spray injectors and tumble generator valves, *electronic drive-by-wire throttle, high-boost turbocharger, intercooler, and manually operated intercooler water spray*

Maximum boost pressure: *14.5 psi*

Fuel requirement: 91-octane minimum

Airflow through this combination: *32-lbs/min*

MEP: 301.6 psi

HP/Liter: 122.1

For this high-output combination, Subaru approached it in the same manner as a good aftermarket tuner. It uses a stiffer engine block to provide durability under higher boost and power conditions. The 2.5-liter horizontally opposed (boxer) 4-cylinder engine is based on a specially reinforced semi-closed-deck engine block with forged aluminum-alloy pistons and forged high-carbon steel connecting rods. The semi-closed deck design provides the same cooling efficiency as an open-deck cylinder block but with the greater strength of a full closed deck. Special reinforcing ribs in the block provide additional strength.

The DOHC cylinder heads use hollow camshafts to reduce mass. Shim-less cam followers likewise reduce valvetrain mass to enhance response. The WRX STi powerplant incorporates Subaru AVCS (Active Valve Control System) variable valve timing technology to optimize the engine's volumetric efficiency throughout the rev band. AVCS adjusts intake camshaft timing to employ the ideal intake and exhaust valve overlap under all engine operating conditions. The system reduces the compromise between low-end torque and high-RPM horsepower and also helps to enhance fuel economy and reduce emissions. AVCS can rotate the intake camshafts through a range of 35 degrees relative to the crankshaft.

The engine control module (ECM) regulates this movement, based on input from various sensors – airflow, engine coolant temperature, throttle position, and camshaft position. The ECM generates an electrical output signal to an oil control valve positioned at each intake camshaft sprocket. Oil pressure is then varied within advance and retard chambers inside the AVCS actuator. The system calls upon computer maps to respond to various driving conditions, providing ideal valve timing for stable engine idling and optimum torque across the engine speed range.

The high-boost turbocharger in the WRX STi 2.5-liter engine produces a maximum of 14.5 psi of boost, compared to 13.5 psi in the standard WRX 2.0-liter engine. Because AVCS allowed Subaru engineers to tune the WRX STi engine to produce greater low-end torque, they could select a turbo optimized for high-end power. This combination effectively addresses an old compromise: smaller turbos require less exhaust energy to achieve boost in response to throttle opening, but as a result of their small size they produce less pressure and therefore lower boost and power. Larger turbos can produce more power but their larger turbines take longer to build boost, resulting in greater lag.

The intercooler in the WRX STi measures 18.5 inches wide versus 16.3 inches for the standard WRX; 7.3 inches long with 33 tubes versus 5.9 inches long and 29 tubes in the WRX. The STi's larger intercooler offers greater heat transfer capacity. This also allows the engine to run more advanced ignition timing (for more power) without causing detonation (knock).

The large-capacity intercooler features a manually operated water spray system to provide additional cooling. Under high-performance driving conditions, the driver can operate the spray to reduce intercooler temperature and therefore keep power and performance more consistent. Pressing the dash-mounted button activates the spray through a single nozzle in two-second bursts. A reservoir is located in the trunk to enhance weight distribution and ensure a cool water supply.

Subaru expects WRX STi owners to take advantage of the engine's high-performance capabilities and so has fine-tuned every detail to provide durability, especially in regard to temperature control. Piston crown thickness was increased to handle high thermal loading. Using technology adapted from racing engines, the exhaust valvestems are sodium-filled to aid valve cooling. Under high temperatures (over 280 degrees Fahrenheit), the sodium melts and splashes up and down in the stem, absorbing heat from the valve head and transferring it to the cooler stem, where it is dissipated into the valve guide and cylinder head.

Iridium-tipped spark plugs provide greater protection from heat than platinum-tipped spark plugs. A precious, silver-white metal, Iridium is one of the densest materials found on Earth. An Iridium-tipped spark plug requires less voltage to spark, burns fuel more efficiently, sparks at leaner air/fuel mixtures, and delivers higher horsepower and better fuel economy.

CHAPTER 9

HISTORY OF TURBOCHARGING AND SUPERCHARGING

TURBO HISTORY

The idea of turbocharging an internal combustion engine is almost as old as that of the internal combustion engine itself. The first efforts were in 1885 and 1896, when Gottlieb Daimler and Rudolf Diesel tested the effectiveness of increasing the power output and reducing the fuel consumption of their engines using pre-compressed combustion air. (Sounds like these guys also laid the groundwork for nitrous oxide as well.) It wasn't until about 1912 that Dr. Alfred J. Büchi of Switzerland developed the first exhaust-driven supercharger. Dr. Büchi, Chief Engineer of Sulzer Brothers Research Department, proposed the first prototype of a turbocharged diesel engine for commercial development in 1915, but his ideas gained little or no acceptance at that time. But by 1925, Büchi demonstrated the advantages of exhaust gas turbocharging by achieving a power increase of more than 40 percent. This was the beginning of the gradual introduction of turbocharging into the automotive industry.

The first turbocharger applications were limited to very large engines, e.g., marine engines, during this time. However, General Electric, with an eye on the emerging aviation industry, began developing this technology as well. Dr. Sanford A. Moss of General Electric proposed a turbocharged engine concept in the late 1910s, and in 1920 took a LePere bi-plane that was equipped with a Liberty engine, fit a hand-built General Electric turbocharger to it, and set a new altitude record of 33,113 feet (10,092 m).

Turbocharging automotive engines started with truck engines in 1938, when the first turbocharged truck engine was built by the Swiss Machine Works Saurer. The beginning of World War II and the need for industrial and transportation power accelerated the development of turbocharger technology.

Here's what the ill-fated Oldsmobile turbo unit looked like. The unit is primitive and inefficient by today's standards, especially on the compressor side.

Perhaps the most glamorous turbo application was to warplanes – notably the high-altitude airplanes, B-17 Flying Fortresses, the B-24 Liberator, the P-38, and the P-47. It was out of this area that the first company dedicated to turbo technology was born. The Garrett Corporation was formed in 1936 by J. C. "Cliff" Garrett in Los Angeles, California. His company supplied the charge air cooler (soon to be called the intercooler) for the B-17, located between the General Electric turbocharger and the Pratt & Whitney engine.

The efficiency and power advantage of turbos was also applied extensively on the less glamorous but equally important production chain. During the war years, turbos began to be used extensively on large marine, industrial, and locomotive diesel engines. But it wasn't until the early 1950s that the current turbocharger industry landscape was set in full relief.

In the early 1950s, Caterpillar Tractor Co. (CAT) began experimenting with turbochargers as a way to get a competitive advantage in developing future heavy-duty earthmoving equipment. CAT designed and built a turbo, then sent it for testing to Garrett. The first unit failed miserably during testing. At that point, CAT decided to let a specialist develop and produce turbos for them. They needed a firm with experience in turbocharged engines as well as with metallurgy, seal, and bearing technology. CAT struck a deal with Garrett, who put a team together to developing a turbo for CAT's equipment. Bob Keller, President of Turbonetics, Inc., says that one of the members of that original team was Hugh McGinnis, who basically told us all how turbochargers work.

During this time, McGinnis and Garrett were refining the design of gas turbine engines and further developed their understanding of the metallurgy of the housings, high-speed seals, radial inflow turbines, and centrifugal compressors. With the CAT contract and a world in full recovery after the war, Cliff Garrett made the decision to separate the turbocharger group from the gas turbine department due to commercial diesel turbocharger opportunities. The new AiResearch Industrial Division for turbocharger design and manufacturing was established September 27, 1954. AiResearch Industrial Division would later be named Garrett Automotive, which is now a subsidiary of Honeywell.

In hindsight, Cliff Garrett's 1954 decision to start a company dedicated to turbocharging was in part a response to the success of a prototype turbo built in 1953, designated the T02. Just to be clear, this is not directly related to current Garrett Automotive T2 series. The T02 prototype performed above expectations for over 1,800 hours without hinting of a failure. From this prototype came the T15. It was less complex yet equally durable, and CAT ordered 5,000 units as a power adder for the CAT D9 tractor.

Garrett wasn't the only company developing turbochargers in the early 1950s. Cummins Engine was using turbos made by Elliot and Schwitzer for its diesel truck engines and even dabbled in producing its own units for a time.

Even with all this corporate effort, in took until the 1960s for turbos to become reliable and essential components of diesel engine design with full acceptance of the trucking industry. By the end of the decade, AiResearch established itself as the leader in turbocharger technology with a broad range of products covering the full spectrum of commercial applications. The firm retains its top position in the industrial market still today, with minor competition from Borg Warner, Schwitzer, Holset, KKK, and several European knock-offs.

The Chevrolet Corvair Monza and the Oldsmobile Jetfire were the first turbo-powered passenger cars, and made their debut on the US market in 1962-63. Despite maximum technical outlay, however, their poor reliability caused them to disappear quickly from the market.

The 1962 Oldsmobile Jetfire, a 215-ci aluminum V-8 with a Garret+AiResearch T5 turbo using what Bob Keller of Turbonetics called "the most complicated application one could imagine," is an example of how clueless even factory engineers were about turbocharging. Mistake number one was that the engine had a 10.25:1 compression ratio. Mistake number two: it was under-carbureted, using only a single-throat side-draft carburetor. Mistake number three was that it employed a complex water-injection system utilizing what the marketing types branded "Rocket Fluid." This was a basic 50/50 mix of water and alcohol that was used to prevent detonation and supply a little more fuel in an attempt to make more power. This system was so unwieldy and complicated that Oldsmobile actually offered to remove the system and replace it with a conventional carburetor for a fee of $50. Obviously, high-tech engineering in the formative years of the musclecar craze had a few teething problems.

Chevrolet, on the other hand, did it much better with the introduction of the turbocharged Corvair. It took a far more elegant approach, using a turbo system designed and built by TRW with input from McGinnis. For the record, it wasn't the turbo system that doomed the Corvair. It had more to do with a certain Mr. Nader's jihad against what he saw as a murderous machine, detailed in his book *Unsafe at Any Speed*. Still, the turbocharged Corvair proved that turbocharging a mass-produced engine could be done successfully and potentially profitably.

The 1960s was an, how to put it ..., an entrepreneurial decade. Horsepower was hot, the baby boomers were in full musclecar mode, and several individuals began to try to master the art of turbocharging. Several tried to ride the wave to a successful aftermarket business along with Vic Edelbrock, Isky, and other businessman/racers, but most failed. But that research and development that these individuals and firms performed are the bedrock that the current OE and aftermarket turbocharger businesses are built on. Turbos reappeared on Indy cars in 1966 and have dominated ever since.

The 1960s ended with Texas-based Rajay Industries purchasing the TRW product line, as well as hiring Mr. McGinnis as chief engineer. Rajay established a Long Beach, California,

Chapter 9

In the 1960s and 1970s, American hot rodders (the forefathers to the tuner crowd) were experimenting with all sorts of wild combinations. This is an Ak Miller turbocharged application to a Ford six-cylinder using propane as fuel. Miller was noted for making power with his ingenious combinations, and this was surely one of them. On occasion, racers still use propane-fueled turbo engines to run Pikes Peak.

Here's another early 1970s turbocharged combo from Ak Miller on a small-block Chevy.

facility and developed the turbocharger market for general aviation, specialty industrial, and automotive performance applications. According to Turbonetics' Bob Keller, probably one of the most significant contributions to the development of a turbocharger aftermarket sector was that Rajay made its products widely available. This, continues Keller, allowed many would-be turbo Einsteins to get their feet wet. Because Rajay sold product to the public, companies such as M&W Gear, Spearco, and Daytona Marine appeared on the scene. Still, Rajay's largest business, by far, was to compete directly with Garrett-AiResearch in the agricultural/industrial diesel market.

After the first oil crisis in 1973, turbocharging became more acceptable in commercial diesel applications. Until then, the high investment costs of turbocharging were offset only by fuel cost savings, which were minimal. Increasingly stringent emission regulations in the late 1980s resulted in an increase in the number of turbocharged truck engines, so that today, virtually every truck engine is turbocharged.

In spite of the competition from Rajay and others, AiResearch was still the leading innovator in turbo technology worldwide. However, the technology still wasn't making its way into the hands of automotive performance enthusiasts until the early 1970s.

In the early 1970s, in part as a response to the oil crisis and stricter environmental standards, the most significant attempt to get turbocharging into the hands of the enthusiast was made by the creation of the TurboSonic product line of retrofit hardware produced by ACCEL, the performance marketing arm of Echlin Corporation. (Bob Keller created TurboSonic product line after Echlin bought out his turbo interests in the original Turbonetics in 1973.) ACCEL had been enjoying a very lucrative business in the performance aftermarket and, through a very ambitious campaign of advertising, feature articles, and nationwide product promotion, it was able move thousands of turbochargers into the hands of energetic consumers who knew nothing at all about what turbos were, how they worked, or how to install them.

In 1976, shortly after the introduction of the ACCEL TurboSonic product line (which utilized Garret+AiResearch turbochargers), Echlin purchased an up-and-coming industrial aftermarket turbocharger "copy-cat" house by the name of Roto-Master in California. Roto-Master had by then established itself as the principal aftermarket source of remanufactured industrial diesel turbochargers and components in the US and probably the world. This purchase enabled ACCEL to produce its own turbos for the TurboSonic product line and firmly establish Roto-Master as the leading producer of aftermarket performance turbochargers. Roto-Master's chief engineer and vice president of engineering was the ubiquitous McGinnes. Keller became Roto-Master's chief engineer of turbocharger systems.

In the late 1970s, Detroit enthusiastically "discovered" turbocharging – the threat of a serious fuel crunch as 1980 approached, as well as the then-severe CAFE requirements imposed by the government, forced automakers to develop small engines that delivered great fuel economy but were woefully underpowered. In order to restore some resemblance of performance to these small-displacement engines, auto manufacturers applied turbochargers in earnest – so much so that by the early 1980s, essentially every auto manufacturer from Ford to Mercedes had multiple families of turbocharged vehicles in their lineup, much to the delight of Garrett-AiResearch, the major supplier at the time.

Aftermarket retrofit and performance turbocharging became more of a political subject than a technical subject when government regulations imposed by the Clean Air Act of 1977 and California's Air Resources Board made it extremely difficult and costly for retrofit turbocharger kit manufacturers to produce economically viable products that could be sold legally. Some houses did take on this challenge, however, and were able to demonstrate that a retrofit turbo could provide that extra desired kick in the pants and satisfy emissions requirements at the same time. Spearco, Dina Engineering, Custom Automotive, Gemini Turbo Systems, BAE, Advanced Turbo Systems, Gale Banks Engineering, Turbonetics (created by Keller after he left Roto-Master in 1978), and others have proved it can be done by obtaining Executive Orders from the California Air Resources

Turbo VWs are perhaps the proto sport compact. This shows a Spearco (yes the intercooler firm) that probably fit to a dune buggy. It's a draw-through carbureted design. Notice how the headers feed the turbine and how the shorty exhaust exits the turbo.

Here's a typical street version of a Spearco turbo Bug. There's just a simple exhaust pipe leading to the turbo. This is a push-through design, where the carburetor is pressurized to provide proper fuel metering.

Chapter 9

Spearco even had a few turbo kits for carbureted Hondas. The blow-through design seemed to work best on carbureted street cars.

Turbo Milestones

- 1905 – Invented by Alfred J. Büchi
- 1903 – First centrifugal supercharged racecar, offered as road car same year
- 1922 – First operational air squadron with turbos
- 1923 – First commercial Diesel marine engine
- 1930 – First turbocharged racecar (Cummins Diesel). Dale Evans drove the Cummins Diesel Racing Car. It was the first diesel racer built in the US. It placed 13th in the Indianapolis 500 of 1930 without making a single stop for fuel, water, or tires
- 1962 – First turbocharged US production car
- 1966 – First spark ignition USAC racecar
- 1968 – First turbocharged-engine win at Indy 500
- 1977 – First turbocharged Formula 1 racecar. Renault 1,492-cc V-6 produced 510 hp. By the early 1980s, the engine made 1,300 hp from 1,492cc.
- 1978 – First turbo-diesel passenger car (Mercedes-Benz)

Board that declared – after extensive testing and engineering review – that the product was in compliance with all emission requirements.

The modern breakthrough in passenger car turbocharging was achieved in 1978 with the introduction of the first turbocharged diesel-engine passenger car, the Mercedes-Benz 300 SD, which was followed by the VW Golf Turbodiesel in 1981. The benefits of the turbo diesel engine was, and still is, that a passenger car's efficiency could be increased beyond that which a gasoline engine can achieve, but it had nearly the same driveability of a gas motor, plus the emissions were significantly reduced.

Today, turbocharging gasoline engines, from the automaker's perspective, is no longer primarily seen as a performance-based marketing tool, but is rather viewed as a means of reducing fuel consumption and, consequently, environmental pollution by way of lower carbon dioxide (CO_2) and other emissions.

Performance turbocharging for legitimate competition was a very frustrating exercise in the 1980s. It seemed that any time an adventurous car builder put together a turbo vehicle that showed some degree of success, he found himself strapped with arbitrary weight and/or displacement penalties or even ruled out of competition. The established success of turbos in Europe and at Indy still had a long way to go to overcome the ignorance of many US sanctioning bodies in discouraging turbos because of their "exorbitant" cost and "unfair" advantage. Formula 1 also began instituting rule changes that penalized turbocharged racing engines.

In the mid 1980s, the aftermarket turbo companies were absorbed into each other. Roto-Master purchased Rajay in 1982, which in turn was bought by Garrett in 1986, giving Garrett a monopoly position in the turbocharger aftermarket. This position in the aftermarket failed to translate to OEM deals, and the company lost ground to Japanese turbo suppliers. Just check under the hood of almost any American turbo car and you'll see Mitsubishi, Hitachi, IHI, etc., turbochargers. Garrett is working its way back into being a viable factory supplier, but it has a long way to go as of this writing.

The 1990s was the decade that turbo technology finally made it to the masses. The transfer of this technology was a result of Honda offering serious performance product (from its successes in F1) mixing with a new generation of American car enthusiasts. The Japanese automakers continued to develop turbocharged vehicles and eventually they began exporting them to the US, where an eager audience of Gen-X and Y motor heads started hot rodding, er... tuning them. The cars performed well mostly because the electronic engine management systems were developed to a point that they actually worked. Combine that with the ability to tune the electronics to various combinations, and it's easy to see why demand was created for retrofit turbos and superchargers for popular sport compacts.

That brings us up to the present. The popularity of Japanese import machines produced a new wave of automotive enthusiasts at least as significant as the first wave that spawned the hot-rod crowd. But for the tuner movement it's all about high tech: electronic fuel injection and engine management, turbochargers, blowers, nitrous, and off-the-hook all-motor combos. Some of these machines are literally street-driven racecars, carbon fiber tubs and all. Racing venues such as the "Battle of the Imports" were established, which recognized turbocharging as an integral part of performance, allowing new companies to spring up to take advantage of this enthusiasm. As Bob Keller of Turbonetics observed, there are more entrepreneurial ventures involving performance turbocharging now than existed in the hot-rod heydays of the 1950s. Major players such as HKS, Trust-GReddy, Turbonetics, and even newer firms such as Innovative Turbo, have found themselves in a demand market that is almost impossible to satisfy. We're sure Bob and company are trying hard to fill the need: the need for speed.

A Short History of Automotive Supercharging

Most types of superchargers, in elementary forms, were used for some other purpose well before cars were invented. They were used to pump water, to be pumped by water (that is, to work as a type of water wheel or mill), or to blow air for ventilation, for furnaces, or for other purposes. The Roots blower design traces its origin to two American brothers, Francis and Philander Roots, who were trying to design a better waterwheel to power their woolen mill in 1854. Their bi-rotor gear pump was not successful as a water mill, but they later found it to be very good for pumping large volumes of air at relatively slow rotor speeds as a blast blower for a foundry furnace. The Roots brothers patented their blower in 1860, updating the design with 16 more patents by 1884. The Roots blower has been used in a wide variety of industrial applications, including blowing fresh air into mine shafts, ever since. The company is still operating as the Roots Division of Dresser, Inc. of Connersville, Indiana.

The first noted example of a blower being fitted to an internal combustion engine was in 1901 when Sir Dugald Clerk, the pioneer of two-stroke engine design, used a pumping device to force more air into the engine to (supposedly) lower the maximum combustion temperature. As we've found out since, blowers actually raise the temperature of inlet air and of combustion in the cylinder; but Clerk found that the blower ultimately increased the power of his two-stroke engine by six percent. Thus, the power-producing capabilities of supercharging were discovered. In 1902, Louis Renault patented a supercharging system in France that used a centrifugal compressor to blow air into the carburetor.

Motorsport and Supercharging Before World War I

The first example of supercharging in the United States, the first supercharged car to win a competitive event, and the first application of a supercharger for production vehicles all belong to Lee Chadwick of Pottstown, Pennsylvania. He had been manufacturing Chadwick automobiles since about 1900. In 1907, he and engineer John Nichols mounted a centrifugal blower to the 1140-ci Great Chadwick Six, producing a certified top speed of over 100 mph. The initial Chadwick design drove the supercharger with a leather belt from the flywheel at nine times crankshaft speed, blowing dry air into the carburetor. A second version used a three-stage centrifugal compressor with

Supercharger development in the United States centered around centrifugal blowers. Blown Duesenberg and Miller straight eights totally dominated the Indy 500 through the 1920s. This is a Goosen-designed, Offenhauser-built Miller 91, circa 1927, showing the flywheel-driven centrifugal blower at the back with a single updraft Miller barrel-valve carb. Note the increasing diameter of the blower scroll housing.

three 10-inch-diameter impellers of 12 blades each (but of increasing widths for three-stage compression). This car won the Wilkes-Barre Hill Climb in 1908, the first event in which a supercharged car was ever entered, and went on to score many other victories before Chadwick ceased production in 1911 after making some 260 cars.

In 1911, a Frenchman named Sizaire carried out experiments with centrifugal blowers. The following year, Marc Birkigtt designed a Hispano-Suiza for the Coupe de l'Auto race that used two of its six cylinders to supercharge the other four (that is, a four-cylinder engine with a built-in two-cylinder compressor for supercharging). This experiment wasn't very successful.

Further automotive applications for superchargers were eclipsed by the outbreak of World War I. This was the first air war, and air superiority relied heavily on supercharging, because the higher an aircraft flies, the less dense the surrounding atmosphere to feed the engine becomes. Supercharging was immediately seen by the Germans as a practical means for maintaining engine power at higher altitudes, by mechanically forcing a denser charge into the cylinders. Similar supercharger development followed in other European countries and in the US.

Naturally, most leading auto designers and manufacturers were involved in the war effort in Germany and elsewhere. Not long after the war's end, superchargers of various types began showing up on racecars.

One of the first companies to use superchargers for automobiles in Germany was Daimler, which made Mercedes cars, and later merged with Benz in 1926. With the assistance of Dr. Porsche, who worked for Daimler at the time, they developed the 28/95 Mercedes six-cylinder, which won the 1921 Coppa Florio – the first victory for a supercharged car since the Chadwick. The 28/95 Mercedes, like several later models including the famous SS and SSKs, used a Roots-type blower mounted vertically at the front of the engine, driven by a bevel gear and cone clutch from the crankshaft. The blower was engaged only at full throttle, and blew into the carburetor. When the blower was engaged, power was reportedly increased 50 percent with a pressure boost of approximately 6 to 7 psi. A considerable amount of Roots-blower technology was compiled by Mercedes-Benz between World War I and World War II.

In 1923, Fiat added a Wittig vane-type supercharger to its eight-cylinder Grand Prix car. The blower was front driven by the crankshaft and, like the Mercedes, blew into the carburetor only at full throttle. This early vane-type blower did not work very well (possibly because oil had to be injected into the blower to lubricate the vanes, causing detonation in the engine). Later the same year, Fiat switched to a Roots blower with an intercooler and did much better, finishing first and second in the Italian Grand Prix and setting a new lap record just shy of 100 mph at Monza.

In 1924, both Sunbeam and Alfa Romeo introduced Roots-blown Grand Prix cars. Sunbeam was first to place the Roots supercharger between the carburetor and the intake manifold (that is, in a draw-through rather than a blow-through arrangement), discovering through testing that this design netted a 20-percent increase in horsepower over the blow-through configuration. The cooling effect of the vaporizing fuel in the blower, plus the better atomization of the fuel particles as they passed through the rotors, were the main factors in the power increase. From then until a rule change in 1952 that virtually banned blowers, supercharged cars totally dominated Grand Prix racing in Europe, and the majority of these cars used Roots-type blowers.

In the United States, by a series of coincidences, supercharger development centered on the city of Indianapolis. Prior to World War I, Dr. Sanford Moss, working for General Electric, had been experimenting with Roots-type blowers and centrifugal turbochargers; he was also a pioneer of the two-stage blower concept. Dr. Moss, as well as Mr. Kerr and Mr. Le Blanc, who were designing a gear-driven centrifugal blower for the Liberty aircraft engine, were working for the US government at McCook Field, near Indianapolis. Allison Engineering, manufacturer of the Liberty engine and other subsequent supercharged aircraft engines, was also located near Indianapolis, and the company's owner, James A. Allison, was one of the founding owners of the Indianapolis Motor Speedway. Thus, much of the pioneering supercharger development in the United States was occurring in the same city as most of our pioneering racecar development, albeit for different reasons.

Meanwhile, brothers Fred and August Duesenberg had opened their new automobile manufacturing company in Indianapolis in 1912 and were involved in building one-off racecars. In 1924, the Duesenbergs fitted a centrifugal supercharger to their already highly successful straight-eight racing engine. The blower was gear- and shaft-driven and was the first recorded example in the US to place the carburetor ahead of the supercharger in a draw-through layout. This supercharged Duesy was a winner, and all subsequent Duesenberg racing engines were similarly supercharged.

After Errett Lobban Cord bought into the Duesenberg company in 1928, as he had with Auburn previously, they introduced the famous J and SJ production models, which came equipped with shaft-driven centrifugal superchargers mounted horizontally above the engine. Models of the Auburn, the V-8 Cord, and the Cord look-alike Graham also came factory-equipped with similar centrifugal blowers.

Shortly after the Duesenbergs unveiled their blown engine at the Indy 500, a Los Angeles-based engine builder and fierce competitor of the Duesenbergs, Harry Miller, came up with a centrifugal supercharger for his straight-eight racing engines. Designed by Leo Goosen and built by Miller machinist Fred Offenhauser, this flywheel-driven blower was relatively advanced for the time (more advanced, in fact, in terms of impeller, diffuser, and scroll-housing design, than some of our recent offerings in aftermarket belt-driven centrifugal blowers).

The most interesting point about this period of supercharger activity in motor sports (roughly between World War I and World War II) is the fact that Roots-type blowers were used almost exclusively in Europe while centrifugal-type blowers were used exclusively in the United States. The Europeans tried other types of blowers to begin with, as did the Americans, but each group soon discovered which type of supercharger worked best for the particular style of racing that was predominant in their part of the world.

In Europe, the Grand Prix, or road racing, was the ultimate in auto competition. The twisting and turning road course required a broad horsepower range, as well as instant throttle response and good low-end torque for accelerating from slow corners. In the United States, however, the ultimate was the Indy 500, a long, fast oval with sweeping curves that kept a racing engine operating in a fairly tight RPM range. From the turn of the century on, auto racing in the US was done primarily on circle, oval, or board tracks, and therefore mostly at wide-open throttle. The Roots blower gave the Europeans

History of Turbocharging and Supercharging

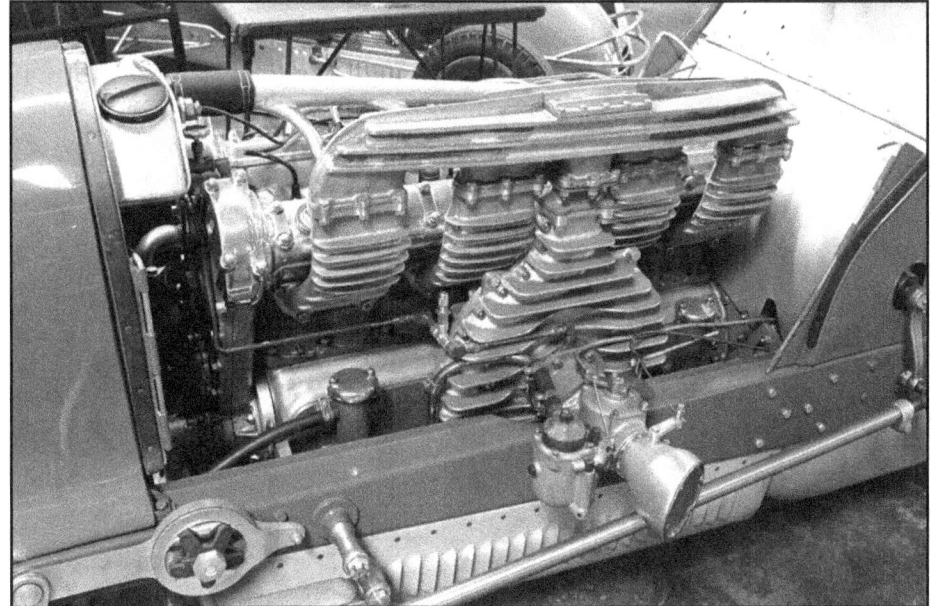

One of the more radical Indy designs was the Duesenberg "side-winder" introduced in 1927, using a side-mounted, shaft-driven centrifugal blower. All of the fins on the blower case and the tall intake manifold weren't just for looks. Their purpose was to dissipate heat generated by the blower — one of the first intercoolers.

The Italians were also big on Roots blowers, and most manufacturers made their own. This straight-eight, single overhead cam '27 Bugatti Type 35B used a side-mounted blower driven by a shaft from the crank gear.

The 1934 MG K-3 Brooklands also used a front-drive Roots type blower (a Marshall) with a single SU carb.

On the 1934 Alfa Romeo Tipo 8 Mille Miglia, the Roots-type blower tucks low on the side of the engine with a big Memini carb just ahead of it. Again, note the use of fins on the manifold for intercooling. This car won Le Mans four times in the 1930s.

the kind of power they needed; the centrifugal blower, which was more efficient in a narrower RPM range, gave the American cars the top-end boost they required.

The period between the two world wars was the heyday of supercharging. Not only did the major racecars of the time run blowers, but, as you might expect, so did several of the more racy production models, both here and in Europe. However, the Great Depression and then World War II finally put an end to supercharged luxury sports cars and, shortly after war's end, rules changes stifled the supercharger's advantage in racing. Consequently, after the 1940s, superchargers virtually disappeared from the automotive scene.

Motorsport and Supercharging After World War II

Just before and after World War II was when hot rodding really began to develop. The young kids who raced stripped-down Model Ts and As on dirt ovals and dry lakebeds were a far cry from the sophisticated European Grand Prix and US Indy racecar builders. However, they had paid close attention to the way the experts built racing engines and they knew the effectiveness of superchargers. In hot-rodding, there was no ban on blowers; the major deterrent

Chapter 9

In the 1920s and 1930s, you could buy several types of supercharged production cars to drive on the street (if you had enough money). One of the most famous in America was the Duesenberg SJ, which used a horizontal, shaft-driven centrifugal blower. This example, a '35 SSJ owned by Gary Cooper, was one of three specially outfitted with two updraft carbs by the factory.

then, even more so than now, was cost.

There were a few early examples of blowers being run on roadsters at the dry lakes, even in the Depression days before the war. A few rodders acquired centrifugal blowers from production American cars such as the Graham, and adapted them to the Ford flathead V-8. However, Graham production blowers produced very little boost; when hot-rodders tried to spin them faster to get more pressure out of them, they usually ended up stripping the blower's step-up drive gears. McCulloch also introduced a centrifugal supercharger as an aftermarket bolt-on kit for the Ford V-8 about this time (probably the first aftermarket blower kit), and some of the more affluent rod builders tried them at the dry lakes.

The first generally noted example of a Roots-type blower being fitted to a hot rod was in the late 1930s when the Spalding Brothers somehow acquired a Mercedes-Benz blower and put it on their flathead Ford. After the war, Don Blair bought a blower from the Spaldings and adapted it to his Goat Unlimited-class roadster for the 1946-47 seasons. Running alcohol through two Stromberg 48 carbs, and driving the blower with two V-belts, the car turned a top speed of 141 mph.

The person usually credited with the first installation of a GMC industrial blower on a hot rod is Barney Navarro. Barney had been aware of blowers for some time, but they were scarce and expensive. Then one day in 1948, Kong Jackson showed up with a 3-71 GMC off a World War II landing craft, and he offered it to Navarro for $60. Barney was manufacturing his own line of V-8 heads and intake manifolds at the time, so he modified one of his manifold patterns to accept the blower and cast an intake manifold for it. He built his own drive using four V-belts and mounted four Stromberg 48 carbs on top of the blower to run alcohol (ethanol). On a destroked, 176-ci V-8 in his '27 T roadster, this early GMC blower setup pumped 16 pounds of boost and pushed the car to 146.9 mph. The only internal modification Barney made to the blower was to bore the case slightly larger for increased rotor-to-housing clearance for higher-RPM use.

Barney not only ran the roadster at the dry lakes, but also raced it on the

During World War II, supercharger development progressed rapidly, but for aircraft engines rather than for automobiles. The huge unit at the front of this Rolls-Royce Merlin V-12 is a two-stage, crank-driven, centrifugal blower. Unfortunately, little of this technology has ever been applied to cars.

dirt circle tracks, possibly the only supercharged hot rod to do so. Although he never had any mechanical problems with the blower, he had plenty of trouble with V-belts, especially on the tracks, since they tended to heat up and disintegrate. Barney solved the problem by drilling a series of holes both vertically and horizontally through the pulleys to cool the belts.

Tom Beatty, who worked for Navarro, built a similar system for his own lakes roadster, adapting a 4-71 GMC to an Oldsmobile OHV V-8 for his belly tank lakester. Beatty eventually manufactured manifolds and drive kits for the GMCs, based on the Navarro V-belt design, and helped pioneer the more widespread use of Jimmies. In fact, back in the 1950s Beatty stuffed one of his blown Olds race engines into his 1940 Ford sedan delivery to use as a street driver and push truck.

Navarro was also one of the first to run a blower at the drag races, since he entered his roadster at the first running of the Santa Ana drags in 1950. However, Barney did not pursue drag racing with a blown engine because, as he put it, "I broke too many quick-change rear ends."

According to hot-rod historian Greg Sharp, the first use of a blower at the drags was actually at one of the very first organized drag meets, held near the Goleta airstrip in 1949. The contest was between Tom Cobbs, who was running a Roots-blown V-8, and Fran Hernandez, who was using a secret new fuel called nitro-methane.

Hernandez won that round. It was drag racing that really pushed the development of GMC blowers in hot rodding. The Roots blower produced gobs of horsepower and torque in the low-RPM ranges, which is exactly what dragsters needed to get off the line – unlike the dry lakes and Bonneville racers who went for top-end speed.

However, the Cobbs/Hernandez duel was also representative of another new element in rodding that affected both drag racing and blower development – nitro. Once the secret of nitro got out, rodders discovered that it gave them even more horsepower than blowers. But it was also very temperamental, literally explosive, stuff. Early experiments with blowers on alcohol or gasoline proved fairly reliable, but combining a blower with nitro usually ended in disaster. So, widespread use of Roots blowers in drag racing had to wait until the racers got the nitro situation sorted out.

This is not to say that some drag racers weren't using GMC blowers right away. One of the first was Ernie Hashim of Bakersfield, California, who mounted a 3-71 GMC on top of a Ford V-8 as early as 1950, and was using it at the lakes as well as to drag race on airfields in the San Joaquin Valley, such as Maricopa and Famoso. He got his 3-71 from partner John Gilbert, who operated heavy equipment in the Northwest and had therefore become acquainted with GMC industrial blowers. By 1955, Hashim had adapted a front-mounted 4-71 GMC to a Chrysler Hemi with a one-off Hilborn two-throat injector, which he ran in a '32 roadster at Bonneville and in a rail at the drags. Shortly

One of the first Roots blowers to be used on a hot rod was a Mercedes unit that Don Blair ran on his modified lakes roadster in 1946. He used it to turn 141 mph with a Ford flathead V-8.

This unidentified photo was taken at the first World Series of Drag Racing in 1954. The GMC-blown Cadillac flathead from Illinois was turning a respectable 110 mph.

Can you guess who's driving this GMC-blown, GMC-six-powered drag roadster at Santa Ana in the early 1950s? None other than "Dyno" Don Nicholson, a famous drag racer who cut his teeth on GMC blowers. Note the chain drive on side-mounted 4-71.

Chapter 9

Oftentimes hot-rodders who tried innovations met with derision from others who didn't understand the principles. Ted Rawleigh fed a crank-driven 6-71 into a belt-driven 4-71 on his Olds-powered dragster in the mid 1950s and got 670 horsepower. However, the car couldn't put the power to the ground, and two-stage supercharging at the drags hasn't been tried since.

 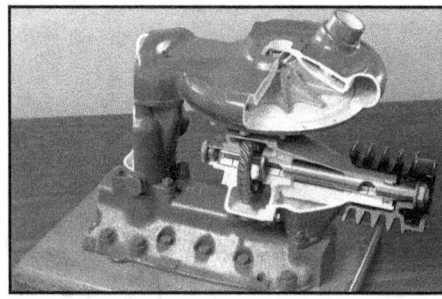

The first aftermarket street blower kit was this centrifugal McCulloch, marketed in the late 1930s. The horizontal blower is driven by a bevel gear shaft. The polished unit on the engine differs from earlier cutaway models.

Another early one-off McCulloch (Paxton) blower is this centrifugal unit made for extremely high boost on the Novi Indy cars.

The year of the first Bakersfield Fuel and Gas Championships, 1959, was the year that the 6-71 GMC-blown Chrysler Hemi came to rule drag racing — and things have changed little since then.

afterwards, Hashim mounted a 6-71 on top of the Chrysler and fabricated one of the first Gilmer belt drives. About the same time, Ed Iskenderian purchased a batch of 6-71 GMC superchargers and hired Hashim to rework them for use on dragsters, which involved reversing the rotors, milling the case, and resetting the clearances. In 1959, Isky introduced its "Forced Induction" blower drive kit for top-mounted 6-71 blowers.

Prior to that time, the most popular blower setup for drags or Bonneville was Chuck Potvin's front-drive for 6-71s. Early versions, introduced in the mid 1950s, were of a "U-Fab" variety, leaving much of the work to the installer; later models used cast aluminum manifolds and drive housings. The big advantage of the front-mount blower, besides the fact that the lower profile was better aerodynamically and gave the driver a better view, was that the direct drive from the crankshaft solved the persistent problem of drive belt slippage when the blower was pumping substantial boost. The toothed Gilmer belt would later solve this problem for top-mounted blowers.

Mickey Thompson gets credit for the first blown Chrysler Hemi. In 1953, he dropped one of the new Hemi-head motors into Bill Burke's old streamlined Bantam coupe *along with* one of his more traditional three-carb Ford flathead V-8s! To this strange marriage, Thompson added a 4-71 Jimmy atop the Chrysler. The first year the blower

History of Turbocharging and Supercharging

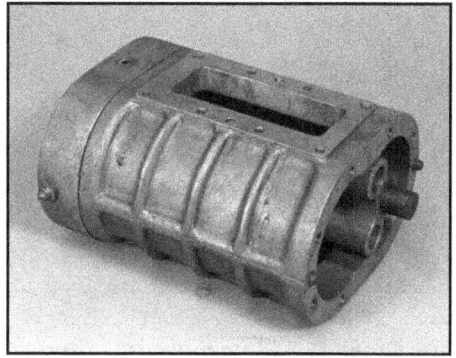

Although tons of these little Pepco Roots-type blowers were made, the only example we could find today is this partial unit with one broken rotor.

The primary Fageol Max 25 installation kits were for Toyota four-cylinders using a Weber two-throat carb (shown), and for Chevy 60-degree V-6s in S-10s, Blazers, and Fieros retaining the factory computer-controlled induction system.

resulted in two melted pistons in the Hemi; later the odd-coupled contraption went well over 190 mph. In 1954, Bruce Crower brought a '49 Hudson to Bonneville, powered by a blown Chrysler, ran 157 mph, and drove it on the street. In 1955, Ernie Hashim and Tony Waters set the fastest speed ever for a stock-bodied roadster with their blown Hemi '32 at 189 mph. That same year, Tom Cobbs switched the homemade front-mount 4-71 from the flathead in his '34 coupe to a brand new Chevy 265-ci V-8, probably the first Jimmy-blown Chevy small-block. Also in 1955, top dragster pilot Calvin Rice was getting a homemade front-drive GMC blown Chrysler Hemi to run faster than his backup flathead in his Nationals-winning rail.

However, the 6-71 blown Hemi didn't become the standard dragster powerplant until about 1959. That was the year of the first Bakersfield Fuel and Gas Championships and the first trip to the West Coast for Don Garlits. When Garlits arrived, he was running his fueler naturally aspirated on eight carburetors, but all of his California competitors had recently begun running the big GMC blowers. After that meet, but before his other two scheduled West Coast appearances, Garlits towed the dragster immediately to Isky to have a 6-71 installed between the Hemi and the eight carbs. Other than developments in fuel-injection systems, alloy blocks, and big-displacement blower cases (8-71s to 14-71s), the story in fuel drag racing has been the same ever since.

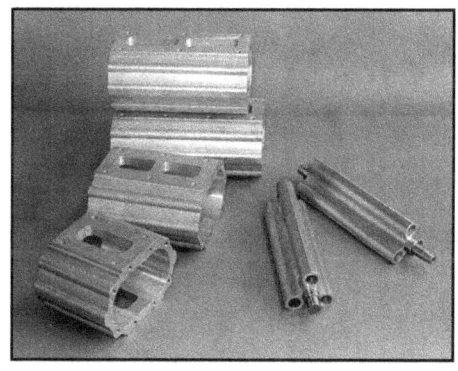

Since both the case and the rotors in the KF Industry blower are made from extrusions, they can be cut to varying lengths to make different sizes of blowers. After they are cut to size, the case and the rotors are finish machined.

This Fageol Max 25 uses cast-aluminum bearing plates and drive snout, press-in bearings and seals, straight cut steel drive gears, an extruded aluminum case, and three-lobe rotors.

Supercharging for the Street

As far as supercharging for street-driven, gasoline-burning automobiles goes, the history is brief. After the prestigious supercharged road cars of the 1920s and 1930s, the next appearance of blowers was a handful of bolt-on supercharger kits that suddenly appeared on the market about 1950. These included the McCulloch, the Frenzel, the S.CO.T/Italmecanica, a few kits based on reworked GMC 3-71s or 4-71s such as the J.E.M. and the Speed-O-Motive, and a bit later the Judson and Latham. These blowers were used primarily in street applications, rather than racing. Because such blower kits were very expensive for the time, not many found their way onto hot rods when they were first introduced.

The next development came in the mid 1950s. After Chevrolet introduced its new small-block V-8 in 1955, Ford

Chapter 9

Jerry Magnuson built his Magna Chargers in several styles and sizes in the 1970s and 1980s. The small 40-, 60-, and 80-ci models were made primarily for motorcycle applications. The larger 110-ci unit is good for four-cylinder, V-6, and small V-8 automotive installations. Note the air divider bars in the inlets of each of these blowers.

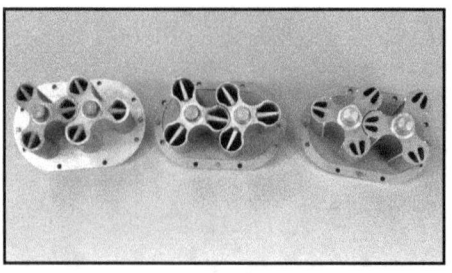

Magna Chargers use three-lobe cast-aluminum rotors. Jerry improved the design several times over the years. Shown here are three generations of rotors, with those on the right being the newest.

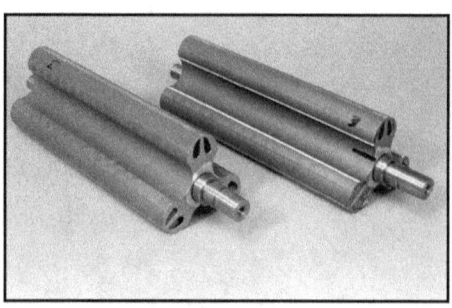

The straight-cut, three-lobe rotor design is basic to the overall design of the Magna Charger. These blowers can also be set up with or without Teflon strips (the rotor on the right has been fitted with Teflon).

The Latham blower consists of a stack of stator fans, with a corresponding stack of rotor fans inside on a revolving shaft. The number of rotor and stator sections could be varied to make the blower larger or smaller. Air was drawn in through the carburetor mounts at the front (top) and emitted into the manifold of the engine at the other end. This unit has been fitted with four Carter YF side-draft carburetors in an unusual arrangement (two facing forward instead of all four mounted to the sides).

The 1989 Ford Thunderbird was the first production car to use the refined Eaton Roots supercharger. Ford, and other manufacturers, have since used Roots and Lysholm superchargers on a number of applications.

and other manufacturers suddenly found themselves in the position of playing catch-up. Since Ford's new Y-block was no match for the Chevy, Ford turned to supercharging as the one sure way to best the Chevys on the NASCAR tracks and on the beach at Daytona. Ford had McCulloch design a special centrifugal blower for the racing Fords, and then offered the standard McCulloch variable-speed, belt-driven blower as optional equipment on '57 Fords and T-Birds. The same year, Studebaker offered the McCulloch on its Golden Hawks and on some of the last Packard models. As late as 1963, the McCulloch/Paxton was used as standard equipment on the Studebaker Avanti. From this time on, until the Eaton Roots-type supercharged '89 Ford Super Coupe, Detroit turned to the turbocharger for boosting production models.

Through the 1960s and early 1970s, there were isolated examples of supercharged street-driven hot rods, but most of these were considered phenomenal at the time. The sight and sound of a working GMC blower on the street, not to mention the potential power on tap, was awe-inspiring. GMC blowers were scarce, parts to

History of Turbocharging and Supercharging

These photos show how the Variable Speed McCulloch blower actually worked. When the pulley flanges were closed, the belt rode on a larger circumference, and the blower turned more slowly in relation to the crankshaft (left). When the pulley opened, however, the belt dropped down, essentially increasing the drive ratio and turning the blower faster. This technology isn't currently in use in any of the sport-compact kits, but history sometimes has a way of repeating itself.

This cutaway of an early Variable Speed McCulloch blower graphically shows that only a small portion of the unit was the actual supercharger — the impeller and scroll housing (1) located at the extreme left. Just behind the impeller are the drive balls, which are held against their races by a strong clutch pack of springs (2). The rest of the case holds the mechanism which changes the pulley ratio, consisting of an electric solenoid (3) triggered by manifold pressure, and a vacuum/pressure-operated diaphragm (4), which pulled the back of the pulley in or out against the tension of the spring in the middle. This area in current Paxton blowers is empty except for the oil reservoir and pump.

adapt them to a street engine were nearly non-existent, and getting one to work right in traffic took lots of trial and error.

Within the last couple of decades, however, blowers came of age for street machines. Old-school rodders have discovered that, with proper clearances, bearings, and drive ratios, there's no reason why a GMC should be any hassle on the street. First a variety of companies offered complete drive kits for GMCs on street motors – kits which incorporated water pumps, fans, alternators, and so on. Then a couple of companies started fabricating or modifying blower manifolds to fit street motors other than small-block Chevys and Chrysler Hemis.

In the 1990s, Oscar Jackson was the first, to our knowledge, to apply

A special Paxton blower, shown on the right in this photo, was made for factory option applications on 1957 Fords and Thunderbirds, but only a few hundred were ever installed. It had an internal system for varying the drive ratio. Even more rare is the larger Phase 1 blower made for NASCAR and Daytona Beach racing '57 Fords, shown on the left.

the new Eaton supercharger units to sport compacts. His success proved there was a market for supercharged high-tech four-cylinder engines. With the market demand proven, several other firms started designing both Eaton-based and centrifugal supercharger kits for this market.

Sport Compact Turbos & Blowers

Appendix A

Turbocharging Source Guide

TURBOCHARGING SOURCES

Aeromotive, Inc.
5400 Merriam Drive
Merriam, KS 66203
Phone: (913) 647-7300
Fax: (913) 647-7207
Email: info@aeromotiveinc.com
Tech Email: tech@aeromotiveinc.com
Website: www.aeromotiveinc.com

Bill Smulo Engineering, Inc.
345 N. Maple Dr., Suite 294
Beverly Hills, CA 90210
Phone: (818) 480-1009
Fax: (310) 777-8754
Warehouse and multi-line distributor of automotive accessories, including superchargers and turbochargers, specializing in Hyundai vehicles.

BorgWarner Turbo Systems
1849 Brevard Rd.
Arden, NC 28704
Phone: (828) 684-4000
Fax: (800) 424-6464
Email: bradh@turbos.bwauto.com
Website: www.turbodriven.com
Manufacturer and supplier of all 3K and Schwitzer performance and replacement turbochargers and parts.

Dream Workes Racing
2451 E. Tremont Ave.
Bronx, NY 10583
Phone: (718) 792-0993
Fax: (718) 409-3762
Email: dreamworkes@aol.com
Website: www.dreamworkesracing.com
Manufacturer of superchargers, turbochargers, and performance brakes, specializing in Infinity and Nissan automobiles and SUVs.

Easy Street Motorsports
11834 & 11836 Vose Street
North Hollywood, CA 91605
Contact: Ali Afshar
Phone: (818) 764-9800
Fax: (818) 764-9805
Email: info@easystreetmotorsports.com
Website: www.easystreetmotorsports.com

Edelbrock
2700 California Street
Torrance, CA 90505
Phone: (800) 416-8628
Website: www.edelbrock.com

Garrett Engine Boosting Systems
Website: www.egarrett.com
Website: www.turbobygarrett.com

Greddy Performance Products
9 Vanderbilt
Irvine, CA 92618
Phone: (949) 588-8300
Fax: (949) 588-6318
Email: info@greddy.com
Website: www.greddy.com

Hahn Racecraft
1981-D Weisbrook
Oswego, IL 60543
Phone: (630) 801-1417
Fax: (253) 830-7558
Email: feedback@turbosystem.com
Email: sales@turbosystems.com
Website: www.hahnracecraft.com
Website: www.turbosystem.com
Manufacturer of turbocharger conversion kits for import and domestic applications, upgrades for OE turbochargers, intercoolers and piping, exhaust and downpipe systems, related support equipment, fuel systems, and upgrades.

Hally Auto Spare Parts LLC
6th Floor, Office Court Bldg., Oud Metha
Dubai, AE
Phone: +971-4-3350585
Fax: +971-4-3350858
Email: info@hallyauto.com
Website: www.hallyauto.com
Wholesaler and multi-line distributor of various high-performance auto parts, including turbochargers and intercoolers from Turbonetics Inc. or Spearco, as well as racing pistons from Ross Racing Pistons.

HKS USA Inc.
13401 S. Main St.
Los Angeles, CA 90061+1613
Phone: (310) 763-9600
Fax: (310) 763-9775
Website: www.hksusa.com
Manufacturer of high-performance intake, exhaust, intercooler, turbocharger, boost-control, fuel management, ignition, engine, drivetrain, suspension, and brake upgrade systems.

Jim Wolf Technology Inc.
212 Millar Ave.
El Cajon, CA 92020
Phone: (619) 442-0680
Fax: (619) 579-8160
Website: www.jimwolftechnology.com
Manufacturer of computer upgrades, air intake systems, turbochargers, nitrous oxide control systems, and other performance products for Japanese vehicles.

Turbocharging Source Guide

Precision Turbo & Engine
616-A S. Main St.
Hebron, IN 46341
Phone: (219) 996-7832
Fax: (219) 996-7749
Email: turbo@precisionturbo.net
Website: www.precisionturbo.net
Manufacturer of aftermarket turbochargers, intercoolers, and related components specializing in high-performance and racing products.

Race-Tech Distributors
Rd. #2 Km. 70.3
Arecibo, PR 00612
Main Phone: (787) 817-7002
Fax: (787) 817-7002
Email: racetech@xsn.net
Website: www.racetechspeedshop.com
Distributor of racing and high-performance products specializing in turbochargers and EFI for import and domestic vehicles.

TEC (Turbo Engineering Corp.)
17222 S. Golden Rd.
Golden, CO 80401+5020
Phone: (303) 271-3997
Fax: (303) 271-3927
Email: inquiries@turboengineering.com
Website: www.turboengineering.com
Manufacturer of turbocharger systems, turbochargers, cartridges, components, systems development and engineering services, and competition turbochargers. Factory-authorized Garrett+AirResearch, Roto-Master, Rajay, Holset, Schwitzer, Mitsubishi, IHI, and K.K.K. dealer.

Tial Products Inc.
615 Cass St.
P.O. Box 1019
Owosso, MI 48867
Phone: (989) 729-8553
Fax: (989) 729-9973
Website: www.tialsport.com
Manufacturer of turbocharging components, including wastegates and blowoff valves.

Turbo Clutch
9820 Owensmouth Ave. Suite #14
Chatsworth, CA 91311
Phone: (818) 993-9174
Fax: (818) 993-9177
Website: www.turboclutch.com

Turbonetics Inc.
2255 Agate Ct.
Simi Valley, CA 93065
Phone: (805) 581-0333
Fax: (805) 584-1913
Email: info@turboneticsinc.com
Website: www.turboneticsinc.com
Manufacturer of performance turbochargers kits, intercoolers, radiators, related controls and components, and engineering and overhaul services. Authorized Garrett, Mitsubishi, Warner-Ishi, and Schwitzer distributor.

XRP, Inc.
5630 Imperial Hwy.
South Gate, CA 90280
Phone: (562) 861-4765
Fax: (562) 861-5503
Email: sales@xrp.com
Website: www.xrp.com

SUPERCHARGING SOURCES

Arizona Speed & Marine
6313 W. Commonwealth Ave.
Chandler, AZ 85226
Phone: (480) 753-0208
Fax: (480) 753-0216
Website: www.azspeed.com
Manufacturer of custom fuel-injection systems, superchargers, and all other performance components.

Avenger Superchargers LLC
Branch Office of Avenger 4WD & Auto Pros
4712 Austin Bluffs Pkwy.
Colorado Springs, CO 80918
Phone: (719) 594-4766
Fax: (719) 278-9290
Email: avengersuperchargers@earthlink.net
Website: www.avengersuperchargers.com

BBK Performance
1871 Delilah St.
Corona, CA 92879+1800
Phone: (909) 735-2400
Fax: (909) 735-8882
Website: www.bbkperformance.com
Manufacturer of performance induction, exhaust, and suspension products, including superchargers, throttle bodies, headers, and lowering springs for today's cars and trucks, plus a line of Mustang products.

Boost Tech Motorsports
4101 1-1/2 Mile Rd.
East Leroy, MI 49051
Email: wemeyer@attglobal.net
www.boosttechmotorsports.com
ATI Procharger superchargers, turbo systems, Electromotive fuel-injection, chassis fabrication, paint and bodywork, engine building, custom intercoolers, chassis, and engine dyno services.

Comptech USA
4717 Golden Foothill Pkwy.
El Dorado Hills, CA 95762
Phone: (916) 939-9118
Fax: (916) 939-9196
Email: info@comptechusa.com
Website: www.comptechusa.com
Manufacturer and distributor of high-performance parts including intakes, exhausts, headers, and superchargers for Acura and Honda vehicles.

Eaton Corporation
Air Management Systems Division
19218 B Drive South
Marshall, Michigan 49068
Website: www.eaton.com

Fuel Injection Specialties
11051 Wye St.
San Antonio, TX 78217+2615
Phone: (210) 654-0774
Fax: (210) 654-0775
Email: fuelinjection@fuelinjection.com
Website: www.fuelinjection.com
Furnisher and installer of computer-controlled wiring harnesses for engines, complete fuel-injection systems, superchargers, and engines. Services and installs all items sold, including ACCEL, Vortech, Carroll superchargers, Holley Performance products, and Fel-Pro fuel-management systems. In-house dyno tuning on late-model GM and Ford performance vehicles.

Gorilla Motorsports LLC
1425 S. Clark Dr.
Tempe, AZ 85281
Phone: (866) 446-7455
Fax: (480) 892-0887
Email: info@gorillallc.com
Website: www.gorilla-motorsports.com
Company specializing in superchargers, custom interior and exterior, performance enhancements, video systems, and audio systems.

Hunter Performance Inc.
9302 Livernois Rd.
Houston, TX 77080+8017
Phone: (713) 461-2596
Distributor of superchargers and related systems, parts and components, hard parts for racing and competition, sport trucks and off-road use, and inline and V-8 engines.

Jackson Racing/Moss Motors
440 Rutherford St.
Goleta, CA 93117
Phone: (805) 967-4546
Fax: (805) 964-0415
Email: jacksonracing@mossmotors.com
Website: www.mossmotors.com
Manufacturer of superchargers, supercharger systems and performance products for selected Acura, Daimler-Chrysler, Ford, Honda, and Mazda automobiles, plus supercharging products for imports and compact cars.

Turbocharging Source Guide

Kenne Bell
10743 Bell Ct.
Rancho Cucamonga, CA 91730+4834
Phone: (909) 941-6646
Fax: (909) 944-4883
Website: www.kennebell.net
Manufacturer of supercharger kits for Ford, Dodge, Chrysler, Mazda, and GM; high-performance chips and modules for late-model and OBD-II vehicles; and fuel pump boosters.

Magnuson Products Inc.
3172 Bunsen Ave.
Ventura, CA 93003
Phone: (805) 642-8833
Fax: (805) 677-4897
Email: info@magnusonproducts.com
Website: www.magnacharger.com
Website: www.magnusonproducts.com
Manufacturer, designer, and engineer of superchargers and Magna Charger supercharger systems, utilizing Eaton superchargers, plus remanufacture of original equipment Eaton superchargers.

Paxton Automotive Corp.
1233 E. Orangethorpe Ave.
Fullerton, CA 92831
Phone: (805) 604-1336
Fax: (805) 604-1337
Email: info@paxtonauto.com
Email: paxtonsc@pacbell.net
Website: www.paxtonauto.com
Manufacturer of gear- and ball-driven centrifugal superchargers, electric fuel pumps, filters, and regulators for fuel-injected and carbureted applications, and a complete line of fourth-generation Camaro and Firebird suspension components.

Performance Engineered Systems
5 Humphreyes Dr.
Ivyland, PA 18974
Phone: (267) 288-0161
Fax: (267) 288-0165
Website: www.pes-tuning.com
Manufacturer of supercharger and turbo systems for European vehicles.

Powerdyne Automotive Products Inc.
104 E. Ave. K-4, Suite C
Lancaster, CA 93535
Phone: (661) 723-2800
Fax: (661) 723-2802
Email: pwrdyne@aol.com
Website: www.powerdyne.com
Manufacturer of centrifugal superchargers featuring SilentDrive™ with no oil lines or reservoir and easier installation, designed to be smog-legal for most vehicles.

Powertrain Dynamics
15628 Graham St.
Huntington Beach, CA 92649
Phone: (714) 373-0068
Fax: (714) 379-0553
Website: www.powertraindynamics.com
Automotive engineering, custom engine, driveline, and chassis work. Custom supercharger kits, sales, and installation of parts. Dynojet and data logging for custom tuning.

Pro Lex Performance
42738 Mayfair Park Ave.
Fremont, CA 94538+4040
Phone: (408) 393-6330
Fax: (408) 435-9413
Email: info@prolexperformance.com
Website: www.prolexperformance.com
Mail-order sales of Lexus high-performance parts including short-shift kits and exhaust systems, engine management, Lexus IS300 superchargers kits, exhaust heat shields, radiators, and underbody panels.

ProCharger (ATI)
14801 W. 114th Terr.
Lenexa, KS 66215
Phone: (913) 338-2886
Fax: (913) 338-2879
Website: www.procharger.com
Manufacture of superchargers and complete supercharger system with or without integrated intercooling for street legal and competition automotive, truck, SUV, sport compact, Harley-Davidson, and marine applications.

RSM Racing Inc.
2355 Derry Rd., Unit 25
Mississauga, ON, CAN L5S 1V6
Phone: (905) 671-9998
Fax: (905) 671-8937
Email: sales@rsmracing.com
Website: www.rsmracing.com
Manufacturer of performance parts for GM and BMW vehicles, including supercharger kits, throttle bodies, strut tower braces, and air intakes.

Rtech Performance
249 Bayshore Blvd.
Churchill, ON, CAN L0L 1K0
Phone: (705) 456-1270
Fax: (705) 456-1271
Website: www.rtechperformance.com
Manufacturer of low restriction intercoolers for supercharger systems.

SA Alpine Developments Inc.
7581 Acacia Ave.
Garden Grove, CA 92841
Phone: (714) 379-8066
Fax: (714) 379-8166
Website: http://www.alpine-developments.us/
Manufacturer of supercharger and turbocharging applications for both the OE and the aftermarket.

Slick Motorsports
3615 Superior Ave., Suite 1001A
Cleveland, OH 44114
Phone: (440) 979-9633
Fax: (509) 472-8783
Website: www.slickmotorsports.com
Retailer and installer of high-performance import parts. Specializing in turbo, supercharger, and engine building. Custom fabrication available.

Unorthodox Racing Inc.
11 Brandywine Dr.
Deer Park, NY 11729
Phone: (631) 586-9525
Fax: (631) 586-2599
Email: info@unorthodoxracing.com
Website: www.unorthodoxracing.com
Manufacturer of high-end lightened underdrive pulleys, lightened adjustable cam sprockets, custom supercharger and turbo kits, aluminum flywheels, and multiple stages of clutches for sport compacts, SUVs, and trucks.

Vortech Engineering Inc.
1650 Pacific Ave.
Channel Islands, CA 93033+9901
Phone: (805) 247-0226
Fax: (805) 247-0669
Email: info@vortechsuperchargers.com
Website: www.vortechsuperchargers.com
Manufacturer of Vortech gear-driven superchargers, complete smog-legal supercharger system components, aftercoolers, and related performance components for automotive and marine applications.

Whipple Industries Inc.
3292 N. Weber
Fresno, CA 93722
Phone: (559) 442-1261
Fax: (559) 442-4153
Email: sales@whipplesuperchargers.com
Website: www.whipplesuperchargers.com
Manufacturer and supplier of the twin-screw Whipple Charger, emissions-legal bolt-on supercharger systems for automotive and marine use, computer bolt-on performance, OBD II engine control solutions, emissions, and performance computer calibrations.

www.ingramcontent.com/pod-product-compliance
Lightning Source LLC
Chambersburg PA
CBHW051417070526
44584CB00023B/3465